Traveling INDIAN ARIZONA

Anne O'Brien

WESTCLIFFE PUBLISHERS

westcliffepublishers.com

International Standard Book Numbers:
ISBN-10: 1-56579-518-0
ISBN-13: 978-1-56579-518-1

Text Copyright: Anne O'Brien, 2006. All rights reserved.
Photography Credits: See p. 284

Editor: Peg Tremper
Design Concept: Sheré Chamness
Final Design and Production: Craig Keyzer

Published By:
Westcliffe Publishers, Inc.
P.O. Box 1261
Englewood, CO 80150

Printed in China through: World Print, Ltd.

Library of Congress Cataloging-in-Publication Data:
O'Brien, Anne (Anne Hughes)
    Traveling Indian Arizona / Anne O'Brien.
        p. cm.
    Includes index.
    ISBN-13: 978-1-56579-518-1
    ISBN-10: 1-56579-518-0
1. Indian reservations--Arizona--Guidebooks. 2. Indians of North America--Arizona--Social life
and customs--Guidebooks. 3. Indians of North America--Arizona--Antiquities--Guidebooks.
4. Automobile travel--Arizona--Guidebooks. 5. Arizona--Antiquities--Guidebooks. I. Title.
    E78.A7027 2005
    305.897'0791--dc22   2005008070

For more information about other fine books and calendars from Westcliffe Publishers, please contact your local bookstore, call us at 1-800-523-3692, or visit us on the Web at **westcliffepublishers.com**.

Please Note: Risk is always a factor in backcountry and high-mountain travel. Many of the activities described in this book can be dangerous, especially when weather is adverse or unpredictable, and when unforeseen events or conditions create a hazardous situation. The author has done her best to provide the reader with accurate information about backcountry travel, as well as to point out some of its potential hazards. It is the responsibility of the users of this guide to learn the necessary skills for safe backcountry travel, and to exercise caution in potentially hazardous areas. The author and publisher disclaim any liability for injury or other damage caused by backcountry traveling or performing any other activity described in this book.

Previous page: (Top left) Everett Pikyavit, a member of the Moapa Paiute Band, keeps his people's traditions alive by creating traditional clothing and basketry; (top right) A life-size petroglyph guards a remote pass in Yavapai country; (bottom) Ga'an Dancers at Fort Apache.

Opposite: Wukoki Ruin at Wupatki National Monument. Ancient dwellings like this one preserve the long history of Arizona's native people.

Acknowledgments

This book had its beginnings in 1948, when on my ninth birthday I was welcomed as a small, curious, skinny, blonde visitor to Acoma Pueblo. Actually, my twin sister and I were welcomed together. Peas in a pod. Whatever happened back then—and it wasn't anything dramatic—neither of us ever lost our interest in the Native cultures that surround us. My first book was one I wrote after that visit to get extra credit in fourth grade.

So many people are contributors to this book in spirit and action. I will always thank Madeleine Blais, who teaches as well as she writes, for giving me the confidence to put words on a page and show them to somebody. I am grateful for my husband Rich's total support and for the staff at the Heard Museum who assisted me. My dogs, Chooser and Duke, were with me the whole way, too.

My experts were mostly people who live with the same sense that I do: The Native peoples of the Americas and their lifeways are to be honored. Some of these people are Native American Indians and some aren't. We all have different ways of showing respect. I believe that we all have something to contribute, whether as insiders, outsiders, or something in between.

Special gratitude goes to Camille Nighthorse, Sara Bird-in-Ground, Raymond Endfield, John Hoopingarner, Sunny Dooley, three Hopi gentlemen whose names are too long to put in here, and Luis Gonzales. Also to Patrick Conley and Ron Hubert in Flagstaff, where I did most of my writing; Michael and Kathy Hard, whose house was often my library; Betsy Stodola, and all the photographers, archivists, and librarians who help to make things easier and more enjoyable.

Opposite: A Pima frybread chef prepares this universal favorite. Topped with beans, cheese, lettuce, and tomato, it would be a Pima taco. Depending on where it was made, it would be a Navajo taco, a Hopi taco, or simply an Indian taco.

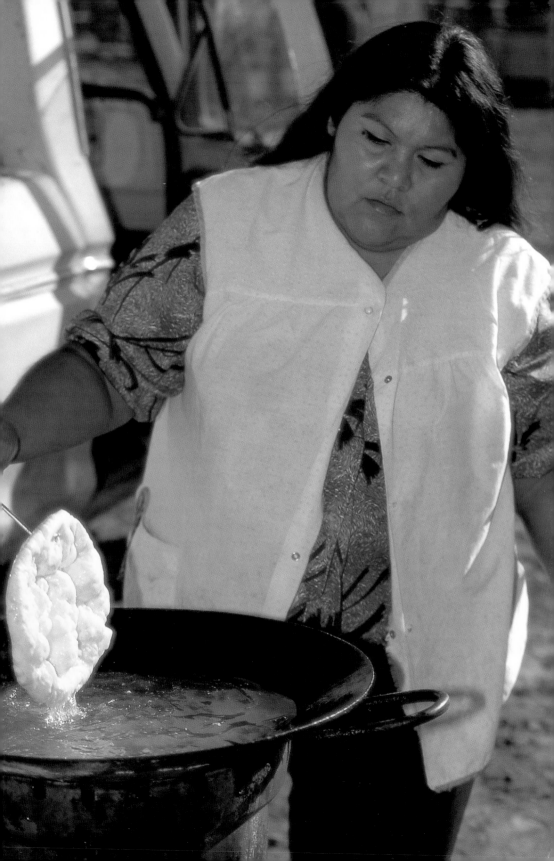

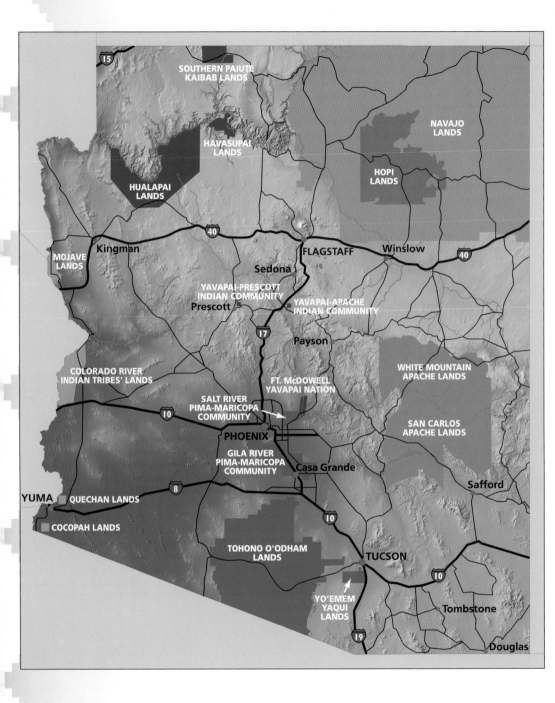

Table of Contents

Foreword

by Ann E. Marshall, Ph.D.

Director of Collections, Education, and Interpretation, Heard Museum, Phoenix

In 1895, Dwight and Maie Heard, a young married couple from Chicago, relocated to Arizona and were quickly drawn to learning about the land and Native cultures of Arizona. From Phoenix, they traveled in all directions around the state, first by horse and buggy and later by car. In the Heard Museum archives, we have photographs of Mrs. Heard standing beside the ancient wall of a cliff dwelling very properly attired in a long skirt, high-necked white shirt-waist blouse and a perfectly centered hat with flowers on it. I have no idea how she climbed up to that cliff dwelling in those clothes and arrived looking so collected. The Heards' excitement with Arizona and the First People of Arizona led them to create an impressive collection and in 1929, to establish the Heard Museum.

Yavapai basket made in the early 1900s. From the collection of the Heard Museum.

Today, many visitors to Arizona share a kinship with Dwight and Maie Heard. Like the Heards, people coming to Arizona and the Southwest recognize that this is a beautiful land where many American Indian people live in the locations they have inhabited for centuries. Within Arizona alone, there are 21 federally recognized tribal communities. The Heard Museum's exhibits and programs are a good way for people to begin learning about the diversity of Native cultures and impressive arts of yesterday and today. Sometimes, a visit to the Heard includes a chance to talk with an artist or one of the many Native people who present the programs here.

Navajo wedding basket from the collection of the Heard Museum.

If we've done our job, the experience whets the visitor's interest in learning more. The volunteers at our information desk field many questions about how to visit Native communities. The questions are about much more than location and directions. Visitors want to know what kinds of experiences they will have when they get there. They want to know about appropriate behavior. We are happy to answer questions, but the discussion only scratches the surface of information that is needed.

Fortunately for Phoenix visitors, they don't have to go far to visit American Indian communities. In recent years, communities—especially those close to urban centers —have developed resorts, golf courses, and gaming facilities. Some communities are near major tourist attractions such as the Grand Canyon or the

Woven Hualapai water bottle sealed with pine pitch and clay. From the collection of the Heard Museum.

Colorado River and travel can often be entwined with ways to learn in greater detail about the art and culture of the community. Most communities have cultural heritage centers; many have well-developed websites. As more people come to Arizona and explore the state, Native communities are working to shape the visitor/community interface in a way that everyone will enjoy.

As we thought of the many questions we receive from visitors, it seemed that Anne O'Brien's book is a good way to help people plan their visits and gain the additional knowledge that ensures great experiences. I am sure the volunteers at our information desk will be citing passages from the book as they field visitor questions.

Preface

This book is for the kind of travelers who venture out to investigate worlds beyond their own. Whether visiting a place for the first or the hundredth time, true travelers approach experience quietly, knowing that something new and fascinating will develop if they are open to seeing, hearing, smelling, or tasting it. There is an art to creating the kind of experience the intrepid traveler seeks, and this book is meant to assist in preparing to make more than a superficial acquaintance with our native Indian communities.

Visitors to Indian lands expect a cultural heritage that is foreign in some respects to their own everyday life. This is true even if the visitor is Native American, since tribes are quite individual. Hopi ways vary significantly from Navajo, and the customs and history of one branch of the Apache or Yavapai people may have as many differences as similarities.

On the other hand, people around the world are touched by common factors and information that allow them to share much in contemporary life. Computers, television, work, education, and transportation have inevitably

blended traditions and perceptions. Still, history provides context for current issues relating to the lands and their people. Both need to be considered as part of the travel experience.

The dry climate and the work of assiduous archaeologists in the southwestern United States make it easy for the traveler to find the ancient next to the modern. Unexpected combinations—whether of food, design, or dress —show the seasoned observer of peoples and places that acculturation is taking place in all

Women add shinglelike bear grass thatch to a traditional Apache dwelling.

directions: tribe-to-tribe, nation-to-nation, person-to-person. People of European, Mexican, and North American Indian backgrounds have adopted and adapted what originally belonged only to one group. Hybrid cultures, the traveler observes, have taken on lives of their own, and are richer for their combinations.

A consequence of this ancient-yet-modern mix, readily visible to the astute traveler, is the question of personal identity. Answers to "Who am I?" can become a matter of individual choice rather than of community tradition. In Indian country, intermarriage and urbanization dilute clan ties and mix languages, religions, and history. The search for identity raises complex emotional issues: "Where do I *feel* I belong? Are my ties closer to reservation lands or to the city where I live? Do I belong with the people of my mother or my father?" Answers require active, often urgent, soul searching. Sometimes no answer emerges. The visitor embraces the human conditions that multiculturalism creates.

In this search for self-definition we see how Indian cultures, rather than disappearing, are continuing to evolve. Although antiquities still tell their story, *contemporary* arts and crafts open another window into Native American cultural regeneration. Ethnologists no longer regard what is created today as a cultural add-on or as a curiosity imitating the past. The artists, of course, never have. The late Lloyd Kiva New, an artist and interpreter of contemporary Indian arts, explained:

> "The arts movement is in a...dynamic state of refinement in which
> the performing and visual arts...are being used to heal old wounds,
> helping individuals and groups move forward with greatly expanded
> levels of personal pride and strengthened identities."

In this spirit, independent explorers of these cultures take authenticity more seriously than resemblance to what "looks Indian." To assist them in appreciation of their search, this book details some of the identifying characteristics of each tribe's artistry.

This book focuses on traditions and practices related to day-to-day life from a contemporary perspective, putting intertribal as well as intercultural military history in the background, for another day, if that is the reader's area of interest.

But whether prospective visitors make one or multiple journeys into the worlds of Arizona Indians, this book will create for them the fascinating experience of pursuing a true traveler's exploration.

Anne O'Brien
Paradise Valley, Arizona
September 2005

How to Use This Guide

The first part of each chapter of *Traveling Indian Arizona* tells you about the cultural heritage of a specific group of American Indians whose lands lie in Arizona. The second part then guides you to places where these cultures can be experienced today. Together, these sections answer basic questions: *who, what, when, where, and why.* They also extend those answers beyond the obvious.

Begin to use the book by looking at the contents page (p. 7). There you will find answers about *who* the Arizona Indians are and *where* their lands lie. You'll see that the chapters are organized according to the location of tribal groups within the state: **Near Phoenix and Tucson, North and East of Flagstaff, Around the Grand Canyon, In the Mountains,** and **On the Lower Colorado River.** A glance at a map reveals that Indian lands exist in every part of Arizona.

This book is meant to be read as background material, and then referred to as a travel guide. Hopefully it will inspire your curiosity and encourage an appreciation of indigenous peoples whose voices strongly influence how the world defines America. Each division is organized under the name of a people, which appears first in the original language and then in English; for instance, *Ndee* is the original name of all tribes called Apache in English. Language and history defines a "people," although individual tribal groups might have broken off long ago.

Next, turn to the beginning of a chapter, where a detailed table of contents outlines the kinds of information within that chapter. An **Introduction to the Culture** explains *why* the people evolved as they did. This opening section offers a brief view into the deep past, including a creation story. Subsections such as **Enduring Lifeways, Daily Living, Foreign Contact,** and **Reservation Life** move history into the present. **Ceremonial Customs** explains traditional spiritual aspects of the culture that the traveler is likely to encounter through artistic expression or direct contact.

Suggestions about how to experience the featured cultures appear in the second part of each chapter, titled **Exploring the Lands.** Tips on *where* to go and *when* to visit are included here. Because cultural heritage experiences range from touring the Heard Museum in Phoenix (which no one should miss!) to driving in remote corners of Arizona's deserts and mountains, the information given here is quite individual. For instance, the chapter on the Yaqui, who live in three villages within urban areas, differs greatly from that about the Navajo, whose homes are spread across 14 million rural acres. The inconsistent levels of organization related to tourism among tribal communities adds to the variability of these sections.

Destinations to visit, found in **Exploring the Lands**, are listed by location in relation to each other and to the nearest city or town. The information here includes directions, operating hours, and short descriptions of points of interest. In addition, sections called either **Along the Way** or **Side Trips**— depending on whether a detour from the direct route to your destination is necessary—call your attention to sites that add depth to your travel experience.

Recommendations for **Dining and Overnight Accommodations** appear in each chapter. Sections titled **Shopping** discuss the kinds of arts and crafts you can expect to see on your trips and teach you how to recognize those that are authentic and representative of the people you are visiting. These sections also suggest places where you can buy with confidence.

Recurring Events tells you about dances, rodeos, fairs, celebrations, activities, and cultural functions that take place annually and are open to the public. They are specific to each tribe, so exact dates must be obtained from tribal offices. But don't stop there: Serendipitous encounters add immeasurably to planned activities. As every experienced traveler knows, you need to "ask around." Particularly where tourism tends not to be organized, friendly people make the best guides of all. See the website www.indianarizona.com as well as the websites of specific communities for dates and other announcements.

A short profile called **Native Voices, Native Lives** ends each chapter. These sketches offer a personal view that answers the question *who*. Each featured individual is a contemporary representative of the community.

In the back of this book are statements by experts on a variety of related subjects: Native medicine, rock art, Arizona antiquities, and even a Native viewpoint on the "Indian Wars." Lists of further reading and emergency contacts organized by chapter conclude the appendix.

Traveling Indian Arizona is like visiting foreign nations. Experienced travelers would not set out for such places without understanding something of the people and their circumstances. This book puts preparatory information at your fingertips, helping you to recognize the incredibly diverse nature of cultural heritage tourism in Indian Country.

Whether from your armchair or in your car, you are about to begin a fascinating adventure!

Travel Tips and Reservation Etiquette

Travel Tips

• Most travelers will drive their own vehicles to these destinations. Before you leave your home base, determine mileages and make plans to gas up at specific places. Distances can be enormous and reservation towns do not necessarily provide the services that city dwellers are used to. A good map such as AAA's "Guide to Indian Country" can be a helpful planning tool.

• Find out what kind of topography to expect. Travelers who don't know Arizona sometimes think it's all desert. In actuality, you may find yourself on the plains or in the mountains. Temperatures and weather depend to a great extent on altitude. Check weather information and prepare accordingly.

• Even in winter, water is a necessity when you're active in the desert. Always take more than you think you'll need, and drink it! It would also be wise to pack a comb, which handily removes cactus spines that might seem to appear from nowhere to cling to your pants, socks, shoes, or boots.

• Arizona's famous rattlesnakes hibernate during the short winter but love to sun themselves in spring, so be alert, walk where you can easily see the path or trail, and don't put your hands where you can't see what's there. Snakes might stretch out or curl up, looking from a distance more like a beanie than a snake.

• Emergency information appears in the back of this book. However, it is important to know that hospitals associated with the Indian Health Service are only permitted to stabilize non-Indians and order transportation to other healthcare sites. Cell phones may not work, so you can't depend on reaching your emergency roadside assistance. Be sure your spare tire has air in it, pack a first-aid kit, and generally be ready to depend on your own resources if you have to.

• The West in general and Arizona in particular are affected by weather patterns that fluctuate wildly. Drought alternates with floods. "Average" takes on new meaning, evening out peaks and valleys on a weather graph but rarely predicting exact conditions. Be prepared!

Etiquette on the Reservation

• Ask someone in authority whether you may take photographs before even taking out a camera. Cameras can be intrusive. Some tribes have a policy against picture-taking, sketching, and recording. Find out first.

• If you have determined that photography is allowed, always ask before taking a photo of a person or a group. If it seems appropriate, ask whether they would like to be paid. Do not photograph a child without parental permission.

The Apaches' Sunrise Dance Ceremony reaffirms
traditional values for all who take part.

• Err on the side of being conservatively dressed. Much of Arizona is hot, but
please wear shirts, shoes, blouses, longer shorts…you get the idea.

• Be conservative in behavior as well. Many Native Americans are not used
to the loud and constant noise that city people have learned to live with.
Keep your voice low. It is more polite to be reserved than to be too friendly.
Shake hands gently. Look down rather than stare.

• Determine what is public and what is private. Stay away from residential
areas, cemeteries, and anything considered sacred.

• If you attend a ceremony, allow community members to stand in front of
you. Don't applaud unless they do. Don't talk to the people performing the
ceremony. Take your cues from the Native people.

• Don't touch anything that looks like archaeology. You don't want to be the
one who damages it after a thousand years!

• You support the people you're visiting when you buy authentic Indian arts
and crafts. Ask who made them. If a retail store displays an IACA sign, it is
a member of the Indian Arts and Crafts Association, which has guidelines
for clearly marking non-authentic merchandise.

• People have differing preferences about being called Native American or
Indian. One is not necessarily more respectful than the other. Much of the
time it's how you say it, not what you say. Use both and be sensitive to an
individual's reaction. Go with what that person seems comfortable with.

• Alcohol and drugs are forbidden.

O'odham: Pima, Maricopa, Tohono O'odham

"From myth to medicine, the Pimas' metaphor of themselves was as part of the desert."

— Amadeo Rea, *At the Desert's Green Edge*

Opposite: A rainbow in Arizona's Sonoran Desert.
Photo by Joe McAuliffe, Desert Botanical Garden, Phoenix.

Introduction to O'odham Culture

In the days when rivers were truly the great arteries of civilization, the Salt and the Gila were the big ones, and they ran year-round through the desert. The groups that lived near their confluence called themselves the Akimel O'odham, or River People. The smaller Santa Cruz and San Pedro rivers flowed north, linking them with the Tohono O'odham, or Desert People, called Papago by the Spanish. Explorers called the northern villagers Pima. They were joined in the early 1800s by a group of Maricopa who came from the greatest river of all, the Colorado, to help defend against common enemies. The rivers have bound these groups together as many generations cooperated to draw sustenance from an otherwise dry land.

Today, a map of the big rivers can mislead those who don't know the territory. Driving I-10 between Phoenix and Tucson, you can miss the Gila River entirely. Since the 1870s, its waters have been dammed upstream to irrigate Euro-American agriculture. The rich floodplain that once nurtured the crops of the River People for centuries appears barren as bone today. The Salt River is also contained, its waters usually visible only in the mountains and the lakes behind the dams. Ironically, some districts west of Tucson where the Desert People live appear green in comparison, rich with a profusion of high desert plants.

Mollie Juana lived in the Salt River area in the 1880s. Clay was used as hair and face adornment for generations by Maricopa, Pima, and Colorado River Indian women.

Enduring Lifeways

Today, these peoples share common memories of both the water and its disappearance. They recall days when the valley of the middle Gila was truly a bread basket, supplementing wild foods gathered from the saguaro, mesquite, and agave with corn, beans, squash, melons, and seeds for meal. Fish and wild game were plentiful. The Tohono O'odham depended on its bounty for some of their food, as the Pima and Maricopa depended on their southern relatives for labor at harvest time. All these communities share customs, songs, stories, and languages that vary only in dialect (although the Maricopa tongue is related to that of Yuman peoples who still live near the Colorado River).

Naming Names

O'odham, meaning, of course, the People, is pronounced *AW-thum* (with a soft "th," as in "the"). Two groups of O'odham live in Arizona. The Salt and Gila River communities near Phoenix are made up of Akimel *(AH-kee-mell)* O'odham who are commonly called Pima. With them live a group of Maricopa people, whose name for themselves is Piipaash *(PEA-posh)*.

In southern Arizona, the People call themselves Tohono *(toe-HOE-no)* O'odham. Until the 1980s the Tohono O'odham were called Papago, which is used as a place name all over the state. The tribe officially changed its title back to Tohono O'odham, so this is the correct way to refer to them now.

The O'odham groups historically were divided into the One Village, Two Village, and No Village people, according to their settlement patterns. The River People stayed in one village because their lands produced plentiful food, game, and water all year. The Desert People lived in *rancherías* all summer, gathering food from the desert and growing corn, beans, and squash in the valley floodplains during the rainy season, late June to September. They moved to camps in the foothills in winter to be near springs and wells. From there they hunted rabbits, mule

Tohono O'odham Community Action (TOCA), based in Sells, encourages farming of traditional foods like tepary beans and squash varieties, which thrive in high summer temperatures.

Fascinating Facts about the O'odham

• The name Arizona is derived from a Pima word, *a'al-sho-shon*, which means "many springs." Tucson got its name from an ancient O'odham village called *Chuk Shon*, meaning "spring at the foot of the black mountain."

• Irrigation canals built by predecessors of the O'odham, the Hohokam, are considered a wonder of the world. Without metal tools, the wheel, or domestic animals, the Hohokam engineered networks of canals whose controlled water flow prevented flooding and silting. To accomplish this feat, they had to design and construct the canals as a total system.

• Gila River Community farms were so productive that the U.S. Army bought 2 million pounds of surplus wheat from the Pimas in 1862 to help feed troops during the Civil War.

• The Gila River people were always known to be peaceful, friendly, and helpful to strangers. No swear words exist in the Pima language.

• The Pima and Maricopa population outnumbered Euro-Americans in the Arizona Territory until 1880.

• The remains of a 170-foot geoglyphic figure popularly called "The Witch" lies at an undisclosed location on Pima/Maricopa land. Made from troughs and stones, it is fully visible only from the air, after a rain. A figure of a small child lies beside it. In legend, Ho'ok, the witch, was said to carry off children from their homes.

• Ira Hayes, from the village of Casa Blanca, is one of the soldiers immortalized in the WWII photograph and sculpture of six Americans raising the flag in victory over the island of Iwo Jima. His family still lives in the community.

• The U.S. government used Gila River lands for Japanese internment camps during WWII. Some 12,000 Japanese citizens lived in two camps on the reservation. The camps no longer exist, and the government has made reparations to the tribe for using its land without authorization.

• Jazz trombonist Russell "Big Chief" Moore grew up on the Gila River reservation. He joined Lionel Hampton's band in 1935 and later became first trombonist with Louis Armstrong.

• The riverless western part of the desert lands of the O'odham receives as few as 4 inches of rain a year. Only 25 plant types grow there.

• Traditional O'odham brush homes were built without the use of any water. Sometimes dirt and clay were placed on top of the structure to gather moisture when it rained, then dry as hard as adobe.

• The Gadsden Purchase carved southern Arizona out of northern Mexico in 1854, dividing O'odham families by political boundary and language. The Tohono O'odham simply constitute that portion of the related groups who live south of the Gila and Salt Rivers.

• The Shadow Wolves is a crack unit of American Indian trackers based in Sells, Arizona. Using skills handed down through generations, they trace international criminal activity from drug and weapons smuggling to finding missing children as part of the U.S. Customs Service.

deer, pronghorn antelope, and javelina and ate crops and cactus fruits preserved from summer. A small group called the Sand Papago or Hia Ced O'odham, the No Village People, essentially camped wherever they could find food and water sources in the driest western part of the Sonoran Desert. The desert dwellers transformed these sparse resources into food, drink, clothing, medicine, and shelter.

The O'odham peoples were not the first to call the Sonoran Desert home. They followed the Hohokam ("those who have gone") onto these lands. Hohokam (or, in the O'odham language, *Huhugam*) civilization dominated the region for nearly 1,500 years, beginning around 400–500. These ancient engineers left hundreds of miles of gravity-flow canals leading out into the desert on both sides of the Gila and the Salt. Their work served as the basis for the irrigation system originally designed for Phoenix.

Remains of fields and dwellings as well as the artifacts from an elaborate agricultural civilization lie scattered about the entire region. Antique copper bells and parrot feathers reveal interaction with people to the south. Pottery and turquoise came via northern groups. Casa Grande Ruin, an imposing citadel preserved from that civilization, stands between Phoenix and Tucson. Its 4-foot-thick adobe walls once stood four stories high. They apparently were built to protect surrounding settlements and to serve as a ceremonial center. At its apex, Hohokam culture covered lands farther south than today's Tucson and as far north as Flagstaff. However, the years between its demise and the time when events began to be recorded by European explorers remain a mystery.

Foreign Contact

Gila country history goes back farther than that of Jamestown, Virginia, where the first British ship landed in 1607. Spanish conquistadores passed through Pimería, as this territory was known on both sides of the U.S.–Mexican border, as early as 1540. Sixteenth-century Spanish records explain that the people they encountered called themselves Ohotoma, which we now spell O'odham. However, the Spanish called the northern group Pima, adapted from the native word *pimtc*, meaning "I don't know," the response explorers received when they posed questions in an unintelligible (to the Ohotoma) language. Papago, the name by which the Tohono O'odham were known outside their own society until 1986, may have come from their word for tepary beans. *Xalychidom Piipaash*, the Maricopa's name for themselves, means "people who live toward the water."

The desire to convert and claim the indigenous people and their land for Spain motivated the Spanish to expand their presence into both Pimerías—Alta (higher, or northern) and Baja (lower, or southern.) The name of Father Eusebio Francisco Kino (1645–1711), a Jesuit priest who arrived in 1687, became synonymous with Roman Catholic missionary work in the borderlands. During the 1700s the padres—first Jesuits and then Franciscans, supported financially by their government—filled the southern river valleys

Ancient Civilization

The term "Hohokam" (pronounced *ho-ho-KAHM,* although today's O'odham pronunciation is closer to *hu-hu-GAM*) describes south-central Arizona's predominant archaeological culture. It is derived from a polite O'odham euphemism used to refer to people who are no longer among us. The early Hohokam constructed pithouses and made pottery decorated in red. Later, after AD 500, they built public structures that archaeologists call platform mounds and ball courts. They preceded today's Pima, Maricopa, and Tohono O'odham on the land.

with missions, some of which remain. The mission San Xavier del Bac, begun in 1692, survived attack during a Pima uprising in 1751 and is used as a parish church today. San Jose de Tumacacori, 35 miles south, was built in 1811 to replace three other small missions and abandoned when it came under Apache attack.

Haciendas to sustain the priests and their converts were built wherever springs rose in the deserts of what is now Mexico and southern Arizona, which often meant they were next to Tohono O'odham villages—including the one for which Tucson is named: *Chuk Shon.* Of course, these were often the best lands, which ultimately they lost to European immigrants. They gained important new crops like wheat and melons. Eventually they began to raise cattle and use horses for transportation and farm work. But by this

San Jose de Tumacacori stands on the site of an O'odham village that was first visited by Spanish missionaries in 1691.

White stucco mission churches established in the early 1900s by Franciscans are distinguished by their artful doors and creative interiors.

time, the missionaries had dominated the land, culture, and religion.

Over time, the Tohono O'odham wove Roman Catholic teachings into traditional practices, using Christian images in ways unique to their worship. Catholicism remains vital in their lands, but echoes of ancient practices are still heard.

Many of the small churches on the reservation, built during the Franciscan revival early in the twentieth century, recall the way that traditional O'odham religious structures were laid out. Indoors, they protected sacred objects. Outdoors, a much larger space was designed for public ceremonies and celebrations. Even today, parishioners pray in the chapel in the presence of the saints and icons, while communal activities take place outside. Dance floors with benches for spectators, a place for musicians (who typically play polka-like music called *waila* or chicken-scratch), and a ramada for food preparation and feasting belong in the churchyard. Community is its focus.

Some O'odham Catholic families still follow the custom of gathering each year to honor St. Francis (the Jesuit and the Franciscan saints have been merged) in Magdalena, Sonora, the town where Father Kino is buried. There, customs are renewed along with family ties in a fiesta atmosphere. Local ceremonies are held for those who can't travel.

Nor did O'odham Christians forget *I'itoi*, the original Creator. Known as *Se'ehe* among the Pimas, he resides within mountains: on Baboquivari Peak, for the Tohono O'odham; in the South Mountains (*Muadagi Doak*), according to the Pima culture. His nature and activities are too sacred to be discussed at length with the outside world, but he remains a benevolent source of spiritual support. Elder Brother, as he is also known, appears at the top of the very popular design known as "The Man in the Maze."

Christianity didn't overtake the River People until Protestants—primarily Presbyterians—came at the turn of the last century, bringing secular education with them. The Spanish *padres*, whose missions and religion dominated their southern relatives, had passed through northern Pimería, restricting their activities to teaching the people to raise stock, grow winter wheat, and

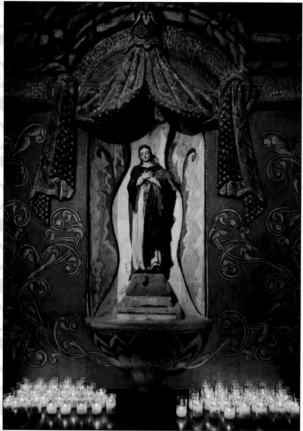

Mary of the Immaculate Conception is one of over 100 figures at San Xavier del Bac. She was carried there from Tumacacori by Tohono O'odham parishioners when their church came under continual Apache attack in the late 1800s.

use metal tools. The Pima recall the Presbyterian missionaries as Americans who came not to acquire land but to lend a hand at a time when their livelihood had vanished with the waters of the river. After decades of starvation, the schools they built on the reservation ushered in a new kind of learning that enabled them to survive.

But that era came long after the domination of the Southwest by the Spanish and then the Mexicans, under whose rule the expensive mission system was abandoned to an unstable civil government. The Mexican-American War ended Mexican rule by drawing new boundaries between the two countries in 1848. For the next six years, the Pimas' section of the Gila River formed the border between the United States and Mexico. In 1853 the United States purchased more land, which was carved from Tohono O'odham territory to accommodate James Gadsden's desire to build a railroad there.

The established pattern was to eradicate, convert, or disperse the native people, then to reorganize them into communities determined by the ruling nationality. The O'odham thus had to adapt to three governments over the years, using Spanish, English, or their own language, as the situation required. Those who wished to escape colonization had to migrate to increasingly remote regions, which resulted in a recombining of different groups who adopted common lifestyles.

Non-religious outside influences came in force to the River People during the Gold Rush, when Forty-Niners and settlers by the thousands passed through Pima territory on their way to California. Always hospitable to travelers along the ancient Gila Trail, they offered them beans, squash, corn, and melons from the bounty of their land, just as they did the Spanish explorers, the American Army, the Pony Express and Butterfield Stage riders, and traders from other Indian lands.

The exception to this rule was the Apache tribes, unrelenting enemies of the O'odham until Geronimo surrendered in 1886. The mountain-based Apache often raided for their livelihood, and the O'odham peoples, particularly those along the river, had a bountiful supply of what they needed. During Arizona's Indian Wars, U.S. troops depended on Pima scouts to fight the Apache. The warrior tradition continued when the mostly Pima-Maricopa Company F, 158th Infantry, 40th Division, refused the option of being discharged at the onset of World War I. They went on to serve with honor and are memorialized at a park on the Gila River reservation. O'odham military service continues into the present.

Daily Living and Reservation Life

Some aspects of traditional life lasted well into the nineteenth century and beyond. The travelers across Gila country found the people living in villages of oval brush dwellings called *olas ki* arranged in patriarchal family compounds, each with its outdoor kitchen and ramada, or *vato*, a large *olla* (pottery jar) of drinking water with a dipping gourd and a small one of *pinole* (meal).

Gold prospectors, like the early, overdressed Spanish soldiers, noted the Pima's way of dressing for desert living in beautifully woven white cotton breech cloths, blankets, or skirts, moving slowly and deliberately and doing much of their work in the early hours of the day.

Lifeways followed many of the old paths until water diversion by settlers began in earnest in the late 1800s. Diminishing water supplies exacerbated the effects of overgrazing by Spanish-introduced livestock. Upstream erosion and downstream flooding ended agriculture as they had known it. Wood used

The Ak-Chin Community

Ak-Chin, the word for the part of a desert wash that can best be planted, served for generations as an O'odham summer camp where crops grew fast during the monsoon. It is still an agricultural community made up of Tohono O'odham and Pima. Together, they formed a community that developed its own dialect.

In addition to farming, the southern people helped out in Pima fields. Times changed quickly. The Southern Pacific Railroad came through with lots of wage-paying jobs. The 21,000-acre reservation was established the same year that Arizona became a state in 1912. Many years later, Ak-Chin Farms, enhanced with Central Arizona Project water, succeeded beyond their expectations. To teach their children community history, the Ak-Chin community has built an eco-museum which keeps tribal records, encourages language teaching, and preserves farming traditions.

A replica of an O'odham harvesting ramada at Phoenix's Desert Botanical Garden stands on twisted mesquite posts. Gourds were hung to dry and later used for dipping, storing, and serving food.

to fuel miners' fires intensified watershed damage. Between the 1920s and the 1940s, the Gila River slowly died. Its disappearance changed forever the *O'odham himdag*, the Pima and Maricopa way of life.

Participating in the wage economy became the only realistic alternative to farming for the Pima and a little later, for the Tohono O'odham. Ranch work, mining, railroad jobs, and cotton harvesting offered work, but not prosperity. Although attempts were made after the 1920s to return Gila River water to the Pima and Maricopa people, their farms were devastated by disuse. Drought further decimated the plan to share water stored behind Coolidge

Feast and Famine in the Desert

People in the desert have co-evolved with their sources of sustenance, where periods of drought alternate with rainy seasons and unusually wet times. Under these conditions, individuals whose metabolisms could utilize nutrition efficiently when it was available and store it for delivery during dry spells survived and thrived. This very ability, however, may contribute to today's high incidence of obesity and diabetes in these communities. Neither of these problems was prevalent before the 1940s. The availability of food 24/7 —especially high-carbohydrate meals—may have turned this survival mechanism into a severe health liability.

Case in point: The Gila monster, a type of lizard that lives in the desert lands of the O'odham, eats only a few times a year. Its pancreas, the organ whose dysfunction is responsible for diabetes, shuts down when it isn't eating but secretes insulin when it is needed to process blood sugar. Two pharmaceutical companies are researching a synthetic form of the hormone that the Gila monster secretes to control insulin production. They expect that it will help them develop a drug to stimulate insulin secretion, inhibit glucose production, and suppress appetite.

Dam. Around the same time, the government took it upon itself to dig wells for the Tohono O'odham, but did not maintain them. A dark time ensued.

The People endured, in spite of conflict over water rights and land distribution. In 1968, farming families in the Pima community combined their traditional plots to establish Gila River Farms, now a completely modern agricultural operation with a $12 million budget. In 1978, Ak-Chin constructed a 15,000-acre community farm after receiving $15 million and 75,000 acre-feet of water. It had the effect of immediately reducing unemployment from 33 to 3 percent.

The Arizona Water Settlement Act, approved at the end of 2004, returned significant water rights to the O'odham peoples. Water, however, whether for agriculture or leasing of water rights to cities, does not entirely resolve the question of sustainable economic development for the O'odham. Laws giving them the ability to lease land helped, bringing security to some after the 1960s.

The legalization of gaming on Arizona reservations in the 1990s has also produced sufficient income to fund some capital-intensive projects. The O'odham—especially those who lived near urban areas—took full advantage of these opportunities, and each community continues to develop its own major projects. They range from telecommunications companies at the Gila and Salt River Communities to shopping centers, industrial parks, and golf courses, social services, and cultural preservation.

Arizona's early inhabitants left grinding stones (metates) at the places where they prepared food. The wooden pestle leaning against this one is typical of those used by O'odham peoples. Mesquite beans were pounded into meal and stored in pottery jars. The meal could then be made into gruel or cakes.

Ceremonial Customs

Before changes wrought by outsiders encroached upon their lives, the O'odham peoples depended on ancient ceremonies to unite natural and spiritual forces with the needs of their communities. These rites are still remembered and respected, though some are no longer performed.

The most sacred and complex ceremony of the Tohono O'odham, the harvest-time *wigida,* is one of these. It once marked every fourth year with several days of elaborate dances involving special regalia and body paint along with prescribed ritual. *Wuaga,* a girl's coming of age rite, is another, as are still others related to hunting, farming, healing, and purification after war.

• **Saguaro Wine Fest:** A summer rain ceremony, the Saguaro Wine Fest had been in decline but is now being revived. It traditionally follows the July saguaro cactus harvest, during which some 450,000 pounds of fruit

were gathered as late as the 1930s. Saguaro fruit can be eaten fresh, dried, ground into meal, or can be boiled into syrup and jam. A portion of each family's syrup was donated to the community to be fermented for two days under the watchful eye of "vintners" in the Rain House, a traditional brush structure built for sacred purposes.

The annual harvesting of juicy red fruit from the giant saguaro cactus precedes the *jujkida* or summer rain ceremony, where *nawait,* ceremonial wine made from its juice, is consumed. It can also be eaten fresh, dried, and made into meal, syrup, and jam.

Fetishes and significant sacred objects collected over the years were, and still are, kept near the fermenting brew in *wacas,* oblong baskets made of yucca fiber. These objects are guarded by specifically authorized individuals. The consequence of disturbing such ceremonial items is believed to be disastrous.

When the wine is ready, men of the village are called to become "well drunk." A night of drinking and vomiting the relatively mild liquor is associated with natural cycles of precipitation and growth. This ritual is called "bringing down the clouds."

• **Skipping Dance:** Another ceremony—one frequently open to the public—is the *chelkona (chell-KO-na).* Known in English as Skipping Dance, it was once common to the Akimel and Tohono O'odham but now is performed primarily by the Tohono O'odham.

Besides its religious significance, the chelkona served as a way of sharing resources and strengthening community. In the old days, a village with

Men work on the roof of a Tohono O'odham ceremonial rainhouse.

abundant crops—the host village—paired with a village needing support. Young men arrived at a designated time, their faces painted black. After a welcoming speech, they would be pelted with fruit and vegetables—a comical gesture that could only be made by those with no lack of food.

The ceremony began with an exchange of formalized speeches. After the dance grounds were cleared of negative spirits, musicians, singers, and dancers found their places. Instruments typically included an inverted basket played as a drum, gourd rattles, and a wooden rasper.

A special leader who had the power to dream such things directed speakers, singers, and dancers in their roles. Long, shiny hair was considered an asset for dancers. Regalia was not considered as important as the *iagta*, ceremonial wands carried by the dancers. Originally made from painted buckskin stretched over wood, iagta presented representations of birds, clouds, and rainbows. A pole on the dance ground was sometimes topped with one of these symbols. The dance itself expressed gratitude for cycles of rain and growth.

Feasting, games, and an exchange of gifts followed the morning Skipping Dance. Runners trained by a *maikai* (doctor) competed in a 15-mile relay race that was the object of significant wagering. Native versions of kickball, field hockey, and other games also became the object of betting, which ultimately amounted to another exchange of property as well as a source of entertainment.

A contemporary chelkona combines the same elements of fun and spirituality. It may be performed on dance grounds beside the village Catholic church or as part of a competition. In either case, it rejuvenates the spirit at many levels.

Storytelling:
Teachings of the Elders

Daniel Lopez of Ge Oidag,
Tohono O'odham Nation

Storytelling for O'odham was done in winter. The people used to say that this was the time when such creatures as the rattlesnake, black widow, and scorpion went into their hiding places for the winter. Also, the cold months were the right time to tell stories because there was not much to do except to stay inside, sit around a warm fire, and listen to them.

In summer, the O'odham were busy planting and harvesting their fields, gathering the wild desert food, and hunting game animals. Most of the crops also had to be dried and stored for winter use. "The dangerous creatures will come after you if you tell stories in the summer," the elders used to tell their little grandchildren.

The *wawhai* (winter villages) were at higher elevations and between mountains, so it was very cold at times. The people stayed inside, and that is when elderly storytellers told the stories. The ancient storytellers had good memories because the stories were only told from winter to winter. They had to remember many stories, and most had songs that were sung by the different characters. Some of the characters were *I'itoi, Ba'ag O'odham, Ho'oki Oks, Ban, Nuwi*, and others. The important creation story, according to some elders, took four nights to tell.

Storytellers always appreciate a good, well-behaved audience, even today. When someone fell asleep, certain storytellers would just stop for the night and then continue the next evening. Of course all the other listeners would be upset at the one who fell asleep. I have also heard that if a child fell asleep, the other people would get some *cu:dagi* or burnt-out coals and blacken the child's face. Just imagine when the little kid came home and everyone laughed at his black face. It was a way of teaching the child to stay awake and listen.

Another thing I heard was that when someone fell asleep, all the others would sneak out and go home. Imagine a child waking up all alone and then walking home in the dark. They say this was really scary for the child, especially during the time when enemy raids were going on.

I once heard that a certain storyteller would start telling stories when the sun came up at a certain point on the horizon. Someone else said that another storyteller would wait until the sun came up on the south side of *Waw Giwulk* Mountain before he told his first story. I guess this all depended on how one learned from his elder.

Storytelling was not just to entertain, but also to teach important values and lessons. From the stories, people learned the value of sharing food and other things. They also learned to have respect for nature, animals, and people. Through storytelling people heard about how things came to be. The children were constantly told, "Don't be silly and lazy like the *ban,* or coyote, and don't eat too much or else people will call you *s-banma* or 'one who eats too much.' " These were just some of the many lessons taught.

Today, storytellers compete with the modern technology of television, Gameboys, and Walkmans. The little children should be told stories at an early age about the values learned from storytelling. Maybe this is how they can learn to value and respect life. This will not be easy to do, but it is something that needs to be done. The reports about children's drinking and taking drugs is not good. O'odham must not give in to the negative influences of the outside world. We need to protect our children, language, and culture.

Our *himdag* (way of living) was given to us for a reason, just as other cultures the world over were given their territories, languages, and cultures. The stories and histories of every culture helped all groups survive for hundreds of years. Because we now live in the age of technology, we should use it to our advantage.

Exploring the O'odham Lands

The lands of the O'odham cover an enormous area (Gila River: 372,000 acres; Salt River: 52,600 acres; Ak-Chin, 22,000 acres; Tohono O'odham: 2.8 million acres, about the size of Delaware), much of which is closed to those who are not community members. A Right of Entry permit from the tribe or district is necessary to enter remote or sensitive areas. Non-members are free to use state and county roads that cross these lands, but otherwise are invited only to visit public buildings and public events. The villages themselves are essentially residential areas, although homes may be clustered or quite distant from one another.

The parts of the Tohono O'odham reservation that border Mexico are particularly heavily patrolled, in order to dissuade drug-runners and illegal border crossings. Despite its large size, the Tohono O'odham reservation population (which is perhaps 3 percent of Delaware's) is widely dispersed, so it's possible not to encounter another car or settlement for long periods of time.

Fortunately, however, these cultures are well documented at a number of easy-to-visit museums, parks, and sites around Phoenix and Tucson. Guided tours and exhibits provide an excellent overview of the O'odham peoples and their history. Museums on the reservations are staffed by knowledgeable community members, so they're always a good place to meet people and learn first-hand. You can also check the noted websites

Tohono O'odham elder Frances Manuel makes winnowing corn look easy.

and www.indianarizona.com (the website related to this book) to find events that are open to the public.

In addition, the creative traveler can use public roads, parks, and scenic lookouts to appreciate the natural beauty of the lands as the O'odham celebrate them in song and story. Some off-reservation destinations such as certain points in Phoenix's South Mountain Park, the scenic viewpoint at the pass on Shea Boulevard between Scottsdale and Fountain Hills and Papago Park offer panoramic looks at the Pima's rich landscape. Seeing the still-flowing Salt and Verde Rivers from Fountain Hills explains better than words the attraction of rivers in the desert. Looking over the Salt River Valley from Papago Park makes it easy for the traveler to imagine how it appeared before settlement, surrounded by mountains, green with lush desert growth, sloping down to what was then a perennially flowing river seeking its confluence with the Gila.

Above: *Toka* (double ball) is a traditional women's game. The ball is thrown past the opponents' goal using bent sticks made of cat's-claw. **Below:** Young people get ready to plant crops using native seed and traditional tools.

In and Around Phoenix

Papago Park

Galvin Pkwy. (64th St.) and McDowell Rd.
www.ci.phoenix.az.us/PARKS/hikepapa.html
Open: Daily from sunrise to sunset

Twelve-hundred-acre Papago Park would draw anyone who lived in the area. Stunning red rock formations overlooking the Salt River Valley set it apart from the surrounding desert. It is not hard to imagine celebrating the sun's

movements at a formation called "Hole-in-the-Rock," which may have been used by ancient astronomers, or orienting a journey by sighting its direction using the mountains that surround it at a distance.

Today you can enjoy the park in many ways. It is possible to get a quick impression of the park's beauty by driving through, but ramadas shelter picnic tables where you can deepen your experience of the place —breathe its air and catch the scent of the desert. Bike

Hole-in-the-Rock is a popular place to visit in Phoenix's Papago Park, which overlooks the Salt River Valley, once a Hohokam urban center.

paths, walks, hikes, and butte-climbing offer further adventure. Parking is ample and well-marked. There is parking on both sides of Galvin Parkway.

Desert Botanical Garden

1201 N. Galvin Pkwy., Papago Park • (480) 941-1225 • www.dbg.org
Open: 8 a.m.–8 p.m. October–April; 7 a.m.–8 p.m. May–September
Closed: July 4, December 25

This 145-acre lease within Papago Park is next on your tour. It offers exhibits that illustrate authentically re-created aspects of traditional O'odham culture. Once inside the garden, a leisurely walk to the well-tended trail called "Plants and People of the Sonoran Desert" will show you why these people chose to live in this environment. Plan about an hour for your visit.

Turning off the main Desert Discovery trail, you will come to a small saguaro forest, where you'll find a replica of an O'odham harvesting ramada built and maintained by Gila River community members. It shelters equipment used to gather ripe fruit from the tops of these giant cactus and to process it into food and ceremonial wine.

A little farther along, at the Desert Oasis, you'll experience the environment that used to characterize the big rivers, where warm-water fish, some of which grew to 6 feet in length, thrived. Huge cottonwood trees, willows, reeds, and cattails along the banks provided materials for building and basketry.

Next you come to a cholla bud roasting pit, built against a background of cholla cactus. Buds were gathered before the spines developed to the uncomfortable proportions you see on mature plants. Small ones were easy to remove. Later, you'll encounter another pit which was used for roasting mescal, the heart of the succulent plant called agave.

The Native Crop Garden illustrates how the O'odham added irrigated agriculture to foods gathered in the wild. In season you'll see varieties of native beans, squash, corn, amaranth, and cotton. Devil's claw, used to make the black design in basketry, is also cultivated there. It is surrounded by an ocotillo fence—traditional except for chicken wire—which was used to keep animals out.

Close to the garden is a replica of an *olas ki* (home to use in rainy or cold weather), *vato* (ramada), and brush kitchen. The climate permitted the O'odham to live most of their lives outside, and a visit to these structures show how practical they were. If you visit on a hot day, you'll better understand the workings of natural air-conditioning.

As you reach the mid-point of the trail, you'll reach the Mesquite Bosque. These small forests were common on the desert before ground and surface water began to be managed by settlers. Mesquite provided food, medicine, dyes, and building materials to native desert people. Near the bosque you can pound mesquite beans to flour with a mesquite pestle in a metate. This is only one of the ways the beans were processed, stored, and eaten.

The rest of this side trail illustrates Spanish and other influences that affected all Arizona natives. Before you leave the mesquite area, take in the view of Hole-in-the-Rock, the nearby butte, and the beautiful desert that still is home to the Gila and Salt River O'odham.

If you decide to add a visit to the Phoenix Zoo (located in Papago Park; (602) 273-1341; www.phoenixzoo.org), its Arizona Trail exhibit offers you a look at the desert's creatures. Like us, the O'odham had (and still have) a healthy respect for Gila monsters, poisonous spiders, scorpions, and rattlesnakes with whom they share the desert. You can see them all behind glass and imagine why the O'odham narrated their most significant legends only during the winter, when snakes hibernate. "The snakes are out!" dictated that only short versions of cultural stories be told, if any.

Pueblo Grande Museum and Archaeological Park

4619 E. Washington St. • (602) 945-0901
www.ci.phoenix.az.us/PARKS/pueblo.html
Open: 9 a.m.–4:45 p.m.; Sunday 1 p.m.–4:45 p.m.

When the Hohokam lived in the Valley, Papago Park would have overlooked the large settlement of Pueblo Grande, where perhaps 1,000 people resided. The people who lived here controlled the headwaters of 19 canals—more than 600 irrigated miles—that served villages as far as 20 miles away. Other settlements such as Snaketown, Mesa Grande, and Pueblo Blanco rose in the area between 450 and 1450, later to be abandoned and dissolve back into desert. The reasons people moved away are still not understood, although severe drought is suspected to be the cause.

Pueblo Grande Museum and Archaeological Park preserves a platform mound, dwellings, and canal channels. Modern canals shown were developed from the footprint of those built by the Hohokam.

Part of a reconstructed Hohokam work compound at
Pueblo Grande Archaeological Park in Phoenix.

The museum is built around Pueblo Grande, an 800-year-old site built on a platform mound situated to oversee the canals. It has been excavated and stabilized so that visitors can learn about its archaeology and imagine a time when such elaborate constructions extended up and down the river.

Permanent exhibits display replicas of Hohokam homes and artifacts such as implements and woven cloth that explain lifeways. A map of the Salt River and the ancient irrigation system related to it illustrates the extent and sophistication of Hohokam engineering, which was implemented without the benefit of the wheel, metal tools, pumping, or domesticated animals.

The intrepid explorer can take a guided tour to the Park of Four Waters, an unimproved field behind the museum where the remains of two original canals are visible. The even more intrepid traveler can call Pueblo Grande to schedule participation in one of their monthly hikes to petroglyph sites in the area.

Above: These Pima baskets incorporate a design popularly called "the Man in the Maze." It pictures Elder Brother, the Creator, and humans' mazelike journey to their final home.

Left: Pee Posh (Maricopa) artists Ida Redbird and Mary Juan created these classic red-on-black bowls in the 1920s and '30s. Water motifs recall the Colorado River roots of the Pee Posh.

Bottom: The Akimel O'odham tradition of finely woven basketry typically uses willow or cottonwood with black Devil's Claw designs.

Heard Museum

2301 N. Central Ave. • (602) 252-8848; Events: (602) 251-0255
www.heard.org • Open: Daily 9:30 a.m.–5 p.m.; Closed: Major holidays

This museum is the place to start for all the tribes. It introduces you to fine examples of Native arts and crafts from ancient to contemporary (see p. 91). It also provides a living perspective on Indian communities today.

Casa Grande Ruins National Monument

1110 Ruins Dr., Coolidge • (520) 723-3172 • www.nps.gov/cagr/
Open: 8 a.m.–5 p.m.; Closed: December 25 • From I-10, take Exit 185 or 194
and follow signs toward Coolidge and the park entrance.

The monument (it's not in the town of Casa Grande) received its name Great House from early Spanish explorers. It retains an ancestral significance to the O'odham and provides inspiration for the architecture of both the Huhugam Heritage Center (see p. 41) and Sheraton Wild Horse Pass Resort (see p. 42).

The remaining walls of an important prehistoric compound surround Casa Grande itself. Now under a protective roof, the Great House is the largest structure known to have been built by the Hohokam. It probably served as both a ceremonial and defensive center for this village and numerous other settlements that lie scattered around the area, unexcavated. Since the entire area was inhabited for at least 10,000 years, artifacts surface with every well, sewer, and new development. The Wal-Mart across from the monument had to shift its planned location three times to accommodate archaeological finds. At its height, circa 1300, 3,000 to 5,000 people probably lived here.

Besides the Great House, some of the features interpreted there include an Aztec-type ball court; openings in walls that align with the sun and moon, perhaps serving as a calendar for the planting and ceremonial year; and the remains of canals and platform mounds.

The architectural design of Wild Horse Pass Resort on the Gila River reservation is patterned after Casa Grande National Monument.

Casa Grande was the nation's first archaeological preserve and displays artifacts and visuals that enhance guided and self-guided tours. Rangers and volunteers are very well informed. A conversation with staff who know the site intimately brings the past to life.

Gila River Arts and Crafts Center

(480) 963-3981 • www.gilaindiancenter.com • Open: Daily 8 a.m.–5 p.m.
Drive about 30 miles southeast from Phoenix on I-10. Go west at Exit 175.
The Center is a white building visible on your right.

The Center is overshadowed by the new Huhugam Heritage Center (opposite), but it's still the place to try a Pima taco. The fry bread and beans are the best (the menu offers many other items as well). The restaurant is a favorite of people from the nearby reservation villages.

The staff is friendly and helpful, and can arrange basket-weaving and pottery-making demonstrations as well as guided tours; just be sure to give them advance notice.

The adjacent park whose purpose is to exhibit examples of traditional native building unfortunately is not currently well maintained. Away from the Center itself you will often find independent roadside dealers of Indian goods, many of which are neither O'odham nor high quality.

Sacaton

Drive about 30 miles southeast from Phoenix on I-10.
Follow signs east from Exit 175.

This is the administrative center of the Gila River Community. Although the village is primarily residential, two public parks honoring military heroes are open to visitors.

To reach Casa Grande Ruins via Sacaton, follow signs to town and then to AZ 87. You will pass fields of cotton, alfalfa, and wheat, testimony to how the irrigated and fertilized desert can produce abundant crops. These fields lie upstream from where the once-flowing Gila left fertile floodplains.

Blackwater Trading Post and Museum

2666 W. Hwy. 87, Coolidge • (520) 923-5516 • Open: Variable hours
Take I-10 east from Phoenix to Exit 185. Follow AZ 387 east to its junction with AZ 87 and turn right (southeast). Casa Grande Ruins National Monument is 3 miles east of the trading post.

The trading post sells practical items like rope, tack, and groceries, but also maintains an informal exhibit of pottery, baskets, arrow and spear points, and other historic and prehistoric artifacts gathered over the years by private individuals. Some are older and rarer than those displayed at the national monument. You have to stop in to ask for a tour, as the museum is locked behind a gate inside the store. Across the road you will see a large agricultural operation owned by the Gila River Community.

Him-Dak EcoMuseum

(520) 568-9480 • Open: Weekdays 9 a.m.–5 p.m. • Take I-10 east from Phoenix to Exit 164. Head south on AZ 347. At the junction of Maricopa and Farrell Roads south of the town of Maricopa, drive 1.8 miles west.

Ak-Chin Community created this small museum to display tribal crafts and photographs and to tell the community its story.

Huhugam Heritage Center

4759 N. Maricopa Rd. • (520) 796-3500
www.Huhugam.com • Open: Call or check the website to confirm times that the museum is open to the public. • Take I-10 east from Phoenix to Exit 164. The museum is visible on your right (north).

Every detail of the Heritage Center was overseen by the Gila River tribal administration. The result is a thoroughly contemporary building that seems to rise naturally out of its desert site. As an institution, it fills a very tall order: it brings together all the traditional requirements of an Akimel O'odham (Pima) and Pee Posh (Maricopa) community gathering and sharing place in one state-of-the-art museum facility, connecting the distant past to the peoples of the Gila and Salt River Communities today. It tells stories through architecture, mural art, exhibitions, collections, and educational programs. From its immense east-facing façade—bermed terraces, a gabion wall reminiscent of hillside agricultural fields, concrete colored like rammed earth—to communal kitchen ramadas interpreted in steel and stucco, an ethnobotanical garden, and references in line and symbol to the Casa Grande compound, this building creates a unique sense of place and people.

Besides providing a site for community activity, the Center honors its predecessors on the land, the Huhugam (Hohokam), serving as a local repository for preserving and studying archaeological and ethnological artifacts. It will hold collections related to the construction of the huge Central Arizona Project (CAP), Snaketown, and other past, current, and future excavations in the area.

Whether or not you plan to visit Casa Grande Ruins (see p. 39), experience the Great Room Gallery, which reflects the design and scale of the original ceremonial

The interior wall of Gila River's Huhugam Heritage Center is reminiscent of the people's terraced farms.

structure. Its architecture recreates a sense of awe that the Hohokam people must have felt when it stood as the center of their part of the world. From the top level, the entire community is visible.

Sheraton Wild Horse Pass Resort

5594 Wild Horse Pass Blvd., Gila River Indian Community, Phoenix (602) 225-0100 • www.sheraton.com/wildhorsepass • Visitors not staying at the hotel may call to make reservations for a cultural tour. • Take I-10 to Exit 162. Follow signs to the resort and spa, not the casino or golf course.

Horses roam the wild desert between the Sierra Estrella and South Mountains within the Gila River Indian Community.

This resort offers a unique kind of cultural experience. A Starwood-managed property owned by the Gila River Community, it showcases the culture of the Pima and Maricopa people in a beautiful, comfortable setting situated on the reservation. Every aspect of the hotel, spa, and grounds was overseen by the Gila River Community. A casino that financed this undertaking is next to (but is completely separate from) the resort.

Besides framing a view of Arizona's legendary sunsets in the V-shaped pass between the Estrella and South Mountains, wild horses roam the unspoiled desert around Wild Horse Pass Resort. These natural assets enhance a very creative experience produced to allow visitors to become acquainted with the River People. Glass cases display authentic cultural icons. References to O'odham traditions are integrated throughout in the architecture, which was patterned on Casa Grande, and interior design, including carpet specially woven in traditional basketry patterns; sconces that resemble devil's claw, a plant used in basketmaking; carved doors with customized hardware; and sheets woven in traditional designs. Signage is in English, O'odham, and Maricopa, and even the food and music take cues from the culture.

The more closely you pay attention to subtle details, the more you will appreciate the cultural experience. Tours are offered daily to guests of the hotel and to visitors. They explain and draw attention to these details, which include themed rooms that recall Pima and Maricopa symbols and legends; displays of seed jars, basketry, antique harvesting tools, and ceremonial objects; paintings, photography, textile pieces, and murals by select Gila River artists; and ceilings reminiscent of traditional willow and mesquite structures. A replica of an *olas ki* home stands near the pool.

A short distance down the miniature river created to recall the Gila of old is a spa called *Aji*, the Pima word used to designate the lone mountains where women and children retreated in times of trouble. A mosaic ceiling dome at its entrance portrays sunrise as one enters and sunset as one departs. It features art illustrating the Pima creation story and ironwork murals of other spiritual legends. Treatments include some influenced by O'odham ethnobotany.

Across the stream from the spa, the Whirlwind Golf Club's courses meander across the desertlike rivers of grass. The Devil's Claw course (or its description) provides an education in Pima/Maricopa culture, since each hole is named for a legend or landmark. The sixth hole, for instance, is "The Home of the Wind." It faces the Estrella Mountains, the legendary source of whirlwinds, or dust devils. The Cattail course features water and deep canyons and reflects the landforms of the area. Both have hosted PGA tour events. Visitors can view the golf courses from small boats that ply the hotel's little river.

The creative traveler will engage appropriate staff in conversation to hear more about the community and its history. Besides the cultural theme manager and guides, Native greeters are often available in the resort lobby. Boatmen are also generally community members, as well.

The active traveler can ride out by horseback from the resort's Equestrian Center. Not only is the open desert scenic, but it's the best way to happen upon the wild horse herd.

A miniature desert river reminiscent of the Gila runs through Wild Horse Pass Resort on the Gila River Reservation.

Hoo-hoogam Ki Museum

10005 E. Osborn Rd., Salt River Pima-Maricopa Indian Community
(480) 850-8190 • www.azcama/museums/hoohoogam.htm
Open: Weekdays 9:30 a.m.–4 p.m. • Follow Osborn Rd. east from Scottsdale.

Museums in which native people tell their own stories remind us that the history and culture of indigenous people is an ongoing, contemporary matter. Often they are oriented toward teaching the younger members of the community about their people. At Hoo-hoogam Ki, visitors and community members alike can see artifacts that recall the roots of today's Pima/Maricopa people. The museum also preserves artifacts from Hohokam settlements in and near the Salt River Community, where it is located. In addition, photographs and artifacts document historical events, including the disappearance of the perennial rivers; farming traditions; and Pima-Maricopa involvement in U.S. military action over the years.

The building itself is patterned after traditional structures, combining contemporary elements with desert woods and adobe. Display cases exhibit reminders of desert river days: pots, practical and plain; baskets whose edges are scarred with use; *manos* (stone implements) worn smooth by hands that ground seeds and corn with them; wooden tools for gathering and processing cactus fruit. Traditional dress is shown. Legends passed down through flood and drought, war and peace, are preserved by storytellers on videotape. A small gift shop offers good-quality baskets, Maricopa pottery, and other items for sale.

In and Around Tucson

Arizona-Sonora Desert Museum

2021 N. Kinney Rd. • (520) 883-2702 • www.desertmuseum.org
Open: 8:30 a.m.–5 p.m., October–February; 7:30 a.m.–5 p.m., March–September
The museum is in Tucson Mountain Park, 14 miles west of Tucson. A scenic route
takes Speedway Blvd. west across Gates Pass. Because this route is steep, large
RVs and trailer-rigs must take I-10 to I-19 south, exiting on Ajo Way and turning
north on Kinney Rd. Conservative drivers might do the same.

The nature of the Tohono O'odham reservation near Tucson is difficult to grasp at a glance. A good scenic overview is available from the Museum. Its exhibits are excellent, too, as are its restaurants. The museum overlooks a huge expanse of Sonoran desert, some parts more arid than others, punctuated by rugged mountains. Tall saguaro cacti punctuate their flanks like giant exclamation points. The narrow route to the Desert Museum through Gates Pass winds through places that will teach you much about the lands the Tohono O'odham have inhabited since their beginnings.

Kitt Peak National Observatory

(520) 318-8726 • www.noao.edu/kpno/
Open: Daily 9 a.m.–4 p.m.; Closed: January 1, Thanksgiving, and December 25
Take I-19 south from Tucson and exit on Ajo Way (AZ 86). Turn left on AZ 386
to Kitt Peak. The trip takes about 90 minutes and climbs to the top of the
6,875-foot peak.

Located atop a 6,800-foot mountain on reservation land, the observatory offers a lofty view of Tohono O'odham country. The highest point on the horizon is the sacred mountain of Baboquivari (*bah-bo-KIV-aree*). At nearly 8,000 feet, its ascent is not only impossible without technical equipment but strongly discouraged by tribal officials. However, a picnic ground and camp on its slopes are open to the public with a paid permit from the Baboquivari District office. The gift shop at Kitt Peak offers Tohono O'odham basketry and crafts.

Baboquivari Peak

(520) 383-2236, District Office (handles fees and permits)
Take I-19 south from Tucson. Exit on Ajo Way (AZ 86). Follow it to Sells and
turn south toward Topawa. At a sign marking the way to the park, turn left and
follow a dirt road 10 miles to a fork. Go right and proceed to the campground.

See the preceding Kitt Peak National Observatory entry.

Opposite: Baboquivari Peak rises majestically
above the Sonoran desert.

Driving on the Tohono O'odham Reservation

The adventurous, very interested traveler can visit Sells, the Tohono O'odham Nation's government center. It is more village than town. A wandering cow or horse may cross your path. You won't pass much that's familiar (no fast food), but you will get an idea how the Desert People live. Traditional ocotillo fences and vatos (ramadas) stand comfortably beside newer housing. You will see a handsome church and visit the Tohono O'odham Community Action office near the tribal government buildings. That is the best place to see authentic arts and crafts and ask questions of the staff. It's a tiny building next to the parking lot where vendors sell food for lunch (including Chinese). Usually the Papago Café is open for lunch, but sometimes not. Some roads off AZ 86 are paved, some aren't. *You will not find a public restroom.*

Unless you plan to cross the reservation on route 86 to Ajo, Sells is as far as you should go. *Only those who know the territory or are guided by someone who knows it can safely venture out to explore side roads.* Routes to the smaller villages are often unpaved and all roads become impassable when it rains. There are no gas stations, restaurants, water, or restrooms, and few passing vehicles. Your cell phone won't work and car problems in the desert, especially in the heat of the summer, mean big trouble. Breathtaking as it is, this is a land better suited to those who have the benefit of generations of knowledge than to strangers.

A cowboy's skills are still important to cattle owners on O'odham Indian lands.

That said, some features of the lifestyle of the people whose homes lie far out on the desert include:

• **Churches:** These are small and were constructed in nearly every village by the Franciscans in the early part of the twentieth century. Church exteriors are generally a similar Mission Revival style, simple white stucco with a bell tower and scalloped roofline centered by a cross. Their interiors, however, take on the personality of the village. Many don't have pews, since feasts and processions take place on the plaza in front. Altars and stations of the cross are unique to each church. A wide variety of icons, *milagros,* candles, devotional objects, framed photographs, seasonal arrangements, and an array of objects significant to those who placed them there decorate the altars. There may be a likeness of Saint Francis, often dressed in specially sewn robes and vestments. Processions held on feast days circle a field cross placed across the plaza in front of the church. A priest may visit weekly. They are not open to the casual visitor.

• **Houses:** Housing ranges from contemporary homes to "sandwich" houses of adobe layered with desert woods. These were encouraged by the U.S. government to speed acculturation when the O'odham continued to live in traditional brush shelters well into modern times. Many villages do not have plumbing or electricity. They represent the *ranchería* type of settlement pattern: houses are spread apart, with no central orientation.

The field cross at classic white mission churches in most O'odham villages defines holy ground and marks the path of religious processions.

• **Shrines:** There are several types to be seen. Some date back to the time of myth, while others memorialize a vow, prayer, a highway death, or pay homage to the *Virgen de Guadalupe,* patron of Mexico and Indian Mesoamerica.

Roadside shrines are built by family groups or individuals. Although they may seem rooted in Catholicism, they are not associated with the Church. Constructed of rock, adobe, or other available materials and decorated with a cross and brightly colored artificial flowers, they serve as places for their creators or passersby to pray. Those who stop sometimes leave notes, gifts, or other mementos.

Along an unpaved road in the desert, one will occasionally come to an elaborate grotto in a rock formation or beside a mountain, furnished with an altar, a statue of the Virgin or a saint, and adorned with religious images and objects. Food preparation, feast ramadas, and decorations left from previous celebrations attest to their use.

Many families maintain a shrine in or just outside their homes. A small structure may protect the altar if it is outdoors.

Ancient shrines used for generations also exist in out-of-the-way places. The Children's Shrine, off-limits to outsiders, recalls a particularly poignant time when a badger (taboo to the Tohono O'odham) took revenge for being attacked by causing water to pour out of a hole it dug in a riverbed. Water

Personal and family shrines are the site of gatherings to celebrate religious occasions. This one was created in a rock outcropping on Tohono O'odham lands. There are often cooking and eating ramadas nearby.

roared out until the land appeared to be in danger of flooding. After unsuccessful attempts to placate the badger, medicine men decided that the people had to sacrifice four of their most beautiful children. Two boys and two girls were chosen and dressed ceremonially, taken to the hole, and slowly lowered into it. As they descended, the water subsided, until the children and the water disappeared. A flat rock and other stones were placed on the spot. Some say that after the sacrifice, the Creator l'itoi took the children to see the world they saved. The Children's Shrine is regularly maintained, and the Flood Children remembered. Those who pray there, as at other shrines, leave offerings that range from personal objects to toys and religious symbols.

I'itoi's Cave on Baboquivari Mountain also serves as a shrine. I'itoi is the Creator in the Tohono O'odham way (he is called Se'ehe by the Pima, and has a home in the South Mountains of Phoenix). Long, long ago he was killed, but came back in the guise of a little old man. He is called upon to help in extreme situations. He was responsible for the plot that killed Ho'ok, the witch who carried off little children, and for the slaying of a monster that threatened the O'odham people.

• **Burial Grounds:** Along the roads lie a few burial grounds, which poignantly combine the old and the new. While many graves are marked with simple white crosses and decorated with the same bright artificial flowers and candles used to adorn shrines, some reflect the traditional style of burial. The grave is defined by rectangular piles of rocks topped with weathered desert wood. Grave markers may or may not include the name of the deceased. The communities are sufficiently close-knit that identification isn't necessary.

Mission San Xavier del Bac

1950 E. San Xavier Road • (520) 294-2624; (520) 294-5727 for special events www.sanxaviermission.org • Open: Daily 8 a.m.–5 p.m. • Take I-19 south to Exit 92, San Xavier Road. Turn right (west) onto W. San Xavier Rd., then right (north) on S. Little Nogales Dr., and right again to the San Xavier Mission parking lot.

The extravagant façade of San Xavier (often pronounced *hah-VEER*), surrounded by the desert, astonishes first-time visitors. And if the Colonial Spanish exterior seems unlikely, the interior will take your breath away. Restored between 1992 and 1997 by an international team of conservators, each detail stands as a testimony to the importance of the beliefs it represents.

The mission, founded originally by Jesuit Father Eusebio Kino in 1692 and replaced between 1783 and 1797 by Franciscans, is still the parish church of Wa:ik, or Bac.

The art that is so lovingly cared for dramatically tells the entire story of Christianity, from the Old Testament to the Roman Papacy. It is meant to teach and the quality of its art work conveys as much as the stories it represents. No expense was spared. Mexican artists were brought to adorn the walls and façade. Hundreds of statues (among them, 182 angels and at least 100 saints) were also imported from Mexican guild workshops. Specialists called *encarnaderos* created lifelike faces and hands. Experts dressed them realistically. Sculptures and paintings were finished with precious pigments of jewel-like colors enhanced with gold.

Take time to see every nook and corner. Read *San Xavier: the Spirit Endures*, by Kathleen Walker; or go to the library and find the October 2002 issue of *Arizona Highways*, which contains an article written by expert Bernard Fontana and illustrated with specially lighted post-restoration photographs. Preparing will be time well spent.

Mission San Xavier del Bac is still the parish church for the village of Wa:ik, or Bac.

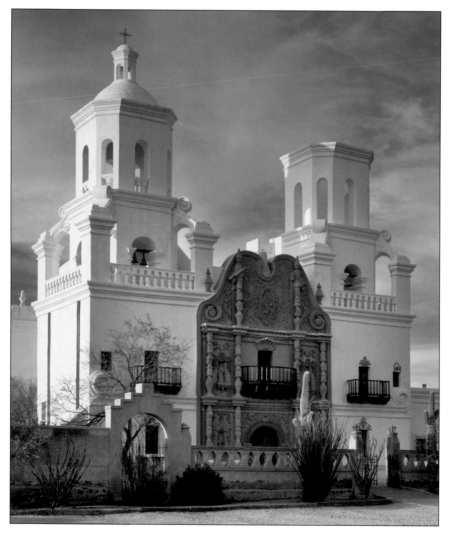

Tumacacori National Historic Park

(520) 398-2341 • www.nps.gov/tuma/ • Open: Daily 8 a.m.–5 p.m.
Take I-19 south to Tumacacori, about 45 miles from Tucson.
Follow signs to the park.

The park preserves the ruins of three early Spanish missions. The oldest and best preserved, San Jose de Tumacacori, was built on the site of an O'odham village. Apache attacks drove them away, but the villagers took some of their most revered religious objects to San Xavier when they left. A fiesta held in December celebrates all the cultures that have come together here.

Arizona State Museum

1013 E. University Blvd., Tucson • (520) 621-6302
www.statemuseum.arizona.edu • Open: Monday–Saturday, 10 a.m.–5 p.m.,
Sunday, noon–5 p.m.
    Parking is available in a garage on the southeast corner of E. 2nd St. and N. Euclid. This museum is near the Arizona Historical Society Museum, so be sure you're at the right one.

This museum, located on the campus of the University of Arizona, focuses on indigenous cultures of the Southwest and northern Mexico. A permanent exhibit, "Paths of Life: American Indians of the Southwest and Northern Mexico," succinctly interprets significant aspects of the cultures of the O'odham, among other groups. Maps, chronologies, and cultural icons such as half-gourd masks for the traditional rain dance, a calendar stick, and an unusual figure of a Nawiju Clown (which the uninitiated would take for a Hopi katsina) are displayed.

    A museum shop and Native Goods Gallery, where original works by Native artists selected for their excellence (some distinctly non-traditional) sells trustworthy arts and crafts. The University of Arizona published an excellent exhibit-related book, *Paths of Life: American Indians of the Southwest and Northern Mexico* in 1996. It is worth finding.

Piecing Together Traditions

The museum's online exhibit titled "Portraits of Cloth: Tohono O'odham Quilts of Goldie Richmond" is a must-see for an insightful, charming overview of that community's life. Visit it at www.statemuseum.arizona.edu/exhibits/goldie/papagolife.shtml.

    Each section of the 30-block quilt created by Goldie, a trader on the reservation for many years, illustrates a traditional activity or an image of daily life. Selecting one brings up an enlarged image of the block paired with a historic photograph of the subject on which she focused.

Hiking

The outdoor enthusiast may well be inspired by the beautiful desert mountains to take a hike. This isn't possible on the spur of the moment, since all the communities and districts require a permit for such activities. (Unfortunately, others have defaced petroglyphs, removed artifacts, built fires, and otherwise made permitting a necessity.) The following areas are near O'odham lands but are open to the public for hiking, walking, picnics, or simple enjoyment of the desert.

South Mountain Park

10919 S. Central Ave., Phoenix • (602) 534-6324
http://phoenix.gov/PARKS (for map and trail guide) • Open: All year

For a great view of the Gila River's former channel and of the reservation, visit Phoenix's 16,000-acre South Mountain Park and hike the Alta Trail from its endpoint to the nearest peak.

Saguaro National Park

2700 N. Kinney Rd., Tucson • (520) 733-5100
www.saguaro.national-park.com; www.desertusa.com
Open: Daily 8:30 a.m.–5 p.m.; Closed: Thanksgiving and December 25

Saguaro (*suh-WAHR-oh*) offers an up-close desert experience. The parks—for there are east and west sections with separate visitor centers—offer an opportunity to experience the Desert People's desert. Saguaro cactus, whose giant humanoid forms and delicious fruits have made them a cultural symbol of the O'odham, can be seen by the hundreds in both sections of this park. Scenic drives, short nature trails, and 150 miles of all levels of hiking trails bring as much of the desert to you as you'd like to experience. All the services you expect of a national park are available.

Dining and Overnight Accommodations

Most visitors to these reservations will stay in one of the big cities, where lodging and dining are not in short supply. All of these reservations have casinos, most with dining and lodging.

Shopping

Basketry expresses the soul of the O'odham people best. While the Pee Posh (Maricopa) are more identified with pottery, both Pima and Tohono O'odham learned everything there was to know about baskets. Mary Paganelli, a writer who works with Tohono O'odham Community Action, explains:

> The history of Tohono O'odham basketry combines utility, ceremony, trade, and artistry. In O'odham culture, basketry traditions and techniques are passed on from one generation to another. When a weaver makes her first basket, she presents it to her teacher in an intimate exchange, thanking her for teaching her this wonderful skill.

> Tohono O'odham baskets are handmade, using the native plants of the Sonoran Desert. No dyes are used and weavers rely solely on the natural colors of desert plants. Collecting basketry materials is a family affair. Generations gather to collect desert willow, cattail, white and green yucca, black devil's claw, and red banana yucca, the fibers that form the foundation of their highly collectible baskets. Gathering, growing, and preparing these natural fibers requires respect for and knowledge of the natural world. Before a weaver places the first stitch, she has to spend countless hours harvesting and preparing her materials.

> Generations ago, making baskets was not only an art but a necessity. Baskets were used for cooking, harvesting, and even carrying water. The Tohono O'odham are renowned for their finely woven baskets, their bold designs and patterns that reflect the natural world around them. Special baskets were also used for traditional ceremonies, dances, and stories.

> In the O'odham language, there is no word for "art." Instead, they have always created artful ways of living, blending beauty and usefulness. Weavers try to live in ways that bring together the material, spiritual, and aesthetic worlds. In basketry, beauty and utility are joined together. Some call it art. Most basketweavers simply call it life.

> The work of a few artists is for sale through retail outlets. Although some still work in clay and others paint, photograph, or use textiles as their medium, sellers are primarily basketmakers, including makers of distinctive wire baskets that are typical of the Tohono O'odham.

• **Wiwpul Du'ag Trading** is a good source and its prices are excellent. It is located at AZ 86, Mile Marker 140, telephone (520) 383-5555.

• **Kitt Peak's Gift Shop** offers some authentic baskets and other items.

• **Tohono O'odham Community Action Center** (TOCA) in Sells has baskets as well as small carved and modeled figures from traditional dances. The shop is open Monday–Friday from 10 a.m. to 5 p.m., or by appointment. You can also buy through the nonprofit **Tohono O'odham Basketry Cooperative** (TOBO) online at www.tocaonline.org.

• **Arizona Museum of History's** gift shop and the **Native Seeds/SEARCH** store at 526 North Fourth Avenue, both in Tucson, carry both baskets and native food items. The **Heard Museum** in Phoenix is also an excellent source.

• For a changing exhibit of crafts, check www.casinoaz.com/arts.asp.

Recurring Events

• **Tribal Fair and Rodeo** *Mul Chu Tha:* Parade, dances, all-Indian rodeo, food, arts and crafts; Sacaton (January or February)

• **O'odham Tash:** Casa Grande "Indian Days" (February)

• **Tohono O'odham Nation Rodeo and Fair:** Sells (February)

• **Iwo Jima Landing Anniversary Celebration:** Sacaton (February)

• **St. John's Indian Mission Festival:** Dances, foods, arts and crafts (first Sunday in March)

• **Waila Festival:** University of Arizona, Tucson (May)

• **Russell Moore Music Fest:** To honor big-band legend Russell "Big Chief" Moore; Sacaton (October)

• **Tohono O'odham Pumpkin Patch Fest** (October)

• **Pima Maricopa Arts Festival** (November)

• The Heard Museum and Tohono O'odham Community Action organize **basketweaving shows** annually. Check with them for dates.

Planting and harvesting bring Tohono O'odham community members of all ages together.

Native Voices, Native Lives: Noland Johnson

Noland Johnson is a Tohono O'odham farmer. He works the land that his grandfather farmed in the 1930s—land that had lain fallow for 50 years until he and a unique nonprofit organization called Tohono O'odham Community Action (TOCA) brought it back to life.

Noland Johnson is keeping alive a long-standing tradition of farming which was almost lost to his community. Many generations ago, the Tohono O'odham farmed and harvested wild foods from their desert lands. In harmony with the seasons, they harvested wild foods like amaranth, saguaro fruit, mesquite beans, prickly pears, and cholla buds, and harnessed monsoon rains with an intricate damming system to water crops like the drought-resistant tepary bean and a fast-growing 60-day corn. Not only were these foods delicious, they were—and are—vital to the health of the O'odham people.

As recently as 1960, Type II diabetes was unknown among the Tohono O'odham. Today more than 60 percent of the population suffers from the disease—the highest rate in the world. Doctors, epidemiologists, and nutritionists have demonstrated that this high rate of diabetes is partly the result of a move from a healthy and traditional diet to a "fast food" diet. Scientists are learning that desert foods have special properties which prevent this devastating disease.

Like many of his generation, Johnson, 30, had completely lost touch with the land and his own agricultural traditions. Although his ancestors were farmers, he had never worked on a farm. But thanks to TOCA's Food Systems Project, which encourages youth to reconnect with their O'odham himdag (Desert Peoples' Way), Johnson learned from the ground up. He consulted with community elders, worked hard hand-planting and hand-harvesting the first crops, and learned the many ceremonial songs and dances that are an integral part of farming in the O'odham culture.

Today the farm is booming. There are acres of white and brown tepary beans, tall stands of 60-day corn, and plots of O'odham squash and melons. Through Johnson's efforts and personal commitment, TOCA has provided tepary beans (once a food staple of the O'odham) to local markets, schools, hospitals, clinics, and elder centers. In addition, TOCA has been instrumental in reinvigorating food-related traditions, including the rain ceremony and the harvesting of saguaro fruit, cholla buds, wild spinach, and acorns.

Johnson is proud of his achievement. He has embraced his past and is helping his community get back on a path to wellness and self-sufficiency.

—Mary Paganelli

Yo'emem: The Yaqui

"The ones that first appeared here, they left this inheritance....Then the Baptized People received it ....Like this, now, it is continued in the songs.... This is cherished and respected. This is all the truth you asked for. Like this it stays in your hands."

—Loretta Salvatierra, in *Yaqui Deer Songs/Maso Bwikam: A Native American Poetry*

Painted wooden masks are worn by pascolas, who amuse participants at religious occasions while reminding them of Yaqui stories and symbols.

Introduction to Yaqui Culture

Yaqui people call themselves Yo'emem, the People. Pascua Yaqui, a Spanish version of their name used by Arizona Yaquis, means the Easter People, reflecting how thoroughly religion pervades Yaqui culture.

Creation Story

From the beginning, the Yo'emem evolved in a close, protective relationship with their creator. He guided them from the beginning when all creatures lived in the ocean through the days of the *sureni*, the ancestors—small and gentle humans who were privileged to come from the sea to live on earth. In those days their land was generous, a flower-filled garden of peace and harmony.

Then one day a miraculous tree spoke through the daughter of Flower Woman, prophesying the advent of Christianity and warning of approaching violence and disorder. It told of the coming of savage invaders. Some sureni were forced to grow larger and learn to fight to the death in order to protect the land that was given to them. They organized families into larger groups necessary to defend themselves. They are today's Yaqui (or *Hiaki*). Scholars say they had accomplished this restructuring by the early 1400s.

Enduring Lifeways

Their beloved land lay around the Yaqui River in what is now Sonora, Mexico. It extended to the coast of the Gulf of California and north past the Gila River, and included some of the most fertile land in that part of Mexico and California. Since perhaps AD 500, this was the region where they hunted game, gathered wild foods, and cultivated corn, beans, and squash. It was blessed with abundant water and year-round warmth. From this place, they traveled to trade desert foods, salt, shells, and furs with the Pueblo and Plains people to the north and with the Aztec and Toltec to the south.

The Language of Flowers

The Yaqui word *sewa*, or *seye*, or *seya*, literally translated, means flower. Flowers are incorporated into so many concepts, however, that even a figurative definition as the symbol of divine grace is inadequate. It means the labor people perform as they participate in religious ceremonies and the blessings that accrue to their dedicated work. Its meaning even extends to the regalia they wear during their service.

Seya aniya is the flower world in which the supernatural deer lives under the dawn, along with the remaining *sureni*, or ancient, unbaptized ones. That world is the source of the deer's music. He is called *sewa yoleme*, flower person, in his songs.

Seyewalio describes the elusive quality of the seya aniya. *Sewa yotume*, growing flower, is an image of the rising sun. *Seyatakaa*, flower body, is a special spiritual power possessed only by certain people, who have it at birth.

Dancing on the Trail of Time

The Deer Dance is perhaps the best known expression of Yaqui culture. The dance and its songs (of which there are more than 300) are ancient. They originated as a way to ask the deer's permission to be hunted and killed. It is likely that the dancer's regalia began as a way to unite the hunter and the hunted.

The dancer's headdress features the head of a deer decorated in red, the color of flowers. His movements mimic the grace and alertness of a deer. Singers sing his ancient song in an archaic form of the Yaqui language, the water drum beats to the beat of his heart, and raspers imitate his breathing. Deer hoof rattles decorate his belt, cocoons click on his ankles like dried grasses beneath his feet. During the long form of the dance he grows from fawn to adult, is hunted, and dies.

Although he dances on other occasions, it is essential that the Deer Dancer participate in Easter season ceremonies. He helps repel the Enemies of Jesus at the church entrance. Always, he represents the amazing, flower-filled world that grew from the blood of Christ's wounds as he hung on the Cross. He also connects the ancient wisdom of nature with the moment. Along with the *pascolas,* the deer creates an environment in which Saint Bullfrog, Saint Horned Toad, Saint Turtle, and Saint Lizard are not forgotten in the Yaquis' ritual performances.

A Deer Dancer and *pahkola* (pascola) dance during an all-night religious occasion.

Foreign Contact

The Yaqui in Mexico were prepared when the first Spaniards came in 1533, trailing behind them the devastation of native people in Michoacán, Jalisco, Zacatecas, and Nayarit. A force of 7,000 men met the soldiers. Violence indeed ensued, as the tree predicted. At the first encounter, a Yaqui leader dressed in pearl-adorned black drew a line on the earth and told the soldiers to stay on the other side of it. They crossed and were defeated. Even when the Mayo and the Lower Pima Indians joined the Spanish as allies, the Yaqui prevailed. They were not as fortunate in resisting new diseases. Measles and smallpox took an enormous toll.

Meanwhile, Jesuit priests arrived from Europe and converted many of the related Mayo to Christianity. Observing the priests' concern for native people,

A woman dressed in a traditional filmy skirt stands in front of her church. Its stagelike entrance provides the setting for dramas played out there during Easter season.

the Yaqui invited them to stay in 1617. Thus began a collaborative relationship lasting 125 years which transformed their lives and their religion.

By 1619, Jesuits reported that 30,000 Yaqui had been baptized. For the Yaqui, baptism signified a metamorphosis beyond the Christian meaning. To be baptized meant to leave the Enchanted World behind and to be subject to death. Salvation for those who chose this path was earned by carrying out a *manda*—a vow to Jesus, Mary, or another holy person. Societies dedicated to such service have developed special roles that are performed on religious occasions throughout the year. In these ways, the Yaqui began to incorporate Christianity into their spiritual lives.

Daily Living

Daily living changed as well. By 1623, the Jesuits had brought the Yaqui, who were used to living in widespread rancherías of earth-covered dwellings, together in eight mission villages about 5 miles apart along the Yaqui River. Each had a church at its center: La Navidad del Senor de *Vikam*, Santa Rosa de *Vahkom*, La Asuncion de Nuestra Senora de *Rahum*, Espiritu Santo at *Ko'okoim*, Santa Barbara de *Wiivisim*, San Ignacio de *Torim*, San Miguel de

---

The Deep Past Meets the Christian Present

A *Pahko* is a religious service held in a Yaqui home. Pahkos are arranged to honor a holy person for help in resolving a difficult situation, for a child's funeral, the anniversary of a death, All Souls' Day, weddings, saints' days, and a number of other occasions. Church groups are invited and everything is prepared as if the home were a church: an altar is built, the path of a procession prepared, and the houseyard cross readied. Food is provided. *Waka vaki,* Yaqui beef stew, is a traditional dish.

The *Pahkome* are the people at whose household a Pahko takes place. They invite men called the *pascolas,* or *pahko'lam* in Yaqui, who perform many roles. A pascola is a keeper of the people's history, which he brings alive through a style of storytelling that helps keep a heavy occasion light. He is a co-host and entertainer at a Pahko.

A pascola wears his hair in a topknot wound with red ribbon, called a flower. His wooden mask is decorated with triangular rays of the sun; small creatures; a Maltese cross-like symbol of the energy of creation; and stars, which represent the home of the ancestors. He is protected from evil by a mother-of-pearl ornament on his necklace. A ritual rattle, sash, bell-adorned belt, and ankle rattles made from the cocoons of silk moths complete his regalia.

Although the pascolas are unrelated to the church, their presence is considered essential. They entertain by clowning around, joking, and dancing animal dances that remind people of their relationship with nature. The symbols they wear refer to mythic times, the plant world, the original villages, and the four directions. Their light-hearted manner of teaching balances the seriousness of the occasion in style, if not content.

Many ceremonies last all night into the morning. Staying for the entire event brings with it the power of spiritual dedication. The pascolas help keep participants involved.

Deep Sea Divers

Yaqui men were known for their skill as pearl divers in Mexico. Their people used pearl and mother-of-pearl as adornment for centuries, so they knew how to find black-lipped oyster shells and tear them free with their bare hands.

They did not always dive willingly for others, however. During the times when Yaquis were used as slave labor, they would be shackled together by night and sent to the pearl beds by day. The work was dangerous. The men's physical strength allowed them to dive down 50 feet or more, holding their breath as they ripped the pearl shells from their beds. Few ordinary men would have survived. Some Yaquis did not.

In the 1800s, capitalistic entrepreneurs employed hundreds of Yaqui pearl-hunters to bring up oysters from the Gulf of California off La Paz and Guaymas, in Mexico. Before the advent of modern equipment, they provided the key to the industry there.

Veenem, and La Santisima Trinidad de *Potam.* Buildings surrounded town plazas and the people set up their dwellings and ramadas nearby. For the first time, the Yaqui went about their daily activities within sight of many others. Their settlements no longer appeared to be seamlessly integrated into the natural world, but took on a separate identity. These eight villages are still considered the sacred homeland.

Before the end of the century, however, their newfound peace began to deteriorate. Silver was discovered in the Yaqui Valley in 1684. Spanish and Mexican miners aggressively claimed it wherever they found it, regardless of who owned the territory. Fertile land invited further incursions by farmers and later *hacendados,* hacienda owners or would-be hacienda owners who resembled feudal lords in their total domination of the people who worked their property. The hacienda economy was based on what the natives had: land and water.

Adding to their loss of control was the increasing authority that the Jesuit organization exercised over the people. When Yaqui leaders Muñi and Bernabé took the people's demands for free elections and respect for land boundaries to local authorities in 1739, the Jesuits had them arrested. This led to the first of a series of revolts and retaliations that lasted into the twentieth century.

Franciscans followed Jesuits, and Mexicans followed Spaniards into power. Around the middle of the 1800s, pressure from Mexican landowners and soldiers intensified. The government employed tactics that ranged from sending troops to "guard" Yaqui pueblos to slavery, execution, and deportation to the Yucatan, Bolivia, Cuba, and the Caribbean. Many Yaqui fled to the mountains or to the United States. Although a peace treaty was signed between the Yaqui people and the Mexican government in 1897, injustices continued. By then, only 4,000 of the perhaps 60,000 who had lived in the Yaqui River region remained.

Labor camps provided homes for Yaquis who came to Phoenix for wage work between the 1920s and '40s. Families often combined the new with the old when constructing their dwellings.

Life in a New Country

The turn of the last century represented a transitional time for the Yaqui. The 1910–1920 Mexican Revolution overturned the heavy-handed government of Porfirio Diaz, whose stated policy was the eradication of the Yaqui. But even without him, chronic conflict led to profound chaos and more families followed those that had already fled to the United States, where they were politically protected as refugees, although few knew it.

Yaquis had inhabited the Gila and Santa Cruz River valleys long before Europeans divided them into two countries. Familiarity with the land itself was far more significant than changing administrative and language boundaries.

By 1900 they had begun to form Guadalupe, near Phoenix. Old Pascua Village, near Tucson, was established a little later, in 1903. Barrio Libre, Pascua Yaqui, and Yoem Pueblo followed.

The Arizona communities continued to provide relatives in Sonora with guns and supplies. As a result, the Arizona Yaqui were the last Indians to fight with the U.S. Cavalry. In 1918 a troop from Fort Huachuca intercepted a group of American Yaqui on their way to help those fighting in Sonora. However, Yaqui encounters with Mexican soldiers continued until 1927. That year, defeat at Cerro del Gallo (Rooster Hill) led to Mexican garrisons being established at all Yaqui pueblos in that country.

Those who escaped turned to wage labor in their new country. Around Phoenix, they provided a work force for the Salt River Valley Water Users Association, which was managing an irrigation system for modern agriculture built on the model of the Hohokam canals. Long experience as farmers in Mexico made the work familiar. Farther south, the Southern Pacific Railroad played a similar role for Yaqui men. Their work often took them far from home. From the 1920s through the labor disputes of the 1930s and 1940s, these two companies employed a large proportion of the wage-earning community. Those who did not work for Salt River or the railroad found employment in agriculture.

Labor camps provided new homes near Phoenix. Some maintained the canals in summer, harvested cotton in fall, and performed other jobs as the seasons made them available. Then came the great wars, in which many Yaqui men served. After the 1950s the people branched out to take other jobs in other places. By this time many were—and continue to be—trilingual, speaking Yaqui (which has borrowed many words from Spanish), Spanish, and English with equal fluency.

Whether in homeland pueblos, labor camps, settlements like Guadalupe, Pascua Yaqui, and Yoem Pueblo, or the urban settings that predominate today, the Yaqui community is bound together by religious ceremony. The church anchors the town physically and the ceremonies performed there strengthen spiritual bonds, especially those conducted during the Easter Season.

Members of Yoem Post 125 of the American Legion are among many Yaqui community members who have proudly served in the U.S. military.

Ceremonial Customs

Modern practices of Yaqui Catholics bear the indelible stamp of ancient history. Long ago, the year was divided into summer and fall, times of rain, growth, and harvest; and winter and spring, months of waiting. A sense of celebration permeated the growing seasons. The fallow months were accompanied by an anxious mood. Echoes of want and plenty, good and evil, creation and destruction are heard as the story of Christ's life, death, and resurrection are re-enacted each Lenten season in every Yaqui community.

Duality prevails in the Lenten dramas. *Matachinim,* men who belong to a society dedicated to the Virgin Mary, dress and dance in ways that represent good. During the year they perform at home-based ritual gatherings, but their essential mission culminates in triumph over the forces of evil on the day before Easter.

Evil and its manifestations are ominously personified by the *kohtumbre ya'ura,* men of "good heart" who perform a different ritual mission. They haunt the streets for 40 days as masked *chapayekas* and aggressive cavalrymen bent on killing Jesus. They frighten children and interfere with church services and personal devotions. Every Friday night during Lent they re-enact their evil pursuits, following the Way of the Cross around the plaza.

On the day before Easter, all the societies, both good and evil, meet at the church entrance. Tension yields to joy as the music of the *Gloria* floats from inside the church and the evildoers are defeated. Jesus lives, and young girls rush out to greet the risen Christ. Masks and ritual weapons that were part of his death are burned. The kohtumbre—*fariseos* and *caballeros*—are received back into the church and forgiven.

The ultimate power to overcome them was given by flowers. The pascola and Deer Dancers were armed with piles of blossoms, greenery, and confetti, which they hurled at the kohtumbre. The Matachin dancers, whose bright-colored headdresses and feathered wands also represent flowers, presented a frightening sight to the Evil Ones. The power of the flowers is enough to destroy negative forces, which disappear for another year.

By the end of the Easter celebration, called *Waehma* in Yaqui, nearly all community members attending have played a role. Ceremonial society members have collected *limosna* (donations). Men and women have performed ritual duties as *maestros* (lay prayer leaders); *cantoras* (women singers); *moros,* event managers who recruit dancers; carriers of the Virgin or a saint; and tenders of the altar. Children in flowered halos have served in the Angel Guard. Men have danced matachin or taken other parts in the dramas of Lent. People have cooked, made and gathered flowers, accompanied the events on the harp, guitar, violin, flute, or drum. No one is simply a bystander.

Next to their vital, uniquely Yaqui religious life, family relationships hold the Yaqui people together today. Although some families dispersed after leaving the Yaqui River, others came together in the same village or community. Along with blood relatives, the people depend on a network of ritual kin that starts with godparents and branches out from there so that a person has multiple mothers, fathers, brothers and sisters, and so on. Many obligations accrue to family life.

Reservation Life

Until the 1960s, the Yaquis' status in the United States was ill-defined. They had not been refugees for generations. They had used the U.S. courts, public health facilities, and other services on many occasions. They attended schools since the 1920s. Were they Mexican immigrants? Were they North American

Holy Ground

A traditional Yaqui church consists of a building with an entrance large enough to accommodate the drama of people and dancers that assemble there. Except for Easter, their doors are never closed—in fact, churches have no doors. Together with the plaza, the entrance appears much like a stage. Shelters where the societies assemble are off the plaza near the building, as well as a kitchen and a fiesta ramada. Inside are statues of the *santora*—the saints, Jesus, and Mary. Outside, across the plaza, is a Great Cross, which marks the beginning of holy ground. Churchgoers cross themselves there before proceeding. Traditional households have their own marker crosses, called a *tevat kus* or houseyard cross. During Lent, more crosses surround the plaza. They serve an important purpose in Yaqui Easter ceremonies and are removed afterward. On special occasions, paper flowers decorate the building.

Flowers, an ancient symbol of power, decorate Yaqui churches on special occasions.

Indians? Euro-Americans, Mexican Americans, and Native Americans disagreed. Even the Yaqui could not reach consensus. They had their own language and customs, although they arrived too late and left behind too many to fit the historical model of an Indian nation.

The question finally was settled in 1978, when the federal government recognized the Pascua Yaqui Tribe of Arizona and added to the 202 acres of land south of Tucson they had received in 1964. They now have a reservation that totals 892 acres and they have the same standing as American Indians. Although the concept of a reservation seemed inconsistent with the scattered Yaqui communities and was not an entirely popular concept with the community, it has allowed them, among other benefits, to have a casino—

Tribal Recognition Day at Pascua Yaqui Village

which came 30 years later. Casino revenue has given the tribe both new options and new problems.

While Old Pascua, Barrio Libre, and Yoem Pueblo in Marana, Arizona are still vital communities, New Pascua has become the largest Yaqui town. Guadalupe, now surrounded by the Phoenix metropolitan area, has its own municipal status and retains its character, including special bus stop shelters built of sun-bleached desert wood and stucco. Guadalupeños tend to be at the liberal end of the Yaqui social and political spectrum, while more rural Yoem Pueblo dwellers are more conservative.

Still, at Easter time, on family occasions, and during visits which Yaquis make to their Sonoran homeland, all are reminded of their Yaqui soul and history. The culture lives and today the tribe has an enrollment of 13,000.

Exploring the Yaqui Lands

The Yaqui villages in Arizona are located, with the exception of Yoem Pueblo, in or very near either Phoenix or Tucson. The time to visit them is during a special occasion to which the public is invited. Best of all is the Easter season, when ceremonies are held each Friday and visitors are welcome. Plan to experience the entire drama, rather than coming and going.

For information about other occasions, as well as Yaqui culture, contact the tribal office at (520) 883-5000, extension 5350 or 5366, or visit their website at www.pascuayaqui-nsn.gov.

Yoem Tekia

7474 S. Camino de Oeste, New Pascua Village • (800) 572-7282
www.pascuayaqui-nsn.gov • Open: Call for days and hours of availability.
Follow I-19 to the Valencia exit. Go west and follow the sign to New Pascua.
The streets are clearly marked.

The tribal museum of Yoem Tekia (*yo-em-TEA-kya*) is located within the village of Pascua Yaqui. It exhibits and interprets the culture from the point of view of the people.

Arizona State Museum

1013 E. University Blvd., Tucson • (520) 621-6302 • www.statemuseum.arizona.edu
Open: Monday–Saturday, 10 a.m.–5 p.m.; Sunday, noon–5 p.m.

Parking is available in a garage on the southeast corner of E. 2nd St. and N. Euclid. This museum is near the Arizona Historical Society Museum, so be sure you're at the right one. The "Paths of Life" exhibit includes an insightful interpretation of Yaqui culture.

Yaqui community members, including "royalty," come together at the New Pascua church to celebrate Tribal Recognition Day.

Dining and Overnight Accommodations

The Yaqui villages are within metropolitan areas so both are easily available. In addition, Pascua Yaqui runs two casinos with restaurants.

Shopping

Wonderful masks are created by some Yaqui artists, but a question always exists as to which masks are appropriate outside a ceremonial context. The tribal museum is the best source of information. Flower-embroidered blouses; "deer's eye" necklaces that absorb negative energy and also may be used as rosaries; transparent skirts that are layered for a distinctive Yaqui women's look; and other items featuring the deer dancer, the Yaqui flag, and other cultural icons are sold at public events.

Recurring Events

• **Lenten Ceremonies:** Friday evenings between Ash Wednesday and Easter Sunday

• **Tribal Recognition Day:** A celebration that takes place at New Pascua annually on September 18.

• **The Holy Day of Saint Francis Xavier:** This event is celebrated with the Tohono O'odham at Mission San Xavier del Bac (see p.49). Yaqui religious society members walk in the procession, dance, and participate in ceremonies. (November)

Native Voices, Native Lives: Guillermo "Bill" Quiroga

A younger Bill Quiroga would have been astonished to know that he would some-day found a company and serve as its president and chief executive officer. In the late 1960s and early 1970s, Quiroga was among the many young people who looked on corporate America as an evil empire.

On the other hand, Native American Botanics isn't just any company. It stands as testimony to Quiroga's discovery—which germinated over a period of many years—that social responsibility and business aren't mutually exclusive terms. Quality, service, job creation, education, and wellness, he found, can belong to the world of profit making and also the nonprofit arena of social service. Even the herbal products—teas and supplements—that the company researches and markets are compatible with his values and traditions.

Quiroga's journey of discovery began in the fields of south central California, where he was raised. He worked at readily available agricultural jobs through-out his school years, and these jobs supported his undergraduate college education. In California, he and his family participated in the formation of Cesar Chavez's United Farm Workers Union, opening the door to Quiroga's days as an activist on behalf of Native American rights. As a young man, he demonstrated at Alcatraz Island, in the Black Hills of South Dakota, and in Guatemala.

Quiroga's travels weren't limited to civil rights demonstrations. He visited and explored the cultures of Native American peoples from Montana to Central America as an independent traveler. Eventually, life demanded a return to finish his education at the University of California at Santa Barbara, where he majored in sociology after working in adult probation, employment counseling, construction, social service program administration, auto mechanics, and his great love, music.

Circumstances brought him to the Yaqui communities in southern Arizona at the end of that period of his life. The leadership qualities he had developed as an activist bore fruit for his community when he served as chairman of the Pascua Yaqui Housing Authority and vice president of the San Ignacio Yaqui Council of Old Pascua Village, both of which have been instrumental in improving housing for Yaqui families. An added benefit to his work was that, in the course of making a difference, he grew closer to his heritage, learning more about traditions as he helped re-establish them. He continues to participate in Yaqui ceremonial activities.

Quiroga's experience led him to consider ways that business principles could be applied to nonprofit management. In order to find out how, he began looking into further education at the University of Arizona. "I looked at public administration versus business, and the difference was day and night," he recalls. "So I applied to business school, where I thought the money was."

He talked his way in, despite needing to make up math requirements before he could be approved as a full student. How many Native American students were in the program? A few. How many from Arizona? None. Quiroga changed that. He studied advanced mathematics, took the GMAT midway into his graduate program, and ended up with multiple scholarships and ultimately an MBA.

During his studies he needed to write a business plan for an entrepreneurship class. While searching for a suitable business to plan, he met his partner, Teena Hayden (now Ph.D.), an agriculture student interested in growing medicinal herbs using hydroponics.

Quiroga brought a desire for Native economic development to the mix, and together they produced the blueprint for Native American Botanics which is still being followed. "We started out with a plan and ended up with a business," he says. The business plan was selected best at the annual business plan competition in 1998. Along the way the plan, the business, Quiroga, and Hayden have won awards nearly every year. In 2001, they were inducted into the Entrepreneurship Hall of Fame at the Karl Eller Center of the University of Arizona.

Today Quiroga functions in management while Teena, who lives in North Carolina, heads up research in the areas of sustainability; efficient water use; and consistency, quality, and the conservation of sacred seed sources. Their geographic combination adds biodiversity to the mix. Recipients of several grants, they recently received an NIH grant to experiment with growing yerba mansa, black cohosh, echinacea, and stinging nettle in an aeroponic environment.

Specialized economic development that Quiroga describes as "helping real Native people deal with the unemployment of isolation on rural reservations" is addressed through outreach, seeking people in such circumstances to act as suppliers and investors. Quiroga, who is descended from a warrior family, sees himself as fighting an economic battle. The part he likes about its outcome is that it's one battle that everyone wins.

Hopi

*"Our ancestral sites are not abandoned,
but are continually remembered
through our ceremonies and songs."*

—Ferrell Secakuku, 1999

Children in Phoenix live their heritage in the Hopi Senom Dance Group.

Introduction to Hopi Culture

Three Mesas: Center of the Hopi World

Nearly invisible on their mesas (high, flat-topped landforms) east of northern Arizona's Painted Desert lies a string of villages with intriguing names like Shungopavi, Mishongnovi, Moenkopi, Walpi. The names of people who live there sound just as exotic to the ears of the rest of the world: Qöyawayma, Lomahongyoma, Kavanghhongevah, Humyumptewa.

This area along AZ 264 was set aside for the Hopi people by an 1882 U.S. government executive order, although they and their ancestors have lived in the region since time out of mind—perhaps for a hundred generations. The traditional Hopi land, or *tutskwa,* is bounded by distant landmarks such as Navajo Mountain (*Toko'navi*), Bill Williams Mountain (*Tusaqtsomo*), the San Francisco Peaks (*Nuvatukya'ovi*), and the rim of the Grand Canyon (*Ongtupqua*). Ritual pilgrimages continue to be made to these distant places to maintain the Hopi's spiritual connection with the land.

The Hopi villages are situated along 90 miles of road that link three mesas on which most of them are located. Two non-Hopi towns terminate the road through the reservation: Keams Canyon at the east end, location of U.S. government administrative offices, a trading post, and some irrigated farms; and Tuba City, at the west end.

Long-distance running is a strong tradition at Hopi.

The region's semi-arid landscape averages about 5,000 feet in altitude. It consists mostly of flat plain sculpted by the elements into canyons, mesas, and buttes. Prominent on the southwestern horizon are the San Francisco Peaks, the sacred mountains north of Flagstaff that are home to spiritual beings represented by Hopi katsina dolls and dancers. Light and weather dramatically change the appearance of this land, so take the time to notice how blues become reds and golden yellows and then fade back to violet again as the sun rises and sets on the serene panorama.

A visit to Hopi, as the area itself is called, offers travelers an opportunity to experience an extraordinarily rich cultural heritage that retains the spirit of its ancient traditions. Without knowing something about their history, however, it would be difficult for the visitor to understand why this relatively small, geographically isolated group has impressed so many for so long. Hardly a famous explorer, missionary, archaeologist, or chronicler of American Indian life has not turned their attention to Hopi, yet the Hopi ways retain an enduring integrity.

Most of the Hopi villages lie on or just below First, Second, and Third Mesas, which were unimaginatively named to describe the order in which they were reached by explorers coming from the east across then-grassland plains. These mesas are really peninsulas jutting out from a larger landform called Black Mesa. The villages grew around sources of water that emerged beneath its cliffs. The first people lived near these springs but moved up to the mesa tops for protection as Spanish and raiding Indian tribes came through in increasing numbers. Tree rings date the oldest excavated houses at around AD 1100. The adobe-plastered stone structures on the mesas, looking much as they did when they were constructed using local earth and rock, are nearly indistinguishable from the rimrock from even a short distance away.

The Hopi Migration

Ancient prophecy preordained the location of Hopi. Their first people emerged from below this world into the current one, which is the Fourth World. In the earliest of times, the Hopi were called to travel in all directions until they reached certain designated points. Like a spiritual relay, the plan then called for them to turn back from their appointed destination and reunite at a site representing the center of existence. This place was the Hopi mesas. The reason for selecting such a demanding environment was to keep the people spiritually attuned, humble, and respectful in their proper dependence on supernatural forces.

Each segment of the people who migrated had a particular function around which the Hopi still organize their rituals. Together with priestly duties, their religious tasks form a cycle that orders life each year from solstice to solstice. Clans, which resemble closely-knit kinship groups, retain today that portion of spiritual responsibility which they took on in those early times. Like a puzzle, each piece is essential to the whole.

Fascinating Facts about the Hopi

• Old Oraibi is generally considered to be the oldest continually inhabited settlement in North America.

• Traditionally, a person is considered to be Hopi if the mother is Hopi. Clan and property pass to children from the mother's side.

• Corn represents the Hopi concept of the cycle of life. The Hopi language uses the same word for a young child and a young corn plant. Another word means both a corn stalk that has dried up and a body when it dies.

• The late Hopi artist Charles Loloma is the father of contemporary Indian jewelry design. In the 1950s he began to create simple, bold shapes with an abstract look, using materials from all over the world.

• The Hopi are known for being long distance runners. Louis Tewanima represented the United States in the 1908 and 1912 Olympics, in which he won a silver medal in the 10,000-meter race and established a record that stood for 52 years. It was said that Tewanima would run barefoot from Hopi to Winslow to watch the trains pass by...then run back, a total of 120 miles.

• Over many generations the Hopi developed cotton and corn species that grow without irrigation in their semi-arid climate, where the average rainfall is between 5 and 12 inches per year (compare that amount of precipitation to the state of New Jersey, which receives an average rainfall of about 45 inches per year).

• Men are traditionally the weavers in Hopi. A groom's male clan relatives make the wedding garments of his bride.

• When a female says "thank you" in the Hopi language, she uses the word *askwali*. Males say *kwakha*.

• The Hopi's reservation is entirely surrounded by that of the Navajo.

Clan membership is passed through the mother and is associated with the mother's home village. Members of each clan know its history and its original function within the tribal ceremonials. In addition to clans, men and women may be initiated into special societies with specific ritual roles.

Each clan has a sign by which it was known: the bear or badger paw for the Bear or Badger Clan; symbolic figures for the Snake, Lizard, Parrot, Eagle, Spider, Bow, Butterfly, and many more—a total of at least 30. These signs, still visible in rock art found in faraway places, provide the Hopi evidence of their migrations. The symbols have been used for generations to document pilgrimages to sacred sites, as well. They are the sources of much artistic design.

Members of the Bear Clan have traditionally been the village leaders, or *mongwi*. When new groups of people came to Hopi, they applied to the *kikmongwi* (the singular form of mongwi), who determined whether they had a role to play in the ritual and daily life at Hopi. A Tewa Pueblo group from the Rio Grande, for instance, whose descendants still live in the village of Tewa, arrived at the end of the 1600s and was invited to stay because they committed to acting as a first line of defense against raids on First Mesa. Even today these Tewa people speak a language related to that spoken by certain of today's Rio Grande pueblos. Hopi is related to the language of the Akimel (Pima) and Tohono O'odham tribes, among others. Villages retain unique characteristics and specialties and speak slightly differing dialects of the Hopi language.

In their own language, the word Hopi is both a noun and an adjective. It is often translated as "peaceful people," describing the nature of the Hopi philosophy of life. It's also been interpreted more broadly to mean "righteous" or "good," alluding to the belief that people who bear this name understand

Ongoing Social Issues

• Traditional and progressive elements disagree on many issues involving change, such as utilizing electricity, non-traditional housing, politics, and spiritual practices.

• Water is at the heart of Hopi tradition and is a giver of life in a land without rivers. Springs that the people have depended on for generations have diminished since the 1960s, when Peabody Coal began mining in the area. Black Mesa serves as a water source due to its geological makeup, and the company uses water that seeps through the mesa to slurry coal over great distances. This continues to concern residents.

• The U.S. government allotted land to the Hopi tribe in 1882, incorporating within the reservation only a small proportion of the area they consider their ancestral territory. The Navajo Nation has come to surround Hopi, and conflicts regularly arise over its use for farming, grazing, and other purposes. In 1974 the Hopi-Navajo Settlement Act partitioned the lands, relocating certain Navajo families. Problems, however, continue among Hopi, Navajo, and United States elements of the negotiations.

the proper rituals and rules of life that perpetuate universal balance. In fact, those who perform ceremonies today do so to benefit not just those who call themselves Hopi, but the entire world.

Ceremonial Customs

Hopi dances, which are really ceremonial occasions, represent a part of the ritual year that non-Hopi may occasionally witness by invitation only. All dances are prayers, although social dances, which celebrate special times such as late-summer harvest, are not as sacred as those in which the *katsinam* (plural of katsina, in Hopi) participate. Outsiders who are privileged to watch them climb smoke-drenched from *kivas* (underground rooms used as ceremonial chambers and meeting rooms);

Hano Clown katsina carved by Lee Grover. Clowns play mischievous tricks on bystanders at Hopi ceremonial occasions.

Spirit of the Dance

The katsina ceremonies essentially consist of dramatized communication between earth people and spirits. Every element is purposeful. They are deeply meaningful ritual works of art, developed over the centuries to include all the senses in their expression.

The Hopi care for the earth and everything on it through their ceremonies. Their religious observances sustain the balance of life: plant, animal, inanimate, and human. Water lies at the heart of it all. Ritual—including sacred, secret preparations and prayers—mediates between earth and the supernatural. Public ceremonies offer the people an opportunity to participate in prayer and meditation already initiated by the priesthood in the kivas. Some ceremonies are solemn, or, like weddings, performed for a purpose; others appear to teach through humor. All are considered spiritual, however, and are worthy of respect by outsiders.

A number of social dances are held in August and September. They are not related to the katsinam, although they have an important purpose: to express gratitude for the blessings of life. The dancing, gestures, and songs are prepared and rehearsed, but all Hopi may join in the celebration. Some dances are designed to honor other tribes and others to invoke other powers. Examples are the Butterfly Dance, the Buffalo Dance, and the Basket Dance. The famous Snake Dance is held every other year and is NOT open to the public.

The Hopi Katsina

Katsina dolls are still given as gifts and used to teach children about the 100-plus katsinam they represent. Although each katsina has a particular ceremonial role and supports Hopi spiritual life, it is perfectly acceptable for a non-Hopi to buy and collect them. The best way to show respect for the cultural significance of katsina dolls is to be sure that those you purchase were carved by Hopi people.

Deer katsinam dance with other animals in summer to encourage good hunting.

Dawa, or Sun, katsinam take part in private rituals around the summer solstice.

These contemporary-style morning katsinam are gracefully carved and colored.

A member of the demanding ogre family.

Crow Mother helps in teaching and blessing new initiates into the katsina culture.

listen to the hypnotic rhythms of chant, rattle, and drum; and experience the power of these supernatural beings usually instinctively respect their meaning. However, the insensitive bystander who fails to display proper etiquette may find himself embarrassingly educated by the antics of Hopi clowns. In the case of gross rulebreaking, the transgressor and all other non-Hopi may be asked to leave.

While those outsiders who are allowed to attend sometimes try to translate Hopi ceremonial symbolism, they are primarily onlookers who can perhaps best sense the meaning of sights, sounds, and movement by quietly taking them in. Given careful attention, the dancing communicates in a direct way to our senses, without labels or explanations.

Although they are among the most spiritual people on earth, the Hopi of course are human, and contentiousness among villages, clans, and even families has occasionally manifested itself in open discord.

Blue Corn

Blue corn meal breads are a traditional specialty at Hopi. A young woman learns to make *piki (BEE-kee)* and *somiviki (so-MEE-vee-kee)* at the time of her Corn Grinding Ceremony, when she is ushered by her relatives into adulthood.

Foreign Contact

Beginning in the sixteenth century, accommodation to the forced presence of Spanish Catholicism at Hopi raised tragic controversy. Although they were initially prepared to welcome the *pahaana* as a white brother who was lost during clan migration times, the idea of generous leadership was dispelled soon after first contact in 1540. In succeeding years, Spaniards returned to the Southwest time after time, claiming the land and the souls of all the Native peoples they encountered. Subjugation and brutality ensued. Ultimately the pueblo groups along the Rio Grande revolted, killing priests, and destroying Spanish missions, records, and influence. Only the cows, sheep, horses, burros, and the crops introduced by the Spanish remained part of everyday life. After the Pueblo Revolt in 1680, the Hopi moved most of their villages up to the mesas to avoid reprisal.

In the early 1800s, the status of a new wave of white men with different religions and further demands became the major issue. In the early 1900s Old Oraibi, then the largest Hopi village, split in a confrontation over association with missionary Christian religions. Various Hopi factions have taken sides over time—conservative versus progressive, religious versus secular —concerning whether or not to adopt the ways of an increasingly dominant European-based culture.

The Tribal Council, formed in 1936 by the U.S. government, frequently served as a lightning rod for this conflict. To this day it is viewed either as helping the people adapt to the modern era or as destroying Hopi practices in favor of the white man's way. Neither extreme has prevailed despite a 500-year history washed over by waves of latecomers from the European continent and Mexico.

Since the Pueblo Revolt, the Hopi have not been involved in significant organized violence. Even in the heat of the Indian Wars of the 1800s, Kit Carson, who etched his name on a rock near Moenkopi, called the Hopi "a peaceable people." Nor have they left their religion in significant numbers. Today, for most Hopi, life is their religion, the earth is a place of worship, and their customs reflect their heritage to a truly extraordinary degree.

Exploring the Hopi Lands

Summer and fall are the best times to visit Hopi. Early spring is windy and winter is cold in this part of Arizona. Summer, even at that altitude, can be uncomfortably hot, although a number of public ceremonial events are held then. Early autumn is ideal. Hats, sun block and sun glasses, extra water to carry with you, and comfortable shoes are a good idea, since you will need to walk to many of the more interesting places.

The Hopi Villages

While the outside world has taken an enormous interest in the Hopi villages, ceremonials, and culture for over a century, tourism as such is not highly developed here. The Hopi people are friendly and helpful in general, and may invite visitors to their homes or social occasions. Storekeepers and service providers often offer useful information. (Most Hopi speak English.)

The Hopi pueblos seem to grow from the earth. Abandoned, they melt back to become part of the mesas. Traditional Hopi villages are made up of a plaza surrounded by compact, multistoried dwellings with shared walls.

Although the villages are clustered on or near the three mesas described in the Introduction to Hopi Culture section, each village is autonomous and has the authority to establish its own policies, which are supported by the Hopi Tribal Council. It is important to be aware of rules and regulations before entering the villages. Look for signs at the entrance to find out where you may park. Some villages may be closed to the public during religious ceremonies.

All archaeological sites must be visited with a tour guide. Certain locations such as the petroglyphs at Pumpkin Seed Hill and Dawa Park may be visited without a guide, but you must have a permit and will need directions. These are issued by the Cultural Preservation Office at the Hopi Tribal Offices in Kykotsmovi on Third Mesa—P.O. Box 123, Kykotsmovi, AZ 86039, (928) 734-3750. It is illegal to remove artifacts or disturb archaeological sites or shrines. For more information on tour guides, see www.hopi.usn.

Demonstrations, home visits, and personalized tours can often be arranged by calling the Hopi Cultural Center (928) 734-2401, Museum (928) 734-6650, or one of the village or tribal offices (see First, Second, and Third Mesa sections beginning on p. 84). Try to organize well ahead of the time you want to visit, since demonstrations are not ongoing. Pottery making,

The San Francisco Peaks are home to the Hopi spiritual beings called katsinam.

basket weaving, and *piki* bread baking introduce you to some traditional specialties of the Hopi villages. Silver overlay jewelry, also a Hopi specialty, is often in progress at the Hopi Cooperative Silvercraft Guild near the Cultural Center. Occasionally it is possible to make arrangements to have a meal in a Hopi home and interact on a personal basis with the family.

Cultural educators work independently and often offer the most effective way to experience the Hopi. For a list of some who may be available to guide you and to arrange for demonstrations and home visits, see this book's website at www.indianarizona.com.

Getting There from Flagstaff

The Hopi Villages lie along AZ 264 between Tuba City and Keams Canyon, Arizona. From Flagstaff, you can take I-40 east past Winslow, turn north at Exit 257 onto AZ 87, and arrive in about 2 hours at its junction with AZ 264 near Second Mesa, location of the Hopi Cultural Center (see p. 87).

The adventurous motorist may choose to drive the back roads (some unpaved) through Cosnino (I-40, Exit 207) and Leupp (I-40, Exit 245) to Indian Route (IR) 2 (Leupp–Oraibi Road), which also leads to Hopi. A sense of the land is the reward for patience and fortitude.

As you approach Hopi lands, why not listen to Hopi radio KUYI (*kuyi* means water in Hopi), 88.1 FM, which plays the most eclectic music on the air.

Once you arrive, the distances between villages is not great. The distance from Kykotsmovi to Second Mesa is about 6 miles; from Second Mesa to Polacca is about 15 miles; and from Polacca to Keams Canyon approximately 11 miles. Services are few and far between, however, so gas up before you leave town. And bring water.

Secrets of Etiquette

No photographs or recordings or sketching are allowed at Walpi. Unless invited, enter only those homes with signs on doors or windows. Do not pick up feathers, which may represent prayers, or disturb pottery shards or other objects. "Bargaining" for art and craft objects is all right, but aggressive arguing is not part of Hopi culture. Even shaking hands is a gentler gesture among these people. Remember that people live here and respect their privacy. Dress conservatively, even on non-ceremonial occasions. Donations left in appreciation of your tour are welcome.

Here, as everywhere in the world, the visitor who is polite and diplomatic can "ask around" to find out what's available. People who man the desks at cultural centers and museums, store owners, and others often know of special events or individuals who enjoy entertaining visitors. An experienced traveler also knows that while this strategy sometimes yields serendipitous rewards, one must be prepared for any answer, including "No."

FIRST MESA

- **Sichomovi** *(seet-CHEW-mo-vee)*   • **Walpi** *(WALL-pea)*
- **Hano (Tewa)** *(HAH-no, TAY-wah)* • **Polacca** *(pole-AH-ka)*

You are driving backward through time as you pass through these villages. Polacca was founded in 1890 by Tom Polaccaca, a resident of Hano. The U.S. government encouraged its growth over the next 10 years by building a day school and houses below the mesa. This was part of an effort to acculturate the Hopi to the ways of the dominant culture. Families of the residents of Polacca are related to those living in the villages above, where kivas and many traditional buildings remain intact.

Hano, which dates from shortly after the Pueblo Revolt of 1680, is indistinguishable to outsiders from Sichomovi, founded when Walpi outgrew its boundaries. Sichomovi, like Polacca but unlike Walpi, has running water and electricity.

Your guide will walk with you toward the tip of First Mesa. This rocky peninsula narrows to only 15 feet before it broadens again to become the picturesque village of Walpi, floating in a sea of land edged by 600-foot cliffs.

Notice the construction of the homes and kivas in Walpi, which closely resemble those of Hopi ancestors whose dwellings you may have seen as you traveled to the reservation—then realize that wood for building had to come

Walpi, at the tip of First Mesa, overlooks the plain in the direction of the sacred San Francisco Peaks.

from trees, of which you see very few in the enormous panoramic distance. Since American Indians did not use the wheel or pack animals until after contact with Europeans, the oldest beams and other wooden elements had to be brought from distant forested mountains by men on foot.

Be sure to take in the setting of this village. Take the time to look off to the horizon in all directions. Watch the sky and the changing light. Artists have painted this landscape in blues, yellows, reds, and shades of black and gray. All of these colorations appear in the course of a day.

First Mesa villages are known for polychrome pottery, katsina dolls, and weavings, and you will find people selling them here, sometimes from their homes (please don't enter unless a sign is posted that invites you in). Now is a good time to start taking a closer look at the arts and crafts for which the Hopi are so well known. Katsina dolls range from old-style, simply painted cottonwood root carvings to exquisite elaborately detailed wood sculpture.

Pottery is also a specialty at First Mesa. Designs inspired by ancient polychrome shards excavated nearby revived that art there in the late 1800s. Nampeyo, a famous potter whose work was marketed by the Fred Harvey Company for the Santa Fe Railroad, worked at Hano. She, her descendants, and many others who work in clay still hand-coil and hand-fire their pottery, and create art in other media as well. So many Hopi are artists that you will easily find a beautiful object in your price range here or at a retail outlet later. Authenticity is assured when you buy from the artist or from a seller with a trustworthy reputation. If you are buying as an investment, don't hesitate to ask for a written statement of authenticity. To see an in-depth look at Nampeyo's work, check out "A Nampeyo Showcase" which can be found at: statemuseum.arizona.edu/nampeyo/index.shtml.

As you leave, take the time to talk to villagers who seem interested in conversation or who offer something for sale. Visit homes that display signs, and look around the public places. This place brings history and heritage alive.

First Mesa Consolidated Tours of Walpi
(928) 737-2262 • http://hopibiz.com • Open: Monday–Friday, 9:30 a.m.–4 p.m.

First Mesa Community Development Office
Polacca • (928) 737-2670 • Open: Monday–Friday, 8 a.m.–5 p.m.

Ponsi Hall Visitor Center
Sichomovi • (928) 737-2262 • Open: 9:30 a.m.–4 p.m. in summer; in winter, call for availability

To get to Ponsi Hall, where you must check in for your walking tour, drive through the community of Polacca at the base of the mesa, climb a steep road to the villages and park. Visitors often find it difficult to distinguish between the three villages, so if you need help finding the parking area, just ask. Your guide will take you to the picturesque village of Walpi.

SECOND MESA

• **Mishongnovi** *(muh-SHONG-no-vee)* • **Sipaulovi** *(shuh-PAUL-oh-vee)*
• **Shungopavi** *(shung-AH-po-vee)*

To begin to explore Second Mesa, drive about 7 miles west of Polacca to South Shungopavi, the "mother village" of Hopi. It was established by the Bear Clan, the first to arrive at the mesas following clan migrations. In the beginning, many clans gathered there, demonstrating their special ceremonial powers—to attract rain, to protect groundwater, to assure germination—in order to assert their eligibility for admission to permanent residency.

The original people of Shungopavi settled at the base of this mesa. They moved the town up for protection after the Pueblo Revolt. Archaeological study of the old site has revealed pottery dating from about 1250–1500. Between 1630 and 1680 the village moved near a Spanish mission, parts of whose walls still remain. Its beams were incorporated into construction in the "new" village above. Sipaulovi was built on the mesa after Shungopavi moved up.

A road to the upper towns turns left across from Second Mesa Day School by a Texaco station; they can also be reached from the Cultural Center. On one of Second Mesa's two fingers lie the villages of Mishongnovi and Sipaulovi. On the other

Alph Secakuku presides over his gallery, Hopi Fine Arts, at Second Mesa.

is "new" Shungopovi, known for producing beautiful silver overlay jewelry and coiled plaques. Sipaulovi was established when a number of clans were sent to help Shungopavi protect Hopi from Spanish reprisal. Mishongnovi was established when the Crow Clan was permitted to act as keepers of the shrine at Corn Rocks, near the base of the mesa. Mishongnovi also relocated around 1700. Like other villages it has melted—roof by roof, room by room—since the days when parts of it were as high as four stories.

Hopi artists, surrounded by tradition, often express their creativity at an early age.

The Second Mesa Community Center, located near Corn Rocks, is a good source of information about visiting. These villages, especially Shungopavi, are quite conservative and are known for desiring privacy. Second Mesa silversmiths may be seen at work back at the Cultural Center, where the Silvercraft Cooperative Guild is located, or at their homes or shops where they exhibit. Again, look for signs or an invitation before entering.

Mishongnovi Community Development Office
(928) 734-2520

Sipaulovi Community Development Office
(928) 734-2570

The designs associated with Hopi pottery were revived by Nampeyo in the late 1800s.

Hopi Cultural Center and Museum
Cultural Center: (928) 734-2401
Museum: (928) 734-6650
www.hopiculturalcenter.com

This is the most easily accessible source of tourism information, as well as the only place to overnight on the reservation. A campground that allows two consecutive overnights is located next to the motel. Reservations are essential, especially in the summer.

THIRD MESA
- **Kykotsmovi** *(kee-COT-smo-vee)* • **Oraibi** *(oh-RYE-bee or -vee)*
- **Bacavi** *(BAH-ko-vee or -bee)* • **Hotevilla** *(hoh-ta-VIL-la)*
- **Moenkopi** *(MOH-en-koh-pea)*

Third Mesa lies 10 miles west of the Cultural Center. The story of its villages stands as testimony to the overwhelming changes that have assaulted the Hopi way of life since contact with Europeans. Established in the last two centuries, each town grew out of dissension between adherents of "progress" and those who espoused the traditional heritage of the Hopi. Third Mesa is best known for its agricultural expertise and fine textiles, wicker baskets, and plaques.

Kykotsmovi, the first village you'll encounter, once was called New Oraibi because it developed when people from Old Oraibi either converted to Christianity or decided to accept "white" education as their new way of life, splitting from the old ways and moving away. However, it is located in an area where many clans gathered long ago while they waited for permission to move into the original village of Oraibi. Kykotsmovi actually means "ruins on the hills," and was so named because there are many sites left from these early settlements in the surrounding hills. It is now the seat of the Hopi Tribal Government.

Two miles away on top of the mesa lies Oraibi, which was established over 1,000 years ago. Sometimes called Old Oraibi (the Hopi name is *Oraivi*) it is generally considered the oldest continuously inhabited settlement in North America.

Oraibi is impressively ancient. Established after the "mother village" of Shungopavi, it surpassed that town in population and for centuries was considered the center of Hopi life. In spite of disease and at least one earthquake, it housed half the people who lived in Hopi at the turn of the last century—perhaps 2,000. But as outside influences proliferated, Oraibi fractured. Elements that opposed cooperation with Christian influences and the U.S. government either were expelled or left.

Today the village of Oraibi is nearly deserted. You must park outside the village and may walk its streets, but it is forbidden to visit the ruins of a church you will see as you visit. The church was established there in 1901 by Mennonite missionaries, blocking the point called Katsina Resting Place. One of its missionaries, Henrich Voth, is remembered for disclosing secret information and offering sacred Hopi objects to the larger world. The church has been struck by lightning twice. It is not considered a safe or appealing place.

Although Moenkopi is 40 miles west of Third Mesa, it is a satellite of Oraibi and is therefore considered one of the Third Mesa villages. Though Moenkopi land lies on ancient clan sites, it served primarily as a farming area for Oraibi until it became a permanent settlement in the early 1900s. This town also fractured along conservative versus progressive lines. A more

Hopi weavers create both coiled and woven baskets and plaques. Decorative plaques are often offered as gifts for special occasions.

traditional life is followed in the lower village, while the upper village has its own constitution. These are the only farms at Hopi where land is irrigated. Ask in town about nearby fossil dinosaur tracks.

In 1906, Hotevilla was also founded as a result of factional disputes in Oraibi. Its terraced gardens show one of the many ways Hopi have farmed, and they are worth seeing. It is known for its dances and basketry. Bacavi, located across the highway from Hotevilla, was established in 1908 when certain clans from Hotevilla tried to return to Oraibi but were not welcomed back.

After bitter disputes had splintered people into these Third Mesa villages, Kykotsmovi, true to its more progressive leanings, became the seat of the U.S. government-created Hopi Tribal Council in the 1930s. The spiritual Hopi world view, with its intricate ritual organization, did not integrate well with the secular order imported by Europeans, and the council was abandoned in the 1940s. But the Tribal Council offered the only available means for the conglomerate of self-governing Hopi villages to interact legally with outside governments, so when politics heated up again in the 1950s over land disputed by Hopi and Navajo, the Council was revived. It continues to serve as a government-to-government entity.

Kykotsmovi Community Development Office

(928) 734-2474; (928) 734-2471
Hopi Tribe Adminstrative Offices: (928) 734-3000

Bacavi Community Development Office

(928) 734-9360

Keams Canyon

You might wish to visit Keams Canyon. You can stop by the trading post there, which has been a landmark since the early 1900s (www.hopiart.com). It passed through the hands of agent Thomas Keam and the famous trader Lorenzo Hubbell to the McGee family, which has owned it since the 1930s. The current generation of McGees was raised on the reservation, and they are a reliable source of information.

Keams Canyon (*Pongsikya* in Hopi; formerly called Peach Orchard Springs in English) is primarily an administrative seat of the U.S. government, and its history reflects government attempts at the turn of the last century to acculturate both Hopi and Navajo. It also witnessed continuing land allocation conflict between the two peoples.

About 1.5 miles north of Keams Canyon, Kit Carson's name is inscribed on canyon rock, dated 1863. That year he was sent to remove the Navajos to Bosque Redondo, New Mexico. To see this inscription, follow the main road through Keams Canyon and look for a shelter a little above the west side of the road, next to the wash. In spite of the fact that he was an officer in the Indian Wars, Carson admired the Hopi people.

Lure of the Grand Canyon

Science tells us that paleo-Indians came to the Grand Canyon region about 11,000 years ago. They were followed by people archaeologists call Archaic, whose era ended about 3,000 years ago. Then came the Ancestral Puebloan people and later the Cohonino. Both lived and traded in the region until about 1500. It is presumed that the prolonged drought of the thirteenth century forced them to leave. Archaeologists say that the Ancestral Pueblo people moved east and became ancestors of the Hopi. The Cohonino apparently moved west, were called the Cerbat and later the Hualapai people. Southern Paiute Indians began making hunting and gathering trips to the canyon's North Rim when the Cerbats inhabited the South Rim. The last native culture to arrive at the Grand Canyon was the Navajo, who have inhabited the area for the past 400 years.

More than 2,000 Ancestral Puebloan sites have been discovered within Grand Canyon National Park's boundaries. The most accessible is Tusayan Ruin and the Tusayan Museum, 21 miles east of the village.

SIDE TRIPS

Discovering the geographical and historical context of the culture is as important for the enjoyment of your visit as arrangements for hospitality. Taking side trips to see museums, artifacts, and architecture along the way; reading books and articles; and visiting the Hopi website (www.hopi.nsn.us) add immeasurably to your experience.

Ancient dwelling places lie not far from the main roads you'll follow on the way to Hopi. Their ties to Hopi and other cultures create a sense of time, place, and architecture that locate today's people within their context. Onsite signs interpret what you are seeing. Visitor centers also offer displays of artifacts and sell books and other merchandise.

The time added to your trip by exploring northern Arizona creates an opportunity to get to know the diverse countryside and to visit museums, parks, and historic and prehistoric places that will help set the stage for Hopi.

Heard Museum

2301 N. Central Ave., Phoenix • (602) 252-8848; Events: (602) 251-0255 www.heard.org • Open: Daily 9:30 a.m.–5 p.m.; Closed: Major holidays

Before going to Hopi, be sure to visit the Hopi display in the Heard's exhibit "Home." The late Senator Barry Goldwater's extensive katsina collection is also housed at the Heard. It is a "must see" as you prepare to visit Hopi. In addition, you will find fine examples of Hopi jewelry, weaving, and basketry in the gift shop as well as in the exhibits. Viewing them will help you to select your own if you plan to shop on the Hopi Mesas.

Museum of Northern Arizona

3101 N. Fort Valley Rd., Flagstaff • (928) 774-5213 • www.musnaz.org Open: Daily 9 a.m.–5 p.m.; Closed: January 1, Thanksgiving, and December 25

Here you will find both historic and prehistoric objects, many from Hopi sources. The founders developed a close relationship with the tribe in the early 1900s and worked with jewelers there to develop the unique Hopi overlay style. You can also see an example of kiva mural painting, an unusual opportunity for a non-Hopi. The museum has an excellent gift and book shop.

Walnut Canyon

(928) 526-3367 • www.nps.gov/waca • Open: Daily 8 a.m.–5 p.m., March–May and September–November; 8 a.m.–6 p.m., June–August; and 9 a.m.–5 p.m., December–February • Leave I-40 east at Exit 204, about 7.5 miles from Flagstaff

Located near Flagstaff, the canyon is a spectacular wooded setting for well-interpreted cliff dwellings from the twelfth and thirteenth centuries. The climb into and out of the deep canyon is somewhat strenuous, although concrete pavement, steps with railings, and benches along the way break up the walk. The canyon can also be viewed from the visitor center at the top.

According to Hopis, the pueblos, field houses, artifacts, and rock art of Wupatki National Monument (*Wupatki* means Big House in Hopi) were made by the *Hisatsinom,* their ancestors, who lived at this trading center in the 12th and 13th centuries.

Wupatki National Monument

(928) 679-2365 • www.nps.gov/wupa/ • Open (visitor center): Daily 8 a.m.–5 p.m., March–May and September–November; 8 a.m.–6 p.m., June–August; and 9 a.m.– 5 p.m., December–February. The pueblo is open from sunrise to sunset. Closed: December 25

Take US 89 about 12 miles north from Flagstaff to FR 545, which loops through the monument.

A short drive from Flagstaff, Wupatki is an example of a large settlement and trading center that is impressive and well-preserved (see p. 142 for details).

Homolovi Prehistoric Park

*(928) 289-4106 • www.pr.state.az.us/Parks/parkhtml/homolovi.html
Open: 9 a.m.–5 p.m. all year • Take I-40 to Exit 253 in Winslow. Signs direct you north on N. Park Dr. about 4.5 miles. Winslow is a good place to gas up and eat if you are planning to continue on AZ 87 to the Hopi Mesas.*

Located near Winslow, this site is the ancestral home of certain Hopi clans. You can see an ancient kiva at Homolovi II and the park offers engaging exhibits, books, and videos. It was occupied in the 13th and 14th centuries.

Tusayan Ruins and Museum

*Grand Canyon National Park • (928) 638-7888
www.cdarc.org/visit/tusayan.html • Open: Daily 9 a.m.–5 p.m.
The ruins are 22 miles west of Grand Canyon Village.*

A self-guiding trail takes you among the ruins of the 800-year-old pueblo, which is interpreted in the museum. Ranger-led tours are also available.

Desert View Watchtower and Hopi House

Open: Daily 9 a.m.–5 p.m. • Desert View is near Tusayan, about 27 miles west of Grand Canyon Village on East Rim Drive. Hopi House is next to the El Tovar Hotel in the historic section of Grand Canyon Village on the South Rim.

Both of these historic buildings imitate the ancient architecture of the Hopi and their ancestors. At Hopi House, architect Mary Elizabeth Jane Colter reproduced a building from the village of Oraibi. At Desert View, she incorporated Hopi symbolism into the design and decoration. The tower's vertical rise and interior paintings depict Hopi emergence from the underworld, an event that took place at a sacred site in the Grand Canyon, which it overlooks.

Mark Tahbo's bowl and jar (above and right) show the influence of traditional pottery decoration. Rainy Naha's designs (below) move toward a different look.

Al Qöyawayma worked with his late aunt, the Hopi potter Elizabeth Q. White, to blend tradition with innovation. His contemporary designs break the surface of the clay with carved and colored renderings of figures.

Dining and Overnight Accommodations

• **Hopi Cultural Center**, (928) 734-2401, has a restaurant serving American and some traditional Hopi food. Try *noqkwivi,* a dish made with mutton and parched corn; or *paatupsuki,* bean and hominy soup. Both are authentically Hopi. Overnight accommodations are also available here. Reservations, especially in summer, are essential because it is the only motel in Hopi.

• **LKD's**, (928) 737-2717, is located at the junction of AZ 264/87.

• **Sekakuku Store**, (928) 737-2632, at this same junction, serves takeout deli items.

• **HildaBurger**, (928) 734-9278, is located in the village of Shungopavi.

• **Korean takeout**, (928) 734-6655, is available from a private home between Shungopavi and the Cultural Center.

• **Kykotsmovi Village Store**, (928) 734-2456, sells groceries and serves pizza, subs, and other deli items.

• **Keams Canyon Cafe**, (928) 738-2296, is located next to McGee's Gallery in the Keams Canyon Shopping Center.

• **Several families in each village serve food from their homes.** Look for signs. Snacks are also available from stores within each village.

• **A picnic is an easy alternative when restaurants are not plentiful.** Many picnic areas are located along AZ 264: adjacent to the Hopi Cultural Center; on the east side of Oraibi Wash a little more than 0.5 mile east of the turnoff to Kykotsmovi; on Pumpkin Seed Hill, 1 mile west of Kykotsmovi on the climb to Oraibi. There are also picnic tables along the wash just north of Keams Canyon adjacent to Beaver Dam and under the cottonwood trees opposite the Keams Canyon Shopping Center.

Because accommodations at Hopi are limited, many visitors begin their drive to the Hopi Reservation from Phoenix, passing through or spending the night in Flagstaff, about 2 hours north on I-17. Route 66, the "Mother Road" before the days of interstates, once passed through Flagstaff and served as the connecting point to Indian Country. Lots of vintage motels are still located along Old Route 66, if you feel nostalgic, or other excellent accommodations are available (www. flagguide.com; www.flagstaff-arizona.com/).

Winslow (www.winslowarizona.org), 60 miles east of Flagstaff on I-40, offers the possibility of a stay at La Posada, "the last of the great railroad hotels," built to serve passengers traveling through Indian country on the Santa Fe Railroad (928) 289-4366; www.laposada.org.

Holbrook (www.wmonline.com/cities/holbrook.htm), also on I-40, offers accommodations of all kinds.

Keams Canyon, Tuba City, Winslow, Holbrook, and Flagstaff are the nearest off-reservation towns offering overnight services.

Shopping

You will want to take some time to shop. There are many places to look, and an array of arts and crafts to buy. You'll gain the greatest satisfaction and get the most for your money if you are knowledgeable about what is offered.

• **Katsina dolls:** By now you have seen quite a few katsina dolls for sale. You may be developing a preference for one kind or another. Unless you are—or want to become—knowledgeable about them (there are many fine books on the subject), what you like dictates your purchase. There are as many ways to carve and decorate as there are artists. The spirit of the katsina will come through in the hands of the most skilled. Traditional katsina dolls are carved from dried cottonwood root, which is much lighter in weight than most woods. While antique or old-style carvings stand on stubby legs or are designed to be hung on the wall, more contemporary pieces are carved with legs and feet and placed in one piece on a stand. They may have wood-burned details and often incorporate brighter colors than the old carvings. While personal preference guides your choice, it is interesting to ask about the katsina represented. Its significance could hold special meaning for you.

• **Jewelry:** Since the 1930s the Hopi have developed the distinctive look of their jewelry, which usually uses the overlay technique. Although many of the patterns are based on designs painted on the same fifteenth-century pottery that inspired Nampeyo, they take on a clean, sophisticated look in silver. The lines tend to be curving and smooth, utilizing ancient motifs such as animal figures, cloud and rain patterns, katsinas, and clan symbols. Few jewelers set turquoise or other stones in their creations.

Two pieces of metal are cut to shape and fused. The top piece expresses an image, while the bottom is finished by oxidation or texturing. Then the top is polished, usually to a matte finish.

Those who are familiar with the finest of Native American jewelry will recognize many Hopi names in the list of celebrated, contemporary artists: Roy Talaheftewa, Watson Honanie, Phil Navasya, and many others. Their creations utilize silver, gold, every imaginable stone, as well as inventive design that suggests tradition but goes

The overlay technique shown in this silver pendant has been used by Hopi silversmiths since the 1930s.

beyond it. You are more likely to find the jewelry of these "stars" of jewelry artistry in museums and galleries rather than in local stores.

If you are buying higher-end art, it will be marked by the artist's name, clan sign, or village. Ask for a receipt detailing its authenticity and the nature of any gemstones if you buy through a second party.

• **Pottery:** Hopi pottery is distinctive in many ways. Clay from traditional Hopi sources is extraordinarily dense and durable. Often neither temper nor slip is necessary, although the potter may use them. During firing, Hopi clay turns to shades of gold and soft oranges. Pieces are typically decorated with colored paints. All are made from clay found in the vicinity of First Mesa, but the red and white pots are covered with slip which colors when fired.

If you were fortunate enough to witness a pottery-making demonstration before shopping, the potter probably will describe digging and preparing clay in age-old ways. It is then coiled in layers by hand and scraped smooth with traditional tools such as a shard of a gourd. When the pot is partly dry, a week or so later, the potter sands and polishes it with a small stone. Then it is painted, using yucca leaf or commercial brushes, the pattern emerging spontaneously as the pot is turned in the artist's hands. Last, they are fired outdoors on a grate over an open fire of burning sheep dung.

Of course pottery, like jewelry, has evolved and can be found in creative contemporary forms that recall tradition without being bound by it. Figures in relief or graffito, a style in which a design is cut out, are an example of

one of the newer forms of expression. Well-known potters include the late Elizabeth White and her nephew Al Qöyawayma, Iris Youvella, Preston Duwyenie, and Steve Lucas. The Nampeyo family, both men and women, continue their traditional excellence.

Beautiful pieces are sold at all price levels. To buy a true souvenir of the Hopi culture, look for authenticity in color and design.

• **Basketry:** Hopi women create a wide variety of unique, colorfully decorated baskets in plaited, wicker, and coiled weaves. The intensity of color in their basketry is not found anywhere else in the Southwest. If

A carver waits outside Garland's Indian Jewelry, an old trading post near Sedona, to market his katsina dolls.

you are offered the opportunity to attend a basket-weaving demonstration, you will have a good understanding of the traditional elements of this art form.

Sumac, rabbitbrush, grasses, and yucca are collected and dyes from native plants and minerals or from commercial sources are used to develop the wide range of color used in Hopi basket design. The dyed plant is smoked with burning sheep's wool to set its tint. Raw materials must be softened in water before they are worked. A great deal of planning and preparation goes into the creation of a basket.

Basketry remains a tradition-based craft at Hopi. Sifter baskets are part of an uninterrupted heritage of basket making that is 15 centuries old.

Coiled baskets are created primarily at the Second Mesa villages. The technique used to make them is a process that resembles sewing as much as weaving. Yucca leaves are finely split and bound into a sort of cable with yucca fiber, then attached tightly in widening circles to form plaques or bowls of various shapes. They also are decorated using shades of white, yellow, green, red, and black.

Wicker baskets, a specialty at Third Mesa, are more highly colored and elaborately decorated, often with many of the themes seen in pottery. Bright yellows and oranges, black, purple, and red make these baskets extremely decorative. They may be woven in the form of a plaque, a bowl, or a deep basket. Plaques are offered on occasions such as weddings and katsina ceremonials. At women's Basket Dances, which are often open to the public, they are given away as gifts—and there is likely to be bold competition for those thrown into the crowd!

When buying baskets, look for appeal, of course, and uniformity in the weave and shape. Fine finish, depth of color, and complexity of decoration all create value in a basket.

• **Other art forms:**
Artists are ubiquitous at Hopi. Once you have become familiar with the themes of Hopi design, you will recognize their work in its many forms wherever you see it.

Weaving is the traditional domain of Hopi men. Embroidery and brocade in spruce green, red, and cloud white often decorate cotton or woolen sashes raining long tassels. Artists: Marvin Pooyouma and Mike Gashwazra.

This bracelet created by the late Hopi artist Charles Loloma shows a contemporary style of jewelry he developed in the 1950s. He used simple, bold shapes that incorporated materials from all over the world.

While katsinas, pottery, and baskets are widely known, it is worthwhile to discover the beautiful weavings traditionally done by Hopi men: red, green, black, and white woolen sashes and the finely woven cotton fabric that is used for wedding garments, baby blankets, and ceremonial kilts, dresses, shawls, and belts. Embroidery and brocade decorate some of these items, often with traditional symbols and colors—spruce green, cloud white raining long tassels, and other designs.

Many visitors to the Southwest aren't aware that weaving is an ancient tradition of the pueblo peoples, including the Hopi. The earliest textiles, found in cave sites in aboriginal Hopi territory, date from between 300–700. Before the invention of the loom the early Hopi produced mats, fur blankets, containers, sandals, and braided sashes. The materials used were plant fibers and animal hair. When the Navajo migrated to the area, they learned weaving from the people who were already there. Today's famous Hopi weaving artists include Ramona Sakiestewa, whose work often abstracts Hopi cultural icons.

Items that began as ceremonial objects are often treated as art. Rattles and drums, dance wands, bullroarers, and lightning sticks are sold to the public as well as being used in ritual. Some express the appealing combination of humor and seriousness typical of the Hopi culture.

Painting and sculpture is, of course, also created by Hopi artists. In fact, Dan Namingha, originally from Polacca, is a famous artist known worldwide primarily as a painter. Thomas Hoving, former director of the Metropolitan Museum of Art in New York, co-authored a book with him, *The Art of Dan Namingha.* These art forms are usually found in off-reservation galleries.

The following list includes shops and galleries located on Hopi lands. Ask for directions to stores if you need to, although most are visible from the road. With the exception of AZ 264, streets at Hopi are not named, so individual assistance is sometimes a necessity. In all the villages, some artists sell directly from their homes; look for a sign before entering any home.

First Mesa

Artists often offer items for sale in the area surrounding Ponsi Hall, near Walpi. Some vendors sit outside, and others leave signs in the windows of their homes inviting buyers to enter.

Second Mesa

- **Hopi Cultural Center**
- **Dawa's Arts and Crafts**, Shungopavi
- **Honani Crafts Gallery**, 0.5 mile west of the turnoff to Mishongnovi
- **Hopi Fine Arts**, Alph H. Secakuku, at the junction of AZ 264/87
- **Nutumya's Hopi Market**
- **Hopi Silvercraft Cooperative Guild**, next to the Cultural Center
- **Iskasokpu Gallery**, 1 mile east of the Cultural Center
- **Selina's Silver Arts and Crafts**
- **Tsakurshovi**, source of ceremonial objects for Hopi and information for visitors

Third Mesa

- **Coolidge Roy Native Art**, Oraibi
- **Calnimptewa Galleria**, Oraibi
- **Hamana So-O's Arts and Crafts**, Oraibi
- **Monongya Gallery**, Oraibi
- **White Bear**, Oraibi
- **Spirit Bear Gifts**, Kykotsmovi
- **Gentle Rain**, Kykotsmovi

Keams Canyon

- **McGee's Indian Art Gallery** is an excellent source of authentic creations and helpful information. It is just off the east end of the reservation.

Recurring Events

Hopi ceremonial occasions, while famous in the outside world, are not always open, public events. Although many visitors hope to witness a ceremonial "dance" when they travel to Hopi, the occasions are no more meant to entertain than is a religious service or ritual surrounding prayer. If you are fortunate enough to be invited to one, it will be a memorable experience, sufficient in itself to justify your trip. You may, of course, ask for permission to attend, but it is not always granted.

Each village sponsors both ceremonial and social dances. Scheduling varies from place to place, and the timing of a number of ceremonies is only determined a few days in advance because it depends on natural influences. The traditional ceremonial calendar is followed in varying fashions in every village.

Since you are an experienced traveler, you will be well prepared to understand and be respectful of what you see if you get to go. Unfortunately, insensitive onlookers have sometimes made themselves unwelcome in the past. The guidelines for good etiquette are both easy and common-sense: no photography or recording of events, dignified dress and behavior, staying in

The Hopi language uses one word that means both a child and a young corn plant. Corn is sacred, for it means life.

the background, and not coming and going in a manner that disrupts either participants or other observers.

Besides lunch, you will want to bring a hat or visor and sunglasses if the weather is sunny and water to drink during the day. Umbrellas are not a good idea if it rains, because they block the view of village participants, but a poncho or rain suit works. Portable seating is also useful.

"On time" is not an important concept in the performance of these ceremonies, so prepare to ignore your watch and appreciate a different approach to life. Relax, and watch with eyes of the ages and generations that created these rituals. Visitors are most welcome at events meant for the public. Check with the Hopi Cultural Center or the tribal offices in Kykotsmovi for dates.

• **Miss Hopi Pageant:** Young Hopi women display traditional knowledge that prepares them to represent the Hopi people as Miss Hopi. Hopi Veteran's Memorial Center. (August)

• **Hopi Leadership Recognition Day:** Honoring decades of Hopi leaders. Hopi Veteran's Memorial Center. (August)

• **Hopi Independence Day Festivities:** Celebrating the Pueblo Revolt. Music, arts and crafts, relay run. Hopi Veteran's Memorial Center. Call (928) 734-6636 for more information. (August)

• **100 Mile Club Run:** Old Oraibi, run begins at 6 p.m. (August)

• **Tuhisma–Hopi Arts and Crafts Market:** The greatest gathering of Hopi-only artists and craftspeople. Featuring the best of Hopi arts and crafts, cultural entertainment and food. Hopi Veteran's Memorial Center. 9 a.m.–4 p.m. (October). For more information call (928) 738-0055 or (928) 738-5667; or see http://hopiartshow.homestead.com/Hopi.html.

• **Social dances:** Visitors may be allowed to visit the Buffalo Dances held in January and the Butterfly, Navajo, and Basket Dances in September, October, and early November.

• **The Tewanima Race:** Named in honor of Olympian Lewis Tewanima, this race is held annually near Labor Day at Shungopavi, his home village.

Native Voices, Native Lives: Keeping Ties to Hopi from the City

Father: I grew up on the Hopi land. My mother and father moved out of there to go where maybe we could do better for ourselves, you know, but we go back and forth. We go to ceremonies and initiations to keep up with all that. We commute back to Hopi land.

Older Brother: The whole family has been back two or three times in the last six years.

Father: Even though we moved to the city, we go out to see my mother and father every year. The kids go out and we try to teach them all the stuff we know. My father teaches them, too. We go for night dances so they can see the katsinas. So they pretty much grew up with the Hopi way. Both my boys got initiated into the katsina society.

Older brother: The uncle does the disciplining out there, especially if he's got chores to do, like cut the weeds in the corn or watermelon fields. If you don't wake up your uncle will come and pour water on you and that will wake you up! If kids are bad, they'll pour water on you. You learn!

Mother: I think what we're doing is we're trying to get both sides. We like to teach so they'll know both. It was easier when our boys were younger because there were a lot more aunts and we went out for whole vacations then. A lot more people were around to do things. Every kid had about a million baby sitters. They never wanted for a lap or somebody to talk to them or take time with them....

Younger Brother: We used to go out every year during the summer, twice a year when it worked out. People knew who we were. I know we knew Hopi, but I don't know it now. Now we go as much as we can, but it's a hundred miles away....

Father: I'd say the most important thing is getting back there. We can drive out there Friday, spend a day and a half, and drive back on Sunday, but at least we were out there to see it as opposed to seeing it in a book. I say, "This is what I did when we were out home, when I was your age."

Younger Brother: I guess through clan ties you're just about related to everyone in the village. You've always got family somewhere, someone you can go talk to or visit. There's always somebody who would like to see you, which is really nice.

Mother: One thing I think was really important was the feeling of freedom that we had a home to go to. You always say, "Okay, we're going out home." And you knew that there was home.

It isn't unusual for Hopis to live away from the mesas while still keeping their ties to family and ceremony.

(*Names withheld at the family's request*)

Diné: The Navajo

"To be Diné is a religion. It is a faith. To really practice our way of life, you have to practice our ceremonies. Hozho is a determined sense of harmony. It comes to you when you are surrounded by the sacred."

—Sunny Dooley

Navajo people sometimes re-occupied prehistoric dwellings originally built by other peoples. This one is Lomaki Pueblo at Wupatki National Monument. One of the four sacred mountains can be seen in the background.

Introduction to Navajo Culture

The vast, dramatic expanse of *Diné Bikeyah (dih-NEH beh-KAY-ah)*, the land of the Navajo, is nothing short of awe-inspiring. Its landforms and landscapes may at first seem vaguely familiar, thanks to western movies and four-wheel-drive vehicle commercials. Yet under a turquoise sky, reaching to the horizon, they compose an even more impressive sight than you might imagine when you see them photographed for staged productions.

Yet the scenery is surprisingly accessible. You can cross the Navajo Nation on I-40. You can travel it on AZ 89A, US 160, or AZ 264, which passes through the tribal capital at Window Rock. You're there when you visit the Painted Desert, Petrified Forest, Lake Powell, and picture-perfect Monument Valley.

From a traditional viewpoint, each rock formation in Monument Valley holds special significance. "The Mittens" and "Merrick Butte" are all that is left of one of the alien monsters that terrorized humans until Monster Slayer rid the land of them. Its head and hands stick out of the sand, reminding us that the bodies of Monster Slayer's victims are strewn about the land of the Navajo.

Navajoland lies deep in Canyon de Chelly, at the foot of Shiprock, New Mexico, and where the Four Corners of Arizona, New Mexico, Utah, and Colorado meet.

But, like all places, Diné Bikeyah is more than the sum of its visible parts. The Navajo homeland just can't be experienced from the window of a speeding car. It is a visually powerful place, larger than 10 of the 50 states and similar to none. Within it, desert blends with grassland, grassland with other-worldly buttes, red and black and gray mesas with forested mountains. Few of its 14 million acres contains a village or town. Many people live in family compounds that are often separated by miles rather than feet. Diné Bikeyah is a place for the senses: it is the grit of sandy canyons, the scent of

Fascinating Facts about the Navajo

• With a population of 200,000 and an area of 14 million acres, the Navajo reservation is the largest and most populous in the United States.

• The Navajo believe an ideal natural human lifespan is 102 years.

• Navajo never reveal a personal name to strangers or enemies, so noteworthy heroes are known in history by their Spanish nicknames: Manuelito, Barboncito, etc. (Approximate translation: Manny, Little Beard—hardly dignified titles for leaders and headmen.)

• When children begin to talk, they are introduced to their relatives by the name of the relationship rather than the name of the individual. A person may have more than one clan mother and father. Clan aunts or uncles may be the same age or younger than their nieces and nephews.

• Some traditional Navajo believe that home should be rooted to the earth. Since mobile homes are not, they believe that the children who grow up in them may not have a strong foundation.

• In the old way, mud toys were put in water when a child was finished with them so that they would turn back to earth.

• The famous Wheelwright Museum of the American Indian in Santa Fe was founded by an heiress and a Navajo medicine man in the 1930s because they believed Diné rituals were dying out. Since Navajo ceremonial life continues to thrive, most of the original objects have been returned to the tribe.

• Traditional Navajo thinking holds that people are part of something much larger than Nature. At death, the good part of the spirit departs but the evil part may remain. Therefore, it is important to avoid the dead and the places where they died.

• When the Navajo were experiencing hard times during the Great Depression, the Gouldings of Gouldings Trading Post in Monument Valley took some Josef Muench photos of the landscape to Hollywood where they convinced director John Ford to use it as a setting for *Stagecoach* and later other films. The Navajo benefited not only from the movies but from resulting tourism.

• The Navajo name for Adolf Hitler was "the man who smells his mustache."

smoldering piñon, the baaing of sheep and goats carried on winds that whirl dust and those that bring snow. You need time to breathe the sage-scented air, listen to thunder in the mountains, hear the soft language of the people for whom the land is life itself.

Despite its accessibility, the sheer size of Diné Bikeyah creates challenging circumstances for the traveler. You'll need to familiarize yourself with the lay of the land and the stories and places you find inspiring. Most travelers have to prioritize cultural and historical interests and experience it in sections. Fortunately, it's easily divided into sub-trips and can be included in travels to other destinations.

How did the Navajo come to occupy this spectacular part of the world? Some time after 1200, circumstances conspired to cause many of the ancient residents of the Southwest to leave elaborately developed sites and settlements like Chaco Canyon, Wupatki, Canyon de Chelly, and Mesa Verde. In some cases they stored their belongings carefully. In others, pots and utensils and even food were left out as if someone would be back to use them. It appears that some people relocated along the Rio Grande River in the pueblos: Jemez, San Juan, San Felipe, and others now called by Spanish names. Some went to Zuni, Hopi, and beyond. Archaeologists believe that the people we call Navajo had not yet arrived.

Canyon de Chelly, seen here from the South Rim drive, has seen at least 1,500 years of human habitation.

Years after the ancients established new homes, a 20-year drought ended. By the mid-1500s, game animals spread across the wide open spaces. Grasslands flourished and springs ran again. Wild foods grew plentiful. It is during this era that historians see the first signs in the Southwest of a group of people who spoke an Athabaskan language. They believe that these people entered the region from the north about the same time as the Spanish explorers came from the south. They say that this small band was made up of early Navajo and Apaches. Their route is unknown, although some archaeologists suggest that they came by way of the Rocky Mountains from the sub-Arctic forests of what is now northwestern Canada and Alaska.

An old postcard shows Government Bridge over the Little Colorado River and sandstone buildings by Cameron Trading Post.

These bands were hunters and gatherers who spread out wherever they needed to go to find plentiful food. They followed game rather than settling in permanent villages like the Pueblos. Over time, they differentiated into the tribes known as the Navajo (*Diné: dih-NEH*) and Apache (*Ndee: n-DEH*). In their own dialects, both words mean "the People." Athabaskan language speakers who still live in the Far North include the *Dene* (den-EH) Nation, whose language can still be understood by the Diné from the United States.

The Diné, whom the Spanish called Navajo, came to fill in the spaces between the Pueblo groups. As the two peoples interacted, they adopted some of each others' customs. The Navajo supplemented hunting and gathering with cultivation of corn, beans, squash, pumpkins, and watermelons (the name Navajo is derived from *navahuu*, a Pueblo word referring to cultivated fields). They learned to weave and make pottery. They were influenced by

Ancient Ancestors

Naming the ancient peoples who built villages here is an ongoing issue. The most commonly used word for them is Anasazi, meaning Enemy Ancestors in Navajo; however, the Hopi use Hisatsinom, their name for themselves. No consensus has been reached by archaeologists or Indian peoples as to how to designate the ancients. The most neutral term in English is Ancestral Puebloans.

certain of the Pueblos' religious rituals and beliefs. But they kept their own customs as well: the pervasive ideal of *Hozho,* universal balance and harmony; the sacred aspects of the eight-sided hogan homes; their myths and symbolic traditions. By the 1700s, Navajo culture had become distinct from that of their linguistic relatives, the Apaches.

The Navajo custom of living at great distances from each other served them well when the Spanish came to the Southwest. It saved them from the secular and religious domination experienced by the Pueblos. *Entradas* made by explorers on the backs of horses and armed with guns soon overcame permanent settlements. But neither soldiers nor priests could track down enough widespread Navajo family groups to influence them, much less conquer them. The Diné instead traded with the Spanish, learned silversmithing from them, and adopted horses, sheep, goats, and cattle without paying the price of losing independence.

After the pueblos revolted against the Spanish in 1680, more people from the pueblos came to live with the Navajo, fearing Spanish reprisal at home. Their presence strengthened blending of the cultures. But the characteristic that has allowed the Navajo to survive and thrive was handed down through their roving ancestors: the ability to adopt new practices without losing the core of their own culture. The binding together of clans and families, the interdependence of men and women, people and the earth—these and other traditions structured how they integrated the old with the new.

The Southwest first introduced crop cultivation to the hunting Diné, but it was sheepherding that came to redefine Navajo life around its core beliefs. By the end of the 1700s, sheep were primary to the economy. They supplied mutton for food and wool for the beautifully woven blankets that constituted the Navajo's most important trade item. The Diné were not limited by ceremonial calendars and fixed villages, so as their herds grew, they freely expanded their territory.

Eventually, they began to bump into another herding culture, the Hispanic New Mexicans. (Remember that everyone in this part of the Southwest was Mexican until 1848, when they all suddenly became Americans.) Conflict over ranges intensified as forage became depleted. One hundred years of mutual

The Slave Trade

Raiding for the purpose of taking captives constituted a serious threat to the Navajo. The Utes were particularly aggressive in this pursuit, although Comanches, Apaches, Mexicans, and occasionally Pueblos also took literally hundreds of women and children whom they sold as slaves to colonial Spaniards, Mexicans, and Americans. The Navajo also raided and took slaves, however. While U.S. treaties included provisions for mutual return of captives, few were ever returned to their people.

Sheep represent the Navajo way of life to many people. Traditional women own them, care for them, prepare their wool, and weave it into an economically important product.

antagonism already existed between the two groups over raiding each other for slaves and later livestock. It left both vulnerable when the U.S. government entered the scene.

Despite frequent warring and mutual raiding, the Navajo grew relatively prosperous. Their numbers increased, and Utes, Paiutes, Mexicans, and more Pueblo people joined their ranks. When Mexico handed over the Southwest to the United States in 1848, the Navajo were a force to be reckoned with.

Resistance

Being perceived as powerful, of course, was not good news for any tribe, since containment was the stated goal for Indians. The Navajo ranged within approximately the boundaries of their Four Sacred Peaks—an enormous area —and numbered 10,000. Their society, like that of the Pai, was incompatible with the concept of containment.

The following year, contingents of the U.S. Army began to take stock of the situation, survey the territory, and inform the Native people that American law now prevailed. A council attended by a group of Navajo headmen led by white-haired Chief Narbona gathered to deal with them. Narbona advocated peace, because he believed that the Americans, victors in the Mexican War, would be natural allies of the Navajo.

These horses, born wild on Coal Mine Mesa, will be trained to compete in informal races that are ubiquitous around the Navajo Nation.

Violence sparked by their raiding past terminated an otherwise productive negotiation. A U.S. volunteer—a Hispanic New Mexican—spotted a Navajo riding a horse he said was stolen from him. His commander, who didn't understand the long history of back-and-forth rustling, ordered his troops to seize any Navajo horse they could, since the rider (or raider) in question had galloped off. When the soldiers charged, the Navajo fled. The soldiers fired, killing Narbona and others.

The Americans ignored this incident and proceeded toward Canyon de Chelly, where they prepared the treaty that Narbona had accepted in concept. It specified that the Navajo would receive presents from the government in exchange for a promise to submit to the law, let the government set their boundaries, and permit the establishment of military posts in their territory. Several headmen made their marks on it and the troops returned to Santa Fe without understanding that only those bands whose leaders signed were bound by the agreement. No single chief spoke for the entire tribe. Not only was the situation unresolved, the soldiers who had fired on the Navajo negotiators left enduring fury in their wake.

Other flashpoints followed. In a grazing dispute in 1858, livestock that belonged to Navajo headman Manuelito were killed near Fort Defiance. The same year, a Navajo killed a black Army slave there. Two years later Navajo attacked the fort and the following year 12 Navajo women and children were shot as a result of a drunken dispute over a horse race.

In 1860, field operations against the Diné began in earnest. In tribal history this era is called *nahndzod*, the Fearing Time. No one felt safe. A reservation was already designated for them, 400 miles from their homeland. Called Bosque Redondo, it consisted of a round forest of cottonwood and mesquite beside the Pecos River in New Mexico.

But rounding up a tribe that was so widely scattered represented an enormous challenge to the Army. How could they move thousands of people distributed over 25,000 square miles to Bosque Redondo, where they would be confined and guarded by a fort? Their homes were scattered across a rugged landscape that offered canyons to hide in, mesas and mountains to ascend, and vast open spaces where an army would be in full view of attackers.

Instead of capturing people, the Army's campaign consisted of ruining the most productive range and farmland in Diné Bikeyah. The destruction of crops and herds, hogans and even peach orchards began at harvest time, leaving the Navajo with no winter supplies or shelter. Troops led by Colonel Kit Carson and supplemented by Ute scouts conducted the devastation. In early 1863, 400 Navajo had been taken to Bosque Redondo. In January 1864, starving and defeated, 2,000 more Navajo surrendered at nearby Forts Defiance and Wingate. The beautiful, verdant Canyon de Chelly system, now a national monument, served as a stronghold for those who were able to hold out in its canyons and caves.

Incarceration

The government was not prepared to feed or house even the first 2,500 Navajo who came in, and their numbers increased. No horses and few wagons were available to take them to Fort Sumner, near Bosque Redondo, so the Navajo

---

Behind Every Great Man...

Manuelito, *Hastiin Ch'ilhaajinii* in his own language, was born in Utah around 1820 and grew up surrounded by Ute and Hispanic raiders. He learned young how to live on the run and was the most successful holdout during the Navajo Wars, living free through three winters. Although history has cast him as a war leader, Manuelito actually served his people in many other ways. As a headman, he was entitled to a number of wives, one of whom was peace chief Narbona's daughter. Another was Juanita, who helped make Navajo weaving known worldwide. He was treated as an authority figure by government agents and officials before and after the Long Walk. The Army made him head of a Navajo force against raiding that operated out of Forts Wingate and Defiance in the 1870s. He met with President Grant in Washington, D.C. as part of a delegation sent to negotiate an expansion of the reservation and spoke out in favor of the American education system as a ladder to a more secure future for his people.

Juanita, wife of Hastiin Ch'ilhaajinii (Manuelito), helped Navajo weaving become known and appreciated at the end of the 1800s.

For centuries, Navajo women have woven blankets and rugs desired for their high quality and great beauty. When the family moved, a loom could be made from locally available materials.

The Speaker of Blessings

Barboncito, whose nickname means "little beard" in Spanish, was born to a Navajo father and a mother from Jemez Pueblo in 1820. His Navajo names reflect his leadership qualities: *Bislahalani,* the Orator; *Hozhooji Naata,* the Blessing Speaker. He was also called He Who Steps Forward. Indeed, his ability to convince Gen. W. T. Sherman to send the Navajo back to their homeland reflects all of these gifts.

Barboncito is remembered as a kind and quiet man who promoted peace. He was a signer of the first treaty between the Navajo and the United States in 1848 after Narbona's death. He traveled to Santa Fe in 1862 to negotiate with General Carlton in an attempt to head off events that led to the Long Walk. No treaty resulted, and Barboncito walked with others to Bosque Redondo. Twice he escaped and twice he returned, finding life on the run impossible.

His role in the encampment then became that of a spiritual leader. He maintained rituals, songs, and prayers that brought the independent Navajo people together in their misery. Before Sherman arrived, Barboncito performed a Coyote Way ceremony out on the prairie beyond camp. The people formed an enormous circle around a coyote, into whose mouth Barboncito was able to insert a white shell bead. The people opened the circle and the coyote went off to the northwest, showing that the Navajo would soon return home.

Empowered by his beliefs, he alone spoke on behalf of the people, saying, "I want to return to my home in the west where the clouds will come and clean the earth, renew the people, and allow the Navajo to survive....I hope (the General) will do all he can for my people. This hope goes in at my feet and out at my mouth....We do not want to go to the right or left, but straight back to our own country."

His dignity and passion prevailed, and Barboncito made his mark on the treaty that allowed the Navajo to return on the condition that they cease warring. In spite of the bitterness of seeing their ruined land, he continued to preach peace. "My kinsmen," he said, "we lost everything and then we promised peace. Tell that to your children. See that they do not fight. See that they work."

Two years after his return, he died at the place of his birth, Canyon de Chelly.

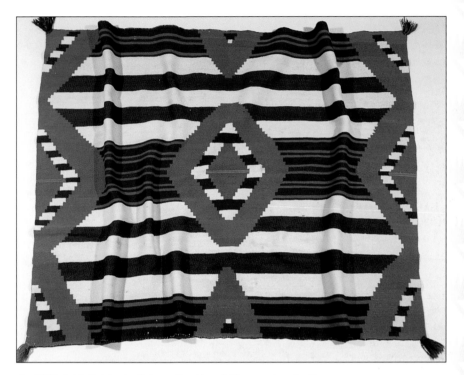

An 1880 "chief's blanket" from the Heard Museum's collection.
No exact counterpart is known outside the Navajo culture for
the classic design of stripes elaborated with geometric designs.

were walked in convoys in late winter across those 400 arduous miles. Those who lagged behind were shot. Some were abducted by Utes and New Mexicans. Many died on the trail.

When they arrived, there was no shelter and little food. Tents had been cut up and used for grain sacks. Food supplies had to be requisitioned from all over New Mexico and as far away as Kansas. The water was bad.

By 1866, nearly 9,000 Navajo had come to Bosque Redondo. For the next four years they tried to grow corn in impossibly wet weather. Ultimately, many fled. Scheme after scheme intended to make the Navajo into farmers—settled and easy to manage like the Pueblos—failed. Their relocation was so clearly unsuccessful that the government was considering moving the people on to Texas or Oklahoma Indian Territory.

No lesser general than William Tecumseh Sherman was sent to negotiate a new treaty. Strongly influenced by Barboncito, one of 12 chiefs who led the Navajo at Bosque Redondo, he was finally authorized to offer the Diné a reservation on their home territory. It encompassed less than half of their original homeland. After later additions, it totaled 25,000 square miles. But this area, figured in acres per capita, was insufficient to support the tribe.

Reservation Life

When the agreement was signed in 1868, the Navajo who survived walked back to Diné Bikeyah. Nearly a fourth of their people were gone. But when they returned, they found a few Navajo who had hidden out and never left.

Back in their homeland, the tribe expanded quickly. Once again, Diné resourcefulness led them to commercialize their traditional skills. They sold lamb, mutton, and wool. The women added rugs created for the tourist market to weaving blankets for themselves and trading tribes. Silver and turquoise jewelry became the signature craft of the men. Trading posts were established and came to play an important part in the economy. Many families depended on the foods the traders exchanged for the women's weavings. The men, who traditionally dealt with the outside world, often conducted negotiations.

To support themselves, however, they needed more grazing land for their livestock. By the end of the nineteenth century 20,000 people were herding more than 1 million sheep and goats. The population doubled again by the 1930s. Sheer numbers of livestock led to severe overgrazing and to a forced government stock reduction program that embittered many Navajo who watched their livelihood disappear before their eyes. Families, especially the women who owned stock, lost the symbols of their position as well as their tangible wealth. This blow followed the years when children were forcibly taken off to boarding school. The culture was stressed. How would they endure?

An eight-sided hogan is the traditional dwelling of the Diné. Its construction is permeated with symbolic meaning.

Again the people adjusted, this time by taking wage work as agricultural workers, in mining, or on the railroad. Men who in the past had been absent, first hunting, then raiding and herding, continued to work away from home. Women bound families together. Their sheep provided wool and their weavings still sold. The discovery of uranium, oil, gas, and coal on the reservation helped the economy. Navajo Forest Products Industries was established. Wartime employment raised the standard of living for some.

Modern Warriors and Their Secret Code

World War II was a turning point for the Navajo, as they were exposed in great numbers to the outside world. Thirty-six hundred young Diné men joined the military, a significant percentage of the eligible population. More than 10,000 were employed in military factories.

Among those who served were the famous Navajo Code Talkers, men who took part in every assault that the U.S. Marines conducted in the Pacific between 1942 and 1945. They telephoned and radioed in a code based on their complicated native language, a code that the Japanese never broke. Their part in the war remained a security secret for many years. Fifty-six years later, in 2001, the original 29 Code Talkers received the Gold Congressional Medal of Honor, many posthumously. The other 400 were awarded the Silver Congressional Medal of Honor.

Preston and Frank Toledo, cousins and WWII PFCs attached to a Marine Artillery Regiment in the South Pacific, relayed orders using the Navajo code.

After World War II, however, many jobs terminated. To assist in alleviating the economic situation, Congress passed the Long Range Program for the Rehabilitation of the Navajo and Hopi in the 1940s. The government spent nearly $89 million to build roads, improve soil and water conservation, strengthen employment circumstances, and advance education. Even so, only half the children of Diné Bikeyah had a school within a reasonable distance from home.

Between government-funded improvements, jobs becoming available on or just off the reservation, and revenue generated on tribal lands, the 1950s brought new hope to the Navajo Nation. As its income and exposure to the world outside increased, the tribe began assuming more and more control over its activities and programs.

The first step was to take over its education programs from the Bureau of Indian Affairs. Incorporating the language and traditions of the tribe into a curriculum that prepares young people to encounter the greater society is a continuing priority for the Navajo.

The tribe established a police and justice system. Programs for health care, law, public works, and community development followed. By the 1960s, the tribe was administered by divisions called chapters, and chapter houses were built in each area of the reservation.

Navajo culture breathes its spirit into daily life, although it continues to be battered by the influences of television and the consumer society. These forces push and pull today's Navajo people in many directions. A family group

A mother arranges her daughter's hair in the traditional Navajo way.

living close together or on the same land may consist of individuals who cover the entire spectrum from traditional to non-traditional. They may come and go, traveling to remote parts of the reservation from transitional towns like Tuba City or from employment centers like Phoenix. Many people work in one place and consider another

A Christian congregation within the Navajo Nation integrates older traditions by building a church in the form of a hogan.

home. Several members of one family group may speak English exclusively or as a first language, while others only speak Navajo. The gap between them can be so large that it creates distrust between the old and the young, the traditional and those who embrace contemporary ways and aspects of the dominant society.

Thus the family compound can represent an amalgamation of lifeways. One or several hogans, sometimes with the addition of a bathroom, will serve as home to elders, a place to store things, or a ceremonial center. A "square house" may be home to mother, father, and children. A family member sooner or later arrives with a mobile home, although because they don't connect with the earth they may be a source of concern to traditionalists. Part of the property is dedicated to sheep and goats. A dog or two strolls around, fed but not treated like a human. Horses and cattle may round out the group, and there's bound to be parking for plenty of the pickup trucks that are needed to haul supplies across unpaved roads.

Such an arrangement allows for flexibility. Someone who is older or not working can stay on the property and do the necessary work. Young family members take care of their elders, who then have an opportunity to share their wisdom. The generations who are being educated bring a different world to the elders.

If you, as a traveler through Diné Bikeyah, make the acquaintance of a Navajo family, it is into this world that you will walk. The opportunity to share a meal, spend the night in a hogan, attend a tribal government meeting, or ride through the abundant scenery with a Native guide will add a dimension to your experience of the landscape that allows you to begin to understand the close attachment of clan and family, earth and the Navajo people.

Navajo Ceremonials

While ceremonial occasions fascinate outsiders, they are not appropriate for visitors to attend. On the other hand, it is important to understand their place in the culture.

Navajo ceremonials form a complex system designed to bring life back into balance. No distinction is made between People and Life. The Creation Myth offers a degree of insight into the symbols used to integrate all things. However, the images, sounds, and rituals that communicate healing to a Navajo are so deeply embedded in ancient beliefs and long-held perceptions that it would be difficult for someone not of the culture to experience them in the same way.

• **Restoring** *Hozho:* Two basic rites address the light and the dark sides of life: the Blessing Way and the Enemy Way. The Blessing Way invokes good and invites prosperity and fortune. It is the matrix that carries songs incorporated throughout Navajo ceremonial life. It may be used to bless and protect a home, a marriage, a baby, or even a job. The Enemy Way is used to ward off evil, violence, and ghostly enemies. It once protected warriors from the spirits of those they had killed in battle.

In addition to rites, the Diné use chants, or Sings, to bless people and endeavors as well as for healing of disease, which can be physical or not. Illness calls for a ceremony because it stands as evidence that the ideal balance of *hozho* isn't fully present. The distinction between rites and chants, according to scholars who have analyzed them (something no Navajo would do) is that rattles accompany singing during chants. A Sing lasts 2 to 9 days, measured from sundown to sundown. It includes elements that attract positive results as well as those that ward off evil.

Most Sings include a consecration of the place where the ceremony is held, often a hogan; one or more sweat baths; a cleansing bath; prayers and offerings to attract good; singing for exorcism of evil; and sandpainting. At the end of the ceremony a final ritual brings closure to the entire process. *Iikaah* (sandpainting) can be translated as "a place where the gods come and go."

In the house made of dawn
In the story made of dawn
On the trail of dawn
O, Talking God
His feet, my feet, restore
His limbs, my limbs, restore
His body, my body, restore
His voice, my voice, restore
His plumes, my plumes, restore.
With beauty before him, with beauty before me
With beauty behind him, with beauty behind me
With beauty above him, with beauty above me
With beauty below him, with beauty below me
With beauty around him, with beauty around me
With pollen beautiful in his voice
With pollen beautiful in my voice.
It is finished in beauty
It is finished in beauty
In the house of evening light
From the story made of evening light
On the trail of evening light.

—"The Breath of Dawn," from *The Night Way*

• **Navajo sandpaintings:** An essential component of healing and blessing ceremonies, sandpaintings are complex symbolic drawings made on the earth by a full medicine man (*hataali*). To create the *iikaah,* he allows colored sand, crushed stones, dried plants and flowers, pollen, cornmeal, and other material to fall through his fingers onto the earth in a precise, elaborate, prescribed design. The colors white, blue, yellow, and black, associated with the directions and sacred mountains, predominate. A pure and sacred sandpainting must be made and destroyed on the same day. It is started at sunrise and completed by sunset. Sandpaintings available for sale are intentionally made incomplete or inaccurate. To sell a perfect *iikaah* would show disrespect for the spiritual power it contains.

Art Etcitty works on the rainbow that protects every sandpainting. He leaves the portion that faces east open, since no evil approaches from that direction.

The pure images for *iikaah* came from the Holy People—First Man, Changing Woman, Monster Slayer and Born of Water, Spider Woman, and others. Their original designs are maintained on sheets of sky, clouds, spider webs, or other appropriate materials. The Diné were given permission to reproduce them when they arrived in the Fourth World in order to call on the deities; however, no image can be preserved lest it be mistreated and thus bring misfortune. The images are swept into a blanket with a feather staff and disposed of carefully with a final prayer.

Once the *iikaah* is ready, the person who is being sung over sits in its center, surrounded by the entire clan family and community. The singer touches ritual items from his medicine bag to parts of the bodies of the Holy People depicted and then to the body of the individual being blessed and healed. *Hozho* is transmitted in this way. Balance is restored.

The ritual ends when the sandpainting is dismantled in reverse order of its creation. The materials are taken off to be buried or scattered to the six directions.

Creation Story

A scientific explanation of Navajo cultural development fulfills the needs of the rational, hemisphere of our brains. The explanation that follows satisfies the holistic, creative side— the part that doesn't analyze, verbalize, criticize, or "make sense" of everything. Instead, it ties together disparate events and gives them meaning. The stories are heard as poetry or music. The Navajo traditions do not separate art or spirituality from everyday life. Instead, they use myth to help integrate their decisions and behavior.

Many versions of these tales were told before Navajo became a written language. They are still taught to children today. Knowledge of the imagery and symbolism set forth in their expanded and various forms (for there are many) introduce the spiritual beings that shape Navajo life.

These paintings created by Navajo artist Harrison Begay illustrate mythical beings, creatures, plants, clouds and other symbols related to the Four Sacred Mountains of the Diné.

In the beginning the Spirit People and the Holy People lived, but the Black World—a dark, wet place—was inhabited only by Insect People and four monsters. They did not have form as we know it. The First World was small. It floated in the mist and its creatures were mist beings. The Insect Beings were able to live there because they understood how to plan and work together. Ant people, dragonflies, and Spider Man and Spider Woman were among them.

First Man and First Woman were created there. First Woman was formed on the western side when a yellow and a blue cloud came together. With her came a perfect ear of yellow corn, white shell, and turquoise. First Man was formed on the eastern side. They agreed in the First World to live together.

Then quarrels led the Water Creature to advise these beings to climb up to the Second World, the Blue World. Blue birds, blue jays, blue herons, and other blue-feathered beings were

already there. Wolves, cougars, badgers, and other animals also lived in the Blue World. They fought constantly. First Man had to kill some of them and then restore them to life because they rewarded him by sharing special songs and prayers. Coyote was already on the scene, and played his part in exploring the Second World.

Again dissension arose. The beings climbed to the Yellow World, home to the Grasshopper People. Still no one had a definite form. In the Third World they found six mountains: east was represented by white shell; south by turquoise; west by abalone shell; north by obsidian; center and east of center also existed. These mountains, directions, and colors still retain their importance. Here Coyote stole Water Monster's baby, which resulted in an enormous flood. He returned it with an offering and the waters receded.

But the beings left for the Fourth World, the Glittering World. Here First Man and First Woman formed the four sacred mountains from soil gathered in the Third World. They traveled by rainbow to plant them: first to the east (Blanca Peak), dressed in white shell; then to the south (Mount Taylor), decorated with turquoise; next to the west (San Francisco Peaks), which received abalone shell; and finally to the north (La Plata Mountains), whose gift was black obsidian. Each was also given a spiritual being who would live inside. Each mountain was covered with a cloud of its color, fastened to the earth by the appropriate method, and assigned a guardian: a bear, a snake, dark wind, and lightning.

First Man and First Woman formed these mountains, along with the life associated with them, under the direction of the Holy People at the genesis of the Fourth World.

In the Glittering World, First Man and First Woman had to create everything under the direction of the Holy People. They communicated for the first time through the *ye'ii*, spiritual helpers like Talking God and Water Bearer. First Man and First Woman learned to make the sun and moon, hogans to live in, rites and chants, seasons—everything. Coyote became impatient as they placed the stars in the sky, so he flipped the star blanket and finished the job as we see it today.

Initially, monsters represented a great challenge in this Fourth World. Fortunately, Changing Woman was soon born of Darkness and Dawn. She in turn gave birth to twin boys, fathered by the Sun. When they grew up, they were instructed by Spider Woman how to go to their father for the power to overcome the monsters. He gave them each lightning to use as a weapon. One by one, the older of the twins slew all the monsters while the younger enacted proper rituals to support him. They became known as Monster Slayer and Child Born of Water.

After this, Changing Woman and her people traveled, first by sun rays, rain trails, and other spiritual means and later by land, on foot. Changing Woman created four clans for the people, each with an animal guardian, and these still exist. Others were added later by the Holy People. The sites they visited fall within and around the Four Sacred Mountains and are recognizable today.

Some of the people dispersed, and are known now as Apaches. A special *ye'ii* protects those who remained within the curve of his body, which extends from Mount Taylor to Blanca Peak, outside the Four Sacred Mountains. The Navajo people risk disharmony with their spiritual past if they go beyond these boundaries.

• **The Wedding Ceremony:** Of course, marriages are performed in innumerable ways in today's world. Traditionally, however, certain customs were followed by the Navajo bride and groom.

The groom and his entire clan family—a clan unrelated to the bride's—would go to the bride's home in the evening, showing respect for the fact that Sun and Changing Woman, the first married couple, were wed during the day. A member of each family made arrangements that included gifts given between the families. The nature of the gifts would carefully avoid any appearance of buying the relationship.

The groom was expected to assess the bride's expectations, attitudes, and standard of living to assure that the couple would be compatible. A relative of the bride would state certain things that were meant to help him: "She never lacked for food or clothing, she never had to be punished and always had something to occupy her." These statements were taken very seriously. If the situation turned out to be misrepresented, the groom's family had the right to come back and complain.

This Edith Johnson weaving portrays ye'ii figures. They represent spiritual beings who carry communications between the Holy People and humans.

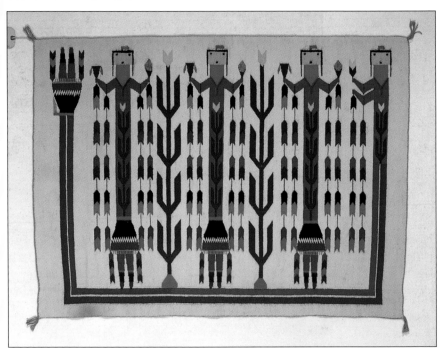

At the time of the wedding, the bride came with white corn and the groom with yellow, symbolizing First Man and First Woman. A well-married relative of the bride poured water over their hands to symbolize life together. Cornmeal with corn pollen brought by the bride would be taken out of the wedding basket from each of the four directions and the middle, the pattern of its opening facing east. The basket was then presented to the groom's mother, a symbol of their contract.

After the ceremony, the bride's family would provide a feast designed to make a good impression on the groom's family. Gifts were presented: cooking pots, towels, soap—practical items for housekeeping. The gifts were taken home to be opened. Specific people were invited to offer advice to the couple, reminding them that they were now partners who no longer should live just for themselves. Typically a well-married older couple, one who set a good example, spoke, along with other relatives.

The speakers might prepare the couple for the time when a child would be on the way. They would remind the mother that during pregnancy she was responsible for behaving well and making sure she did not associate with negative influences. Lack of harmony would show in the health and attitudes of the little one. The first relative to make the baby laugh was expected to give a feast, setting an example of generosity.

When the baby was born, the umbilical cord would be saved and put into the earth in a special place symbolizing the baby's connection with Earth and Sky, the mother and father. In the old days, this would be the place where the person would want to die, completing the circle of life.

• **The *Kinaalda*:** The *kinaalda* is part of the Blessing Way. Changing Woman, giver of life and fertility to the earth and its creatures, performed the first kinaalda, whose story is retold. This ceremony is performed to mark the transition from girlhood to womanhood. When a Navajo girl experiences her first menses she is given a four-day kinaalda. The meaning of the word refers both to the girl and to the ceremony and celebrates the power of the female to bring new life into the world.

During this ceremony, older women relatives prepare the girl to be a contributing member of adult society. She learns that she is a small part of a network that will support her. With them, she will never be alone in her role in the community.

As a woman she will go forward with the knowledge she needs to be educated, polite, hospitable, and a good wife and mother when the time comes. Other people will treat her differently after her kinaalda. It marks her last day as a child.

Exploring the Diné Lands

"I'm Navajo: fry bread and mutton are my specialty."

— Luci Tapahonso, *A Breeze Swept Through*

Navajo comfort food is only one of the experiences that will delight your senses as you travel the Navajo Nation. Its landscape is diverse and its scale is vast—in fact, it is so extensive that travelers who want to explore and experience the land of the Navajo may need to make more than one trip. Four trips are described here, each with places to visit along the way. Trip #4 also contains several side trips for visitors to these lands.

All directions for traveling the Diné lands begin in Flagstaff. I-40 and AZ 89, the two main roads to the Navajo reservation in Arizona, can be picked up from there.

TRIP #1: FLAGSTAFF TO WINDOW ROCK

There are two ways to get to Window Rock from Flagstaff. Both are listed below and each one has interesting places to visit along the way.

Via IR 12: Take I-40 east toward Winslow/Albuquerque. From the Interstate, you will have two choices. You can take the shortest route, which is to leave I-40 at Indian Route (IR) 12 N (Exit 357) and go 24 miles to Window Rock. The total distance is about 162 miles.

Via US 191 to Ganado and AZ 264: The other alternative is to travel via US 191 (Exit 333 off I-40) to Ganado, where you turn right at its junction with AZ 264 and follow it to Window Rock.

Petrified Forest National Park and the Painted Desert
lie on the southern edge of the Navajo Nation.

Via IR 12: Petrified Forest National Park

At Holbrook, take Exit 285, and go south on US 180 to the park entrance.
(928) 524-6228 • www.nps.gov/pefo • Open: 7 a.m.–7 p.m. through Labor Day.
The park maintains transitional hours during the fall and spring months.
Winter hours are 8 a.m.–5 p.m.; Closed: December 25

Your detour takes you into the Painted Desert, which rims the Navajo Nation's southern border, although this part is off the reservation. You will arrive at the south entrance, in the Rainbow Forest area where some of the best-preserved logs are scattered across the desert. You can also visit a museum and follow a short trail that winds past some of the biggest logs in the park. Agate House, a partially restored Native-built structure constructed before 1400 entirely of petrified wood, is also nearby and worth a visit.

Via IR 12: R. B. Burnham and Co. Trading Post

Sanders • (928) 688-2777 • Open: Variable hours
Sanders is located just south of the junction of I-40 and US 191. Take Exit 339.

Although their building is just over 25 years old, Bruce and Virginia Burnham's business began generations ago. In the late 1800s George Franklin Burnham founded it after he came, like many other traders, as a missionary of the Church of Jesus Christ of Latter-Day Saints. Virginia is Diné. Both are very well informed. If you are interested in buying a weaving, jewelry, or another Navajo creation, they can help you find an authentic, high quality piece. You can also order Navajo moccasins made to fit your feet.

Navajo people are the primary clients of this trading post. Travelers are the exception. The store's stock provides an education in the daily lives of the people who shop there. The collection of colorful yarns, the array of weavings, a particular scent of wool and old silver, smoke, wood, and earth becomes a sensory memory of an authentic trading post.

Tourism

Navajoland Tourism offers a source of information about any aspect of visiting the reservation. They can be reached at (928) 871-7371 or (928) 871-6436; Fax: (928) 871-7381; or through http://www.discovernavajo.com or www.navajocentral.com.

Indian Nations are sovereign governments, even though this one rests within three separate state jurisdictions—Arizona, New Mexico, and Utah. It provides a broad range of services on tribal lands, including law enforcement, environmental protection, emergency response, education, health care, and basic infrastructure. Through the Nation's tourism programs, you will be welcomed as honored guests.

When you are traveling, remember that the Navajo Nation observes Mountain Daylight Saving Time during the summer and the rest of Arizona observes Mountain Standard Time year round.

Via IR 12: Lupton

Take Exit 357 at Lupton

The Arizona Office of Tourism maintains a Welcome Center in Lupton. Besides area information, it offers a rotating exhibit maintained by the Navajo Arts and Crafts Enterprise.

Via US 191: Hubbell Trading Post National Historic Site

Ganado • (928) 755-3475 • www.nps.gov/hutr • Open: Daily 8 a.m.–6 p.m.;
8 a.m.–5 p.m., winter; Closed: January 1, Thanksgiving, and December 25
Take Exit 333 and follow US 191 north to Ganado. The historic site is
on the left just after the road heads northwest toward Chinle.

Hubbell's hacienda was a center of activity for both Navajo and others during its heyday in the late 1800s. J. L. Hubbell himself made sure of it. And the Trading Ranch—much more than a post—is still active. Many of the colorful rugs displayed in the old stone building are woven recently, using older designs. Back in the days of the harnesses, saddles, and wooden boxes that are mixed in with today's necessities, rugs were sold by the pound. Hubbell's house, where he often hosted famous artists, is authentically furnished and crowded with paintings that would be the pride of a museum. Don't miss the barn, either. Every building represents a piece of history.

"Hubbell prospected Indian country much as a gold miner would, looking for spots that lent themselves to other ventures," says Martha Blue in *Indian Trader: The Life & Times of J. L. Hubbell.* "With tokens, Mexican silver dollars,

Hubbell Trading Post National Historic Site, which opened in the late 1800s, is still active.

groceries, and occasionally a little cash he wrapped his Indian customers and laborers in a tight economic warp. He spared no effort in developing a dependent community around him, both at Ganado and at his other trading posts."

Via US 191: Sage Memorial Hospital

Ganado • (928) 755-3411 The hospital is about a mile east of the Hubbell Trading Post on the north side of AZ 264, the road to Window Rock.

Sage Memorial Hospital is the only hospital in the region that is able to treat non-Indians. Indian Health Service hospitals are permitted to stabilize patients but must then transport them to other institutions.

Many of the buildings from the late 1800s remain at Hubbell Trading Post National Historic Site.

The Navajo Tribe, with philanthropist Olivia Sage, funded the initial construction of Sage Hospital in 1929. Many Navajo received their first exposure to modern medicine here. Dr. Clarence Salisbury, a missionary surgeon who came on a short assignment to help with a diphtheria epidemic, risked his life by staying and treating people who did not understand his methods. When one of his first patients died, a trusted medicine man had to restrain people who believed that he was responsible for the death. Over his 21-year tenure, Salisbury grew to be part of the community. He later founded the first Native American Nursing School Program there. The complex still serves as a private teaching institution.

Nearby Ganado Mission was the first health care establishment in Ganado. It opened in 1911 with only one doctor. Presbyterian missionaries expanded and ran it until the 1960s.

The historic stone buildings on both campuses are worthy of note.

Via US 191: St. Michaels Mission and Indian School, St. Michaels Museum

St. Michaels • (928) 871-4171 • www.rc.net/gallup/stmichael
Open: Memorial Day to Labor Day, 10 a.m.–5 p.m.
There is no fee but etiquette suggests a donation. The town of
St. Michaels is about 25 miles east of Ganado on AZ 264

Mother Katharine Drexel, an heiress who became a Roman Catholic missionary, came here in 1896 to buy the property for a mission. She amassed 160 acres of land altogether. It was not then on the reservation. Two Ohio Franciscans came to Arizona Territory to manage her project. They studied Navajo with the local trader and incorporated Diné tradition into their ministry, which began during the difficult years just after the people returned from the Long Walk.

The Franciscans who came to St. Michaels ultimately played an important part in the development of reservation life. Father Berard Haile became a student of the culture. He helped create an orthography for the Navajo language and published a Diné dictionary in 1910. In the mid-1800s Father Anselm Weber worked with the people to negotiate for additional reservation land to accommodate their expanding population. Over a million acres were added to the original reservation with his assistance.

In 1902, Katharine Drexel and the Sisters of the Blessed Sacrament from Philadelphia founded the school as an elementary and industrial boarding school for Navajo children. At that time, many Navajo parents feared education, because the government had forced their children to attend boarding schools far from home. Consequently, some stayed with their children at St. Michaels day after day to be sure they were treated well.

The high school opened in 1950, and in the early 1980s boarding was phased out. Today the high school offers a college preparatory curriculum. Over 90 percent of its graduates go on to college or other higher education. St. Michaels' students have also distinguished themselves in boys' and girls' basketball, cross country running, and football. More than 400 students, K–12, of all creeds, attend SMIS. More than 90 percent are Native American; of these, 95 percent are Navajo. The rest come from other tribes in the Southwest.

A prayer chapel on the grounds has an unusual carving of Christ being taken from the Cross. It was fashioned from a tree trunk by a Navajo artist.

Saint Katharine Drexel

Katharine was born into a wealthy family in Philadelphia in 1858. Her family believed that their wealth was meant to be shared with others, especially the poor. Katharine's travels took her to Indian reservations early in her life. Seeing a need, she personally began to finance mission schools and ultimately built 50 missions on 18 reservations. On October 1, 2000, Pope John Paul II proclaimed her Saint Katharine Drexel.

(Remember that this school is in operation during the school year.)

Early in the twentieth century, a Franciscan father photographed people native to the area, and the small St. Michaels Museum (open during weekdays seasonally) offers an opportunity to view his historic photos. It also chronicles the lives of the monks who established a mission in this area in the 1670s. A striking church stands next to the museum.

WINDOW ROCK

Window Rock is the capital of the Navajo Nation and home to impressive tribal headquarters as well as a museum, arts and crafts enterprise, and a small zoo. Diné College, which provides both lodging and an interesting look at contemporary issues and Diné history, is located in Tsaile. The drive between the two has been designated as an Arizona Scenic Byway. It passes from limestone arches through desert and forested mountains that hide secrets of history and prehistory within their canyons.

Window Rock is not large, so specific directions may be obtained from the Visitor Center when you arrive.

The Nation's capital, Window Rock, is named after this opening in the rocks.

Friday Night Lights

If you're traveling the Navajo Nation during the school year, check out a football or basketball game at any of the high schools on Friday nights. They're good games—many of the teams make the state playoffs—and you will participate in a level of excitement you may not have experienced since your own high school days.

Navajo Tribal Museum and Zoo

(928) 871-6574

The Visitor Center welcomes you just inside the very contemporary Museum building. Its entrance faces surrounding rock formations and an authentic hogan. Besides permanent exhibits, many of which refer to the Long Walk and history leading to reservation life (including the 1849 treaty between the Navajo people and the U.S. government), you'll find a hall for changing exhibits and a gift shop.

This furnished hogan, outside the entrance to the Navajo Tribal Museum in Window Rock, is open to the public.

Hidden in the far reaches of the museum is an engaging interpretation related to the Miss Navajo Pageant. Rather than a thinly-veiled beauty contest, the Miss Navajo Pageant celebrates accomplishment and familiarity with both contemporary and traditional issues. Contestants must perform half of their presentation in English and the other half in Navajo. Miss Navajo becomes a spokeswoman for her nation—a natural position for a woman in a matriarchal society. Photographs explain the cultural importance of the competition. You can also see the silver, coral, and turquoise crowns that have been retired.

Outside the museum is a small zoo where wild and domestic animals important to the Navajo culture reside in natural habitats. Some of the animals arrived as orphans. The birds of prey have permanent injuries that prevent their return to the wild. Signage explains their significance.

Navajo Arts and Crafts Enterprise

(928) 871-4090

This coral-colored building houses the main arts and crafts center (the others in Arizona are located in Chinle, Kayenta, and Cameron). Here you can peruse a variety of Navajo-made art and buy with confidence that it is authentic.

Tribal Chambers

(928) 871-6417 • www.opvp.navajo.org/contact.htm

The Nation's legislators deliberate and decide matters of law at the Navajo Nation Council Chambers. The circular Chambers feature murals depicting the history of the Nation and its way of life. Tours may be arranged in advance by calling.

Veterans Memorial Park

At the base of Window Rock a park has been created to honor Navajo military personnel, past and present. The Navajo Code Talkers are the best known of

Rodeos and Beauty Queens: The Navajo Nation Fair

"When the wind is blowing and the sun is hot, it's fair time! Put on your cowboy boots and ribbon shirts and get in the nearest pickup. It's time to go to the Navajo Nation Fair in Window Rock!" says Kathleen Lampert, Diné.

Although the Nation's capital and museum are worth visiting any time of year, Fair Time—usually in September, the first weekend after Labor Day—is a special cultural experience.

The five-day Navajo Nation Fair offers a variety of events including a rodeo, horseracing, an intertribal powwow, arts and crafts exhibits, concerts, a song and dance competition, the Miss Navajo Pageant, native foods and a fry bread contest, livestock and agricultural exhibits, and the Navajo Nation parade. "Come early and bring your folding chairs or a blanket to sit along the road and enjoy the floats, rodeo horses, native dancers, the World War II Navajo Code Talkers, distinguished guests, and Miss Navajo with her court," suggests Lampert. "Proceed on to the fairgrounds and plan to spend all day to take in the many sights."

For information on the Navajo Nation Fair in Window Rock, call the fair office at (928) 871-6647 or visit the website online at www.navajonationfair.com. The fairgrounds are located just outside of Window Rock.

Miss Navajo is crowned at the Navajo Nation Fair. Candidates are subjected to stringent requirements related to understanding Diné language and culture.

hundreds who have served their country over the years. The park contains 16 steel pillars memorializing war veterans and a healing sanctuary for visitors to reflect on their service.

The area around Window Rock was important to the Diné before it was designated as the tribal capital. Near here was a place to obtain ceremonial water. The remains of ancient structures lie in the vicinity. If you are interested in walking to the natural arch, inquire at the Visitor Center about permits and guides.

TRIP #2: WINDOW ROCK TO TSAILE

Leave Window Rock and travel north on IR 12 toward Fort Defiance. This area is closely linked to Navajo history and the Long Walk.

You'll pass rolling hills and red rock cliffs. Be on the alert for livestock. The Navajo Nation is an open range area, and horses, cattle, sheep, and goats have the right-of-way. If you see animals, you are likely to see their herders accompanied by a dog who is, of course, the assistant herder.

On weekends it is not unusual to see Navajo men in bright ribbon shirts riding along on horseback. They may be on their way to a traditional gathering called a squaw dance (you'll see signs announcing the dance, too, whose makers seem unconcerned about the political correctness of the word "squaw"). If the site of the ceremony is close to the road, you may catch a glimpse of a shade house, a wooden structure covered with branches and leaves, where participants gather.

Before you reach Wheatfields Lake you'll pass through New Mexico as the road winds in and out of two states. A few miles down the road you are back in Arizona. Ponderosa pines soon let you know that you're climbing to a higher elevation.

Wheatfields Lake

About 48 miles north of Window Rock you will pass this 270-plus-acre lake set against the Chuska Mountains. It offers campsites with picnic tables and

fireboxes under cool Douglas firs. The small general store is usually open 7 days a week for supplies and light food items. Fishing licenses can be purchased there as well.

Dinner could be trout or sunfish. If you don't have your own fishing gear, you can rent a boat and tackle; or you could just try your luck from shore. A launch ramp is available for boats (electric motors only). Ice fishing is a possibility during the winter months.

Diné College

Tsaile • (928) 724-6654 • www.dinecollege.edu
Open: Monday–Friday for arranged tours. Call for hours and availability of accommodations, which depends on school schedules.

Diné College is dedicated to transmitting the Navajo culture. It was the first tribal college established in the United States and is the largest controlled by a Native tribe. The curriculum offers higher learning with a bicultural emphasis. Instruction combines Navajo language, history, culture, and philosophy with Western disciplines.

Visitors are welcomed at the college, and cultural experiences are available to non-students. Please call in advance for a guided tour; or you may visit independently.

You will see beautiful murals in the student union; the Ned Hatathlii Cultural Center, a museum and gallery of Navajo arts and crafts; and a ceremonial hogan nestled inside the six-story mega-hogan housing the Cultural Center. The inner hogan may be in use, so if you visit on your own, you will, of course, respect the privacy of anyone who is there. The college bookstore is also worth a look. You'll find books there you won't see anywhere else.

If space is available, you may, for a reasonable price, dine with the students and sleep in dorm rooms. You may use the kitchen area to prepare your own food when the cafeteria isn't open.

Diné College in Tsaile, its mega-hogan looming against the Chuska Mountains, offers education in contemporary issues and Diné history for Navajos and visitors.

TRIP #3: CANYON de CHELLY NATIONAL MONUMENT

Chinle • (928) 674-5500 • www.nps.gov/cach
Open: Daily October–April, 8 a.m.–5 p.m.; May–September, 8 a.m.–6 p.m.
From I-40, take Exit 333. Follow US 191 north to Chinle.

The National Monument itself is managed by the Navajo Nation, although the National Park Service maintains the roads and the visitor center. A museum constructed as a replica of a hogan offers cultural demonstrations, exhibits, relevant books, and a ranger-staffed information desk. Facilities include parking, restrooms, and concessions for canyon trips by car, horseback, or on foot.

Rangers organize daily activities from May to September. They include a morning orientation, canyon hikes, natural history presentations, and campfire programs at the Campground Amphitheater. Navajo presenters offer educational talks centering on Diné history and culture every Saturday, May to September.

It is difficult to convey a sense of Canyon de Chelly Monument, even through the many beautiful photographic images it has inspired. It appears in Patricia Schultz's *1,000 Places to See Before You Die,* along with Machu Picchu, Ankor Wat, and Pompeii. Formed by three connected canyons—de Chelly *(duh-SHAY)*, del Muerto *(MWAIR-toe)*, and Monument—the place is truly exceptional, at once subtle, spiritual, and dramatic. It is still alive, home to Navajo families, but preserves a past that goes back before our era. Canyon de Chelly has

Chinle Creek flows toward Monument Valley out of Canyon de Chelly.

been compared to Egypt's Valley of the Nile for the spirit of antiquity that it evokes.

Sheer red walls enclose 83,840 acres where water from meandering streams greens the canyon floor. It is easy to see why it has been home to many peoples for hundreds of generations. Sites exhibit more than 1,500 years of human occupation, from the time of pithouses to cliff dwellings, pueblos, and contemporary Navajo hogans. Today Navajo raise flocks of sheep and goats and farm here in season. They live quite traditionally, without what city people call infrastructure. Scholars believe that Navajo first settled here about 300 years after the ancients departed.

The remains of more than 800 dwellings built perhaps between 350 and 1300 are sheltered in sandstone caves and under overhangs. Some of the finest rock art in the Southwest—both petroglyphs and pictographs—remind us that we are in the presence of the ancient peoples who created them: handprints, running antelope, a fish created from natural weathering, a pictorial record of a Spanish entrada and a Ute raid. Thousands of pages have been written about this place so rich with history. A few unforgettable high points include these sites:

Antelope House

Pictographs painted high on the walls give this pueblo its name. It is built into an alcove on the floor of Canyon del Muerto. Beneath what you see, archaeologists have uncovered structures going back at least to the eighth

Adventures on the Edge

If gazing over and into canyons appeals to you, two scenic drives offer panoramic perspectives of Canyon de Chelly, to the north, and Canyon del Muerto, to the south. From either the north or south edge, the canyons orient you to the scale of their famous sites. Ledge Ruin, Antelope House, Navajo Fortress, Mummy Cave, Spider Rock, and Massacre Cave appear differently proportioned when they are viewed as a small part of the landscape. Some of the views are just plain beautiful, while a few could inspire acrophobia in the most stoic visitor.

At monument headquarters near Chinle you'll find brochures and maps that describe the routes. Allow at least an hour to explore the north rim and two hours for the south rim.

The south rim drive follows Canyon de Chelly and is paved except where it forks to the right onto the reservation (you'll fork left). Its eight overlooks include White House Ruin trailhead, the only hike into the canyon that doesn't require a permit. At Spider Rock Overlook, the final vista, you can peer a thousand feet down to the base of the formation where Spider Woman taught the art of weaving.

The north rim drive—actually IR 64—follows Canyon del Muerto from Chinle toward Tsaile. Short detours from the main road overlook Antelope House Ruins and Massacre Cave, and you'll find wonderful views in between.

A closer look at White House Pueblo reveals extraordinary rock art.

century. Antelope House artifacts create a record of the life of people who lived there—woven cotton, pottery, the remains of food and firewood, all contributed to a picture of the environmental conditions that prevailed during their residence.

Mummy Cave

Two caves deep in Canyon del Muerto are connected by a ledge on which stands Tower House, a well-preserved three-story structure from the thirteenth century that was one of the last to be built before the ancients left the canyon. The caves themselves shelter much older ruins and artifacts, some dated around 400. The pueblo included at least 80 rooms and three kivas. Mummified bodies still wrapped in yucca fiber were found there in 1882 and they gave it its name.

Spanish Influence

The name de Chelly, like del Muerto, reflects Spanish influence here. Tsegi, (tsay-YEE) a Navajo name which means "rock canyon," sounded to the Spanish ear like "shay," which they spelled Chelly. "Del muerto," meaning "of death," was named to commemorate the deaths of Navajo women and children who were massacred there by a group led by Spanish soldiers. The men were away, hunting in the Lukachukai Mountains.

Navajo Fortress Rock

Navajo continually fought enemies after they became established here—other tribes as well as Hispanic and white settlers. Raids and counter-raids were the norm for at least 200 years and the final fights were against Kit Carson's forces. Fortress Rock provided an emergency escape. Notched poles and climbing ropes were placed there so that people could climb, pull up their equipment, and stay until danger had passed.

White House Ruin

Two levels of dwellings make this the largest site you will see. The rooms at the base of the cliff give access to its second level. They are surrounded by extraordinary rock art.

Spider Rock

Canyon de Chelly and Monument Canyon meet at this point. Spider Rock is 800 feet high and stands next to a somewhat shorter spire. It is said to be the home of Spider Woman, who taught Changing Woman to weave on a secret loom. Her crosspoles were made from sky and earth, her warp sticks from sunrays, and her heddles from rock crystal and lightning. She used a batten

800-foot-high Spider Rock marks the spot where Canyon de Chelly meets Monument Canyon. Here Spider Woman taught Changing Woman to weave on a secret loom.

stick created from sun halo and a comb made of white shell. She passed this knowledge on to Diné women.

Visiting the Canyon

To experience Canyon de Chelly is to go back in time. You'll be surrounded by reminders of the vitality of ancient civilizations. It requires at least one full day of exploration and the patience to take it all in. Your need for overnight accommodations will depend on where you came from and where you are going. Especially during summer, the vacation season, it is essential to make reservations ahead of time, for it is a popular destination for people from all over the world.

In summer and winter, be prepared for heat or cold. One reason the canyon is not crowded in winter is that it can be very chilly at 5,500 feet. Summer can mean temperatures above 90 degrees, and the rock walls retain both extremes.

Most visitors want to experience the connected inner canyons from the ground. Reservations and prior arrangements for all activities are highly recommended. Along with Visitor Center resources, four-wheel-drive tours are available through Thunderbird Lodge (see Dining and Overnight Accommodations, p. 144), which is open all year and offers lodging and meals. Other Chinle motels also issue permits and provide information. A vehicle can be rented with a guide, or you may drive your own SUV and hire a guide separately. You must have a four-wheel-drive vehicle, a Park Service permit, and an authorized Navajo guide. Well-informed guides enhance your experience. Each may lead up to 15 people. Horseback rides are also available.

Hiking within the canyon requires a Park Service permit and an authorized Navajo guide, with one exception. White House Ruins Trail, which descends 600 feet to the canyon floor, can be negotiated on your own. The trailhead is 7 miles down the south rim drive. Some places are steep but not extremely difficult. Expect to hike for about 30 minutes, one way.

Loads of Loot

At the turn of the last century, looting ruins was a common practice. When Charles Day built a trading post at Chinle in 1902, the Department of Interior appointed him caretaker of Canyon de Chelly and Canyon del Muerto. He excavated and removed artifacts from many sites. In 1906, he and his son sold a large collection to the Brooklyn Museum of Natural History, where it has occasionally been exhibited since. That same year the American Antiquities Act was passed, finally providing protection for Southwest antiquities and nurturing the new scientific discipline of archaeology. Still, in the 1920s and 1930s, trainloads of artifacts collected by archaeologist Earl Morris were sent to the American Museum of Natural History. A few went to the University of Colorado Natural History Museum in Boulder.

The magic of Monument Valley is revealed at sunrise and sunset.

TRIP #4: MONUMENT VALLEY TRIBAL PARK

*(928) 871-6656 • www.navajonationparks.org • Open: May–September, 8 a.m.–
7 p.m.; October–April, 8 a.m.–5 p.m.; Closed: Thanksgiving and December 25.*

*From Flagstaff, take US 89 north to US 160. Turn east toward Tuba City and
Kayenta, where gas and food are available. Take US 163 north from Kayenta
about 24 miles. Monument Valley Tribal Park lies on the Arizona–Utah border.
The visitor center is about 1 mile east of the road.*

*Visitor services include a cafeteria that serves drinks and meals, a gift shop,
and a museum interpreting the area's history. Commercial guides offer four-wheel-
drive and horseback tours. Check at the visitor center or area lodging for a list.*

Monument Valley is pure natural beauty. It is a tribal park made of sandstone
wind-sculpted into enormous masterpieces, some rising 400–1,000 feet high.
They are set against neutral, softly textured desert onto which the light of
cloud shadows and sun play shape-shifting tricks on the eye. Mesas and buttes,
sagebrush, and sand stretch beyond the horizon.

Sunrise and sunset are the times to be there. The circle road around
Rain God Mesa takes you by spectacular scenery, but passing through at
noon doesn't compare with stopping to take in the changing light. A tour
with a good guide adds color of a different kind.

TRIP #4: SIDE TRIPS

Between Flagstaff and Monument Valley—but not necessarily along the way—
lie a number of destinations that are well worth a detour. While the ancient
dwellings at Wupatki and Navajo National Monuments were not originally
built by the Diné people, they have played a part in their history. Two trading
posts—Cameron and Shonto—are more than places to shop: They have the
look and feel of old times. And the landscapes of the Painted Desert and
Sunset Crater are unique in the United States.

The following points of interest along the route from Flagstaff to Monument Valley are listed in the order in which you encounter them along US 89
north and US 160 northeast. Plan an hour, more or less, for a stop at any one
of them (with the exception of the Painted Desert, which you can see from
your car).

Wupatki National Monument and Sunset Crater

These places are worth a day trip in themselves, although you can swing
through and get back on US 89. They're located on a 20-mile loop, FR 545.
Enter at the first entrance, about 12 miles north of Flagstaff.

Wupatki was an important trade center less than 800 years ago. Perhaps
100 people lived there and 1,000 more lived within a day's walk. The remains
of other pueblos like Wukoki and Citadel surround it. Archaeological evidence
such as the remains of parrots, copper bells, and a ballcourt suggest that its
residents traded with people to the south. Navajo came to live there in the
1870s. It is claimed as hereditary ground by Hopi of the Snake Clan and by
the Havasupai.

Sunset Crater is an extinct volcano, one of 200 in the region. It last erupted
around 800. Cinders cover the ground around Wupatki, while ice caves, lava
beds, and other reminders of that time are scattered for miles around Flagstaff.
It is said to have been a stopping place for Navajo western water clans.

Cameron Trading Post

(800) 338-7385, (928) 679-2231 • www.camerontradingpost.com

This historic lodge, gallery, and trading post on US 89 overlooks the gorge of
the Little Colorado River. It was established in 1911, the year Government
Bridge was built there. The rooms and dining facilities are excellent and the
trading post offers both authentic arts and crafts and inexpensive souvenir
items. The gallery, located in a separate building, sells very high-end antique
and contemporary baskets, pottery, jewelry, traditional clothing, blankets,
rugs—excellent examples of nearly every Indian art or craft. It is beautifully
restored, a virtual museum.

The Navajo Nation maintains two overlook points on the Little Colorado
River Gorge. Cameron is also the site of a Navajo Arts and Crafts Enterprise.

Painted Desert

The Navajo name for the area that you will drive through when you turn off US 89 toward Tuba City is *halchiitah*, "amid the colors," a beautiful term for the badlands that define the southern edge of the reservation. You will see a small sign that points to a dinosaur trackway on the left side of the road. It's there. This area was once home to prehistoric creatures of all kinds.

Navajo National Monument

Shonto • (928) 672-2700
www.nps.gov/nava
Open: Daily 8 a.m.–5 p.m.
Between Tuba City and Kayenta,
go about 10 miles north on AZ 564

Three ancient pueblos are sheltered in the rock here. The Visitor Center overlooks Keet Seel, a thirteenth-century dwelling that is nearly intact. You can also walk a 1-mile

The colorful badlands of the Painted Desert

trail to view Betatakin, a structure from the same period, or hike in and camp overnight with advance reservations and a guide. Call WAY ahead. Overnighters are limited and tours are popular. Round trip, the hike is 17 miles. A visit to nearby Shonto Trading Post is worth a short detour. Ask for directions at the monument.

Kayenta

Monument Valley is now in sight, 24 miles north. The town of Kayenta offers services like gas, food, and lodging that are few and far between in the area. An unexpected pleasure at the local Burger King is a well-organized exhibit related to the Navajo Code Talkers. Who would guess? A branch of the Navajo Arts and Crafts Enterprise is also located in town.

Dining and Overnight Accommodations

Advance reservations are strongly recommended everywhere, especially during the summer. This includes rooms as well as popular activities.

Trip #1: Flagstaff to Window Rock

http://hotel-guides.us/arizona/saint-michaels-az-hotels.html
http://az.allpages.com/window-rock/travel-tourism/lodging/

There is no overnight lodging in Ganado. Food and lodging are both available in **St. Michaels** and **Window Rock**. It's a good idea to make reservations ahead, especially during the travel season.

Trip #2: Window Rock to Tsaile

Diné College, Tsaile • *(928) 724-6654* • *www.dinecollege.edu*

If space is available, you may dine with the students, sleep in the dorm, or use the kitchen to prepare your own food when the cafeteria is closed. Call ahead to check prices and availability.

Trip #3 Canyon de Chelly National Monument

• **Thunderbird Lodge** offers food and lodging and has four-wheel-drive tours. P.O. Box 548, Chinle, AZ 86503; (800) 679-2473, (928) 674-5841; www.tbirdlodge.com.

• **Spider Rock Campground** offers camping (ask about forked stick hogans) and has RV parking. (928) 674-8261, (877) 910-2267; http://home.earthlink.net/~spiderrock/contact.htm.

• **Cottonwood Campground** offers camping and has free RV parking. (928) 674-5500. Located in Canyon de Chelly near the visitor center. Open year-round on a first-come basis. 96 sites; restroom; no showers or hook-ups.

• **Holiday Inn Chinle-Garcia Trading Post**
IR 7, Chinle, AZ 86503; (928) 674-5000

• **Best Western Canyon de Chelly Inn**
100 Main St., Chinle, AZ 86503; (928) 674-5874

Trip #4: Monument Valley Tribal Park

There is no lodging available within Monument Valley, but options are available in **Kayenta** (http://hotel-guides.us/arizona/kayenta).

The nearest town is Goulding, Utah, a small town established in 1923 as a trading post. **Gouldings Lodge** is still a place to stay, eat, see a Monument Valley video, and visit the museum, which displays both Indian artifacts and memorabilia related to the Hollywood movies made in Monument Valley. It offers rooms and a pool, a restaurant, and campgrounds with RV hookups, and it books four-wheel-drive and horseback tours into Monument Valley. Contact them at (435) 727-3231; www.gouldings.com.

Shopping

Because the Navajo reservation is so large, shopping takes place wherever you are visiting. Official Navajo Arts and Crafts Enterprise outlets, museums, and trading posts are the best places to find authentic arts and crafts. The occasional roadside vendor may offer something inexpensive and attractive, such as cedar bead necklaces, but the selection is usually limited. A little research goes a long way in helping you take home something that is truly Navajo.

Diné identity revolves around the spirit of *hozho,* beauty and harmony, which expresses itself in the arts that are inseparable from life itself. The process of creation needs to be as balanced as the object created.

The arts have blessed the Diné spiritually and support them economically. Navajo weavings, jewelry, baskets, pottery, and other expressions of their culture are appreciated worldwide by collectors and more casual buyers.

Weaving is probably most frequently associated with the Navajo. Silversmithing is almost equally well known. Less identified with the Diné are leather working, painting, and sculpture. Navajo Folk Art has also become popular in recent years. It ranges from whimsical mud toys and fancifully decorated chickens with straw tails to the serious spirit carvings of the Willetto family.

Art forms whose roots lie in ritual and ceremony have also been adapted for secular audiences. Examples are sand paintings and carvings depicting supernatural subjects. (Katsinas are Hopi. The Navajo have their own Holy People.) In many cases, the artists have broken taboos to bring these representations to the commercial world, sometimes with unusual consequences.

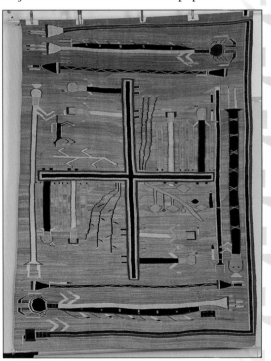

Hosteen Klah, a respected medicine man who worked in the 1920s and '30s, wove sacred symbols into textiles, like this pattern from the Night Chant. He deliberately included errors to avoid showing disrespect for the Holy People.

• **Weaving:** One tradition tells of Spider Woman weaving first with a pueblo dweller who was instructed to take that art to the Diné. In the beginning, they wove with cotton. When churro sheep arrived with Spanish explorers, they began to also use wool.

Designs changed with times, dye technology, and the market. Although some weavers still use natural vegetal dyes, the bright colors associated with many patterns were originally imported from Europe: indigo from Spain; reds, blues, and other colors from German aniline dyes.

The earliest Navajo weavings made on an upright loom using geometric patterns date from the sixteenth and seventeenth centuries. After 1850, hand-spun yarn was augmented with colored thread unraveled from imported fabric. The famous chief's blanket of horizontal stripes alternating black, white, and red began to be accented with diamonds, rectangles, bars, and zigzag shapes about the middle of the nineteenth century. At the same time, traders introduced weavers to oriental rug designs, and the distinctive creations which resulted were very popular with tourists and turned a profit for both weavers and traders.

Railroad travel exponentially increased commercial outlets for Indian art, but buyers were unsophisticated and willing to accept weavings made with coarse imported yarns and inferior dyes. By the end of the nineteenth century, Navajo weavers shifted from making blankets to making rugs for this market. Weavers were paid by the pound for their creations, regardless of quality.

The Fred Harvey Company, which joined the Santa Fe Railroad in making Indian arts and crafts an integral part of their promotion, used its influence to raise standards of raw materials and encourage new patterns early in the twentieth century. The trend toward excellent quality in Navajo weaving has continued. Particular patterns and colors characteristic of areas on the reservation are easily recognizable to the trained eye: Wide Ruins, Chinle, Two Gray Hills, and Ganado Red are named after places where they originated. The best authentic Navajo weavings command prices in keeping with the high level of textile art. Ask for proof of authenticity if you want the real thing. For a cultural experience and an education in Navajo textiles and their pricing, consider attending one of the monthly auctions held at Crown Point, New Mexico.

• **Silversmithing:** The *plateros,* Hispanic New Mexicans living in the upper Rio Grande Valley, first showed the Diné how silver could be crafted. By the

mid-1800s, Navajo were producing jewelry using designs stamped into the piece with dies. They added skills of hammering and casting the metal, then soldering. Bracelets, *ketohs* (bow guards), *concho* belts, necklaces, brooches, rings,

Ketohs began as wrist protection for men when bows and arrows were used. They have evolved to become ornate bracelets worn on special occasions. This silver and turquoise ketoh was made about 1900.

Silver conchos were first used for adornment outside the Southwest. Today's Navajo silversmiths use them most often laced onto leather belts.

flatware, and hollowware all were created by early silversmiths.

Always resourceful, early craftsmen chiseled designs with files on found objects such as the ends of rivets or nail sets, then stamped them into the heated silver. Soft, easily carved sandstone and tuff were made into casting molds. An old rail might serve as an anvil. Early equipment used to soften the metal consisted of a tin bucket and goatskin bellows. The silver itself came from coins and from American and Mexican mining sources. Today's Diné silversmiths purchase jewelry-making tools at stores or trading posts, although some still choose to make their own tools. Silver workers began to add turquoise near the end of the 1800s. The stones were hand-cut and hand-polished then. In some cases, Pueblo people exchanged the stones for silver jewelry.

Commercialization and quantity production encouraged by railroad tourism led to downgrading of quality around the 1920s. Jewelry was often produced for the undiscriminating customer who simply wanted a souvenir. Lightweight pins and bracelets using uninspired, stereotyped designs were bought by the ounce by traders who provided the makers with raw materials.

The Navajo, however, continued to create for themselves heavy silver necklaces and bracelets weighted with enormous stones of variegated turquoise. They represented wearable wealth and could be pawned with traders between lambing and shearing times as a sort of bridge loan.

Currently, mass production of Navajo-like jewelry utilizing stabilized or faux stones has given buyers responsibility for knowing the quality and source of their purchases. If you are interested in real jewelry rather than souvenir curios, ask the seller to put in writing who made the piece, where it was made, and a statement concerning the authenticity of the stones used.

• **Painting and sculpture:** Both have departed from traditional, identifiable styles. Excellent Navajo artists are working in every medium, expressing themselves in a range of genres. Gallery owners can guide you to the best.

• **Sandpainting:** The reproduction of sandpaintings for the secular market began at the turn of the last century. Many Navajo viewed the practice with apprehension since the images represented parts of ceremonials. Hosteen Klah, a respected weaver and medicine man, his family, and others who wove the symbols into textiles avoided the risks involved by including deliberate errors and modifications to avoid showing disrespect for the Holy People.

A commercial sandpainting may be as simple as one figure or as complex as those used for healing. An intricate sandpainting will usually be protected from three sides by a rainbow deity, garlands, connected arrows, feathers, or other designs. The fourth side is assumed to face east, from where no evil can enter. Mother Earth carries sacred plants in her body; Father Sky holds the constellations: everything is symbolic.

Today commercial sandpaintings are most often made on particle board. The base is covered with a thin layer of glue. A design is drawn in glue with a fine brush, section by section. Depending on the quality of the product, colored sand, crushed limestone, sandstone, even turquoise and natural pigment may be used. The skill of the artist comes into play as he trickles the sand evenly through his hand onto the wet surface on which he may or may not have sketched his design. The final step in production is to finish the piece with a fixative spray.

A collection of colorful yarns and beads, an array of weavings, a particular scent of wool and old silver, smoke, wood, and earth suggest an authentic trading post where Navajo people are the main clientele.

Roadside vendors may offer attractive and inexpensive items such as the cedar and glass bead necklaces that Irene Tom and her family make for sale.

Typical Navajo Jewelry

Concho belts (or conchas, from the Spanish word for seashell) originated outside the Southwest. Early conchos were circular forms, hammered and stamped with designs. They were used as hair ornaments, buttons, and brooches by Plains Indians. Today they most often decorate belts and may be made in any shape or size. They are laced onto the leather and often have fancy buckles.

Bracelets are made for both women and men in an infinite variety of designs, with and without stones. Stamped, chiseled, twisted, overlaid, sand cast, ridged, filed, soldered—all are authentically Navajo. Turquoise or many other gems may be used to enhance the design.

Necklaces were first made of round beads soldered together. Later, the beads were oval or fluted. The "squash blossom" necklace is the most widely known Navajo design. It consists of a crescent-shaped pendant (*naja*, adapted from a bridle ornament), sand cast or hammered, which may be silver or inlaid with stones, hung from a sometimes-elaborate necklace.

Buttons for women's clothing and moccasins are more common than those that men used to wear on their leather pants and moccasins, before jeans and boots became the norm. Brooches often adorn women's traditional velvet blouses.

Ranger sets are silver buckles and tips added to men's or women's plain leather belts.

Ketohs were made for wrist protection when bows and arrows were used. They have evolved into ornate pieces worn on special occasions.

Earrings are worn by both men and women. Traditional men sometimes wear turquoise nuggets strung through the ear lobes, but today every imaginable kind of earring is available. They include traditional *jacla* earrings that were tied as ornaments on a necklace when they weren't being worn as earrings.

Recurring Events

- **Fourth of July Celebration**: Window Rock, Fairgrounds
- **Sheep is Life**: Diné College, Tsaile. Sheep is Life honors the central role that sheep play in Navajo spirituality, philosophy, and daily life. (July)
- **Navajo Nation Fairs**: Eastern: Crownpoint (August); Central: Chinle (August) and Window Rock (September); Southwestern: Dilkon (September); Northern: Shiprock (October); Western: Tuba City (October)
- **Navajo Nation Library Arts and Crafts Exhibit**: Window Rock (December)
- **All-Indian Rodeos**: All summer there are rodeos in every part of the Navajo Nation. Even during the winter months, Navajo continue team roping and bull riding competitions. The Navajo Nation Rodeo Cowboys Association and the All-Indian Rodeo Cowboys Association have lots of Navajo members.

Rodeo is a big part of the Navajo Nation Fair. Smaller rodeos are held in towns all over the Nation during the summer.

Native Voices, Native Lives: Ed Singer

I'm an artist, mostly self-taught although I went to San Francisco Art Institute. I'm an "artist's artist." I paint for myself and don't compromise to be "Native American." Soutine and Lucien Freud have influenced me. I call my work surrealism, although it doesn't have anything to do with the movement in the 1930s and 1940s. Being Native American today is such an absurd experience that it's surrealistic. We have all these empty obligations. No one else has treaties with the United States. We are so marginalized that we're off the page. You hear about racism regarding Blacks and Hispanics, but we're a drop in the bucket.

From that is born stereotyping. People off the reservation have so many misconceptions, things they think we're entitled to. You can be working a construction job in Flagstaff or Phoenix and other workers ask, "What are you doing bustin' your hump here when you can just collect your check from the government or your casino?" They think you can walk onto any reservation anywhere, ask, "Is this house being used?" and if it isn't, walk in. People think that the reason Navajo buy a new pickup truck every two years is because the government pays for them. I say, "You have to haul firewood and water on the reservation. You need a truck. You have to drive a long way out. It's easy to put 100,000 miles a year on a truck."

Artist Ed Singer's pastel, *French Postcard,* shows a Navajo man sitting on a sheepskin inside his hogan under a postcard of Ingres' painting, *l'Odalisque.*

My paintings may posture to be pretty pictures, but they always have an edge to them…something that will make people think. I express a lot by the juxtaposition of things observed or imagined. This pastel, called "French Postcard," shows a Navajo man sitting inside his hogan with a postcard of Ingres' painting, *l'Odalisque,* on the wall. It's the best-selling postcard from the Louvre. People ask, "What is that doing in a hogan?" Well, it's probably happened before and will happen again. Maybe his brother's in the service. Maybe he saw it and liked it and put it up.

Nuwuvi: The Southern Paiute

*"It is said that the plants, animals, and...
everything on this land understands the
Paiute language; and when one listens
closely and intently enough, there is
affirmation and a sense of understanding."*

—Kaibab Paiute Tribal Member

Spectacular geology on the plateaus and in the canyons north of
Grand Canyon safeguards the artifacts of Paiute ancestors who
lived there for hundreds of generations before Europeans arrived.

Introduction to Paiute Culture

They call themselves the People, *Nuwuvi*. The Colorado River divides them from the neighboring Pai peoples, who, in spite of the similarity of their English name and geographical proximity, come from entirely different roots. The Paiute language is more closely related to certain Hopi and O'odham dialects than to that of the Pai. The Nuwuvi have given names to places in the area around the Grand Canyon that make some Paiute words familiar to map-readers: *Kaibab, Shivwits, Kaiparowits, Uinkaret.*

The Southern Paiute have lived in what is now southern Utah, northern Arizona, southern Nevada, and a piece of California. Their traditional territory spread north from the Colorado River into the Utah desert, including Bryce and Zion Canyons; west to Death Valley; and south to the Painted Desert. They moved from the canyons into the mountains and back as the seasons led them.

Always learning from the people they met, those who lived north and east took on Plains customs such as erecting tepees instead of building earth-covered lodges and using buckskin for clothing. After the Spanish came, they adopted horses. Some borrowed characteristics of nearby Pai cultures. They carried on a lively trade with the Havasupai, Hopi, and Mojave.

Eventually the Chemehuevi branch broke away altogether. They moved near their allies, the Mojave, along the Colorado River where they reside today. Over generations, this group adopted floodplain farming, earth-covered houses, ritual warfare, shamanic dreaming, and the mourning ceremony described in the section on the Colorado River Tribes (see p. 232).

A diorama at Pipe Spring National Monument's museum shows life in a prehistoric pueblo. The people occupying it are called *E'nengweng* by Paiutes.

Eventually the Southern Paiute formed into 16 bands. As they dispersed across the land, moving with the sun and rain, they carried only light and essential belongings. Wild foods and game made up most of their diet. Rabbits and prairie dogs, birds, insects, and mice supplemented the roots, seeds, and plants they gathered for food and medicine. Wasting nothing, the Southern Paiute crushed and ate the bones of game animals. Corn, beans, squash, amaranth, wild grapes, and sunflowers were cultivated by women in places where enough water flowed to sustain them. Men dug dams and ditches to irrigate the crops. Some bands fished as well, such as those at Fish Lake; for others, like the Chemehuevi, fish are taboo.

The Paiutes' skill at basketry was highly developed. They wove tools for seed-beating, carrying, winnowing, and parching. Pitch-sealed basketry held water and was lighter and less fragile than pottery. Basket weavers even extended their expertise to fashion. Cone-shaped woven hats were a favorite of women, while men wore skin caps. Either went nicely with beautifully tanned leather garments and rabbit robes that were favored by both sexes.

The basketmakers used willow, yucca, and other fibers to create not only light, utilitarian baskets but beautifully decorated pieces that are still collected around the world. The materials used in them are the same as those found in ancient baskets and twig figures that lay preserved in the dry caves of their homeland.

In fact, the land of the Paiute is everywhere marked with the remains of older civilizations. Some of them go back 9,000 years. The spectacular geology of the areas around Bryce and Zion Canyons, the north rim of the Grand Canyon, Cedar Breaks National Monument, and Grand Staircase–Escalante National Monument safeguards the evidence of lives lived there over many generations, long before any Europeans arrived.

At contact, the Southern Paiute had no general tribal organization, but gathered together as families or groups of families for special occasions such

A Kaibab Paiute woman wears a dress of beautifully tanned, fringed leather. A cradleboard lies on the ground beside her.

as harvesting, dancing, and funeral ceremonies. Certain rights such as the use of a particular spring went with relationship. Each group was self-sufficient, although they cooperated when it was necessary. Only consensus constituted a decision. The 16 bands did not organize until they were needed to defend against cultural intrusion. Headmen were not designated until Euro-Americans needed an authority figure to deal with.

Nuwuvi Creation Story

Ocean Woman first created a place for the Nuwuvi as she floated on the water, bits of her skin coming together to form land. Coyote then became her courier. He was given a tightly woven water jar to carry across the desert to a land where Wolf and Rabbit lived. When he arrived, these wiser creatures would give him further instructions, meanwhile he had been explicitly told not to open the container he carried, under any circumstances. However, being Coyote, he became so curious when he heard sounds coming from within it that he decided to take a peek. When he removed the stopper, human beings flew out in all directions. Wolf and Rabbit came to take charge of the situation. They were able to select the correct beginnings for the very best people. They became the Southern Paiute.

Perhaps as a result of their independent lifeways, the U.S. government, when it entered the picture, treated each group of Southern Paiute as a separate entity. Initially described as peaceful people who welcomed strangers, they lost their lands by attrition rather than through violent conflict. Trappers brought measles and smallpox. When westward trails passed through, travelers used their rivers and springs and livestock damaged the food supply. Slave traders continued to steal their children until the middle of the nineteenth century. Southern Paiute numbers declined along with their power to overcome wave after wave of challenge, as their homeland was overrun. Mormon settlement in the late 1800s virtually ended their ability to be self-sufficient.

Between the 1860s and 1940s, a variety of reservations and settlements was established, the largest one along the Santa Clara River in Utah. Even so, a number of bands lived or worked off the reservation, depending primarily on Mormon employers to make a living. One of these was the Arizona Kaibab Paiute, who in 1907 received a 216-square-mile reservation at Moccasin Spring.

In 1957 the government terminated the status of Southern Paiute groups in Utah, which meant they had no land base, health services, educational programs, government employment, or job training. After confusing political maneuvering, their status was restored in 1980 and five groups united to become the Paiute Indian Tribe of Utah. The problems faced by other Paiute during these years ranged from the city of Las Vegas sprawling into their land to the opposite situation: isolation and lack of services and employment. The damming of Glen Canyon in the late 1950s flooded ancestral sites. Cultural regeneration suffered from struggle and constant change. However, in 1990,

Two Dances

Around the early 1900s, the Paiute adopted the Ute Bear Dance, which became a festive social occasion. Women directed the dance itself, as well as selecting their partners. All Bear Dance songs began with the noise of thunder, played to awaken the bears in their caves, where they were waiting for spring to arrive. The dance put the bear in a better mood than he would otherwise be as he went out from winter hibernation to feed.

A Paiute named Wovoka introduced the Ghost Dance, a ceremony that spread rapidly within Indian nations around the 1890s. It offered hope, passed along by dead relatives who promised to restore to the Indians the land and resources that they were losing at an increasingly rapid rate. Their communication predicted that the year following the dances, the earth would be covered with new soil, grasses, trees, and running water. The great herds of buffalo would return. All those who danced the dance would return with the ancestors to live with the great herds of bison. They would live peacefully once more.

U.S. government attempts to eliminate the Ghost Dance led to the massacre at Wounded Knee, South Dakota, in 1890.

This dance is no longer practiced.

the tribe was recognized, finally, as the 509th Indian nation. The Southern Paiute had returned from a figurative Trail of Tears.

Two Southern Paiute bands—the San Juan and Kaibab Paiute—live in Arizona today. The communities of the San Juan group, who inhabited the area between the Colorado and San Juan Rivers for several hundred years, lie on the Navajo reservation, at Willow Springs and Paiute Canyon/Navajo Mountain. The reservation of the Kaibab Paiute, established in 1907, runs along Kanab Creek on the Arizona-Utah border. Today it consists of more than 120,000 acres of scenic open land in the area called the Arizona Strip, the northwestern part of Arizona separated from the rest of the state by the Grand Canyon.

Tourism is an important aspect of the Kaibab Paiute economy. The main road between Las Vegas and Lake Powell, AZ 389, crosses their territory, bringing the majority of their visitors to a museum at Pipe Spring National Monument, which is a cooperative effort of the Kaibab Band of Paiute Indians and the National Park Service. The tribe also engages in agriculture and raises livestock.

Cone-shaped woven hats were a favorite of women, while men preferred skin caps. Both used rabbit-fur capes to keep warm.

Exploring the Southern Paiute Lands

Pipe Spring National Monument

*406 N. Pipe Spring Rd., Fredonia • (928) 643-7260; (928) 643-7105
www.nps.gov/pisp • Open: Park and Visitor Center, 8 a.m.–4:30 p.m. daily;
the historic buildings close at 4 p.m.; Closed: January 1, Thanksgiving, and
December 25*

*Guided tours of the fort and outer buildings are offered daily year-round.
Living history demonstrations, ranger talks, and guided walks are offered daily
during the summer.*

*The monument is 14 miles west of Fredonia, but a long way from most other
places. From Flagstaff, follow US 89 to US 89A, which goes straight north at
Bitter Springs (US 89 heads slightly east toward Page). Take US 89A to AZ 389
in Fredonia. Follow it toward Moccasin and Colorado City and turn north up
Pipe Spring Rd. Count on over 4 hours of driving time, without extended stops.*

The monument is *the* cultural heritage destination on the Arizona Strip. It has
an excellent indoor/outdoor historical museum. The park was established 16
years after the Kaibab Paiutes received their reservation, when the National
Park Service bought an island of private ranch land surrounding Pipe Spring.

Museum exhibits inside interpret
human habitation in the area from
the earliest times. As the site of one
of the few reliable water sources in
the area, Pipe Spring attracted many
generations of native people, the first
Spanish explorers, and early settlers.

With the arrival of the Mormon
pioneers to the Arizona Strip and the
building of a fort over the spring
in 1872, the Kaibab Paiute were
displaced from Pipe Spring. The fort
was built by the Church of Jesus
Christ of Latter-day Saints as the
headquarters of a tithing ranch on
the Arizona Strip (a place to gather
up cattle donated to the church) and
was fortified for protection against
raiding Navajo. The church sold Pipe

Kaibab Paiute elders participated in an
ethnographic assessment of Pipe Spring
National Monument and Zion National
Park, their ancestral homeland.

Spring in 1898 and it has had several private owners. Anson Perry Winsor, for whom "Winsor Castle" at the monument is named, was the property's first owner. Pipe Spring became a national monument in 1923 and offers a glimpse into American Indian and pioneer life in the Old West.

The museum's displays offer insight into the viewpoint of the Southern Paiute people. They include a diorama showing life in a prehistoric pueblo. The people occupying it are called *E'nengweng* by Paiutes, *Anasazi* by Navajos, and *Hisatsinom* by Hopis.

Another display showcases several generations of water jars used at the spring. Others explain the diversity and uses of plants and animals of the region as part of information about Kaibab Paiute lifeways. All this leads you to a quiet place of meditation near the exit. It is designed to allow visitors to contemplate history from the diverse points of view represented by the people who have taken water from Pipe Spring.

Muuputs Canyon

Hikers will enjoy a 1-mile round trip (with a local guide) on the reservation. There is also a booklet that interprets the natural history along the trail. Reservations are required and can be arranged at the tribal headquarters, (928) 643-7245.

Hunting

Permits to take mule deer in season are available from the tribe. Contact the tribal headquarters, (928) 643-7245.

Water vessels on display at the Pipe Spring National Monument Museum remind visitors of the many generations who've used Pipe Spring as an important water source in this dry region.

Along the Way

A trip to Pipe Spring takes you past a lot of Arizona's history and prehistory. Ancient dwellings are set against geological wonders, including the Grand Canyon. You will follow the Vermilion Cliffs past the Paria, Kaibab, and Kanab Plateaus; travel through House Rock Valley, Jacob Lake, and past the LaFevre Lookout. You get the idea—these are the wide open spaces, Grand Canyon Country, a landscape that defies description. The following points of interest are listed in the order in which you'll encounter them.

Navajo Bridge

This old bridge takes you off Navajo Nation lands and spans the Colorado River 500 feet below. The narrow first bridge, completed in 1928, rendered historic Lees Ferry obsolete. A wider bridge spans Marble Canyon now and carries vehicle traffic. You can walk the old bridge, often seeing river runners' boats passing below.

House Rock Valley Overlook

This overlook provides a panoramic view across the plain to the walls of Marble Canyon, the Kaibab Plateau, and part of the Echo Cliffs. In the distance is the Grand Staircase–Escalante National Monument.

LaFevre Overlook, just north of Jacob Lake, offers a panoramic view toward Grand Staircase–Escalante National Monument. All this country is the hereditary land of Southern Paiutes.

A Note on Climate

Don't confuse this part of Arizona with the deserts. Winter comes to the Arizona Strip, complete with cold and snow, especially at higher altitudes. Late spring, fall, and even summer are the preferred times to drive these roads.

The Vermilion Cliffs

These red and buff rock formations rise beside the highway. They are scenic attractions today, but represented impenetrable barriers to prehistoric and historic peoples. The cliffs anchor Vermilion Cliffs National Monument, a 294,000-acre showcase of geological possibilities.

Dominguez-Escalante Interpretive Site

A historical marker 29 miles east of Jacob Lake identifies where the first Spanish explorers in the area camped in 1776. It offers interpretive material about the history and geology of the region.

Sage-covered plains give way to high desert chaparral, then juniper and piñon woodlands, then ponderosa pine forest as you climb the Kaibab Plateau into the beautiful Jacob Lake area.

The Vermilion Cliffs area has sheltered humans for more than 12,000 years.

Jacob Lake Area

This remote region is the gateway to the North Rim of Grand Canyon National Park, 45 miles to the south. Here you will find lodging, food, camping, and information about the region. The Kaibab Plateau Visitor Center is open spring through fall.

Dining and Overnight Accommodations

Food is available at the Monument in a café operated by the Zion Natural History Association and also at the Kaibab Paiute campground. Restaurants and markets can be found in Fredonia and Kanab.

There is no lodging at the Monument. Motels and restaurants are located in Fredonia and Kanab, Utah. Camping is available near the Monument in a campground operated by the Kaibab-Paiute tribe. RV Parking is available.

Shopping

Few arts and crafts are being made by the Southern Paiute people; however, you can occasionally find wonderful basketry, new or old (see Native Voices, Native Lives, opposite page). Traditional cradleboards sometimes come on the market as well. They are woven or made with softly tanned hide, occasionally beaded.

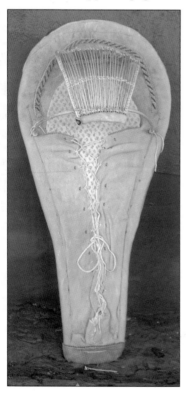

Recurring Events

• **Kaibab Paiute Heritage Day Celebration** (September)

Butter-soft hide, expert weaving, and beaded adornment mark this cradleboard as a Southern Paiute work of art.

Native Voices, Native Lives: Everett Don Pikyavit

I was born in Las Vegas, Nevada, and am an enrolled member of the Moapa Band of Paiutes. I am proud to be part of a very long tradition of basket weavers from the southern portion of the Great Basin.

While I was influenced and inspired by many Southern Paiute weavers of the past, it was my paternal grandmother, Lila Benson Rogers, who inspired me the most. I used to play with my toys at her feet as she was weaving, and that planted the seeds for me to make baskets, too.

My interest developed while I did other things. I am a graduate of Sherman Indian High School in Riverside, California. I worked as a firefighter and went on to continue my education. Recently I graduated with an Associate of Arts and Associate of Science degree specializing in geology from Riverside Community College. I plan to continue my education in the field of natural sciences in the Las Vegas area.

I began exploring my Paiute roots when I was in my 30s. I picked up basketweaving technique easily then. I believe it was in my blood. My work now includes all traditional Southern Paiute and Goshute basketry styles. Some forms I create are winnowers, cone burden baskets, seedbeaters, women's hats, water jugs, cradleboards, as well as various sizes and styles of coiled baskets. Some of the materials I use are devil's claw; yucca roots, leaves, and fiber; junco grass; sumac; desert willow; red willow; and bird feathers. These native fibers are and were used in our basketry of the past. I've found the Creator in these things.

I am one of the only Southern Paiute weavers north of the Grand Canyon who is actively producing and selling. I am a board member of the newly-created Great Basin Native Basketweavers Association and belong to the Moapa Valley Art Guild. I also work in oils, acrylic, pastel, and pen-and-ink mediums and create traditional clothing: beaded buckskin attire, bows and arrows, and feathered hats.

I recently started passing on my knowledge to other Southern Paiute individuals. I encourage them to follow traditional Southern Paiute basket designs, styles, materials, and thought in their individual basketry. I teach them the tradition of leaving something in gratitude to the plant that has provided us with materials: a bead, an arrowhead, pot, or pendant. I try to encourage young weavers to stick with their task. I believe that if I teach people now, they will return to it later. By doing this, I hope to ensure that this ancient art form continues on.

AROUND THE GRAND CANYON

Pai: Hualapai, Havasupai, Yavapai

"Our names are carved upon the cliffs of stone that guarded our retreat into the mother's womb...and planted our hearts in the flowering hills that cradled us within the boundaries of the canyons."

—Roy Purcell, *Long Journey from Wikame*

Opposite: The Hualapai and Havasupai people are the Keepers of the Canyons. The Havasupai, People of the Blue-Green Water, live along Havasu Creek, which flows over four enormous falls on its way to the Colorado River.

Introduction to Pai Culture

The Pai peoples came to the plateaus and canyons of their homelands according to the instructions of their creator. The ancient wisdom given along with the land has been passed down through the generations in a Yuman language similar to that of the Mojave and other Colorado River tribes. Of course, it has been transformed into dialects as people moved about the world, living different lives.

Even before beautiful Matawedita Canyon nurtured the people called Hualapai, the creator gave them life at *Wikame,* or Spirit Mountain. In Matawedita, *Tochopa* protected them and showed them how to live properly. He taught them songs and ceremonies. But as the canyon became crowded and the people quarrelsome, he sent some of them into the greater world. The Havasupai came from spiritual beginnings at Red Butte near the Grand Canyon, while the Yavapai are descended from *Kamalapukwia,* First Woman, who went out from *Ahaghskiaywa,* now called Montezuma's Well, to the Red Rock country.

Western archaeology says that there were 13 original Pai bands. Eventually they became three separate tribes: Hualapai, Havasupai, and Yavapai, all of which continue to reside on portions of their ancestral territory in Arizona.

Pai groups of old spread into side canyons of the Colorado River.

> ## Investing in Eagles
>
> Eagles were very valuable in traditional Pai society. Their feathers were bought and sold. Rights to eagles and their nests went with rights to the land. Often young eagles were taken from the nest and kept in special houses in camp until they were well-feathered. Then they were plucked and turned loose.

The Hualapai, or People of the Tall Pine (*Hwal'bay* in their own language) spread out where the Colorado River makes a long east-west rush through what we now call the Grand Canyon. They populated the deserts, piñon and juniper-covered plateaus, mesas, and pine-forested mountains that form giant steps rising to its rim. They became the keepers of the region they call *hakataya*, the backbone of the river, which includes many side canyons connected to the Grand. At least one conceals an ancient cave in which fossils dating to the Ice Age have been found.

One day far into a future the ancient Pai peoples couldn't have envisioned, Capt. John G. Bourke would describe their country in a U.S. Army report: "No words can do justice to the profundity of (these) cañons. They are as rough and precipitous as any section of the Andes or the Himalayas." Since he wrote these words, the canyons have been given American names like Quartermaster, Mohawk, Meriwhitica, Spencer, National, Havasu, and Peach Springs. The Hualapai language describes them by their special attributes.

The Canyon Keepers

Undaunted by geography, the Pai of old gravitated to creeks within these rugged canyon walls and found perennial springs in the mountains and desert valleys. Ranging north of the Bill Williams River, they gained altitude to hunt in piñon and juniper forests which even today nurture deer, elk, antelope, enormous jackrabbits, and other game. They harvested the nuts of the piñon, one of the native pines that gave the Hualapai their name. They followed the seasons from warm valleys to cool mountains, gathering the fruit of the agave and cactus, the nutritious seeds of grasses and grains, walnuts, acorns, and mesquite beans. They knew and understood the webs of life on the canyon floors, on the mountains and mesas, and at every level in between. A few Pai groups also grew crops, planting pumpkins, lima beans, and other foods near dependable water sources.

Everyone traveled in order to subsist. Bands divided into smaller groups of perhaps 25 relatives because they required large areas to collect enough food. Need determined how and where a group hunted and gathered. The groups followed regular circuits, each using a particular range within the larger tribal boundaries. Some were sufficiently predictable for the travelers to leave fragile pots and heavy grinding stones in place for the next season.

Sometimes land use overlapped. Yet all understood which springs, valleys, and mountains were theirs. While historians sometimes use the word wander to describe their semi-nomadic life, Pai family travels were far from aimless. Their lives depended on being in the right place at the right time and not running afoul of enemies in the process.

Late fall was a season that brought visiting and occasional festivities. People gathered together to settle in for the winter. Bands and sub-tribes joined each other at designated places. Old Yuman customs—the three-day Mourning Ceremony (*nemitiawak:* meet to cry) with its ritual bonfire, painting and tattooing, songs, and stories—were remembered and renewed.

Groups of Pai men tracked large game or organized rabbit drives. The hunt was conducted within bounds prescribed by oral tradition, and boys learned the customs of hunting from their tribe uncles: give away your first kill; offer proper prayers for success and for thanks to the animal; use every part; share.

This was also the time when marriages took place, if young men were successful in offering meat, buckskin, and other valuable gifts to the parents of the desired young women. Shelters of earth, cedar, juniper, and brush were built and rabbit-fur blankets brought out. The men built their sweat house. Buckskin clothing replaced bark aprons and breechclouts. Game animals supplemented stored food until again in early spring each family unit would

This Havasupai dwelling, called a *hawa,* was built of sticks and timbers covered with brush. These were distinguished from the more substantial *wa jmatv,* a log frame sealed with earth.

go its separate way, following the ripening plants from low, warm valleys to cooler mountain slopes.

These bands, which were isolated from one another during most of the year, honored the tribal tradition of leadership that was flexible but pragmatic and proven. Like their relatives to the west, the Pai tended to follow men who merited following. Pai bands had confidence in those who spoke well, hunted successfully, and fought bravely. A leader was expected to be related by birth to a prior headman and to share his wisdom about how to conduct

Passing the Torch of Leadership

Excerpts from a speech on leadership given February, 2004 by Jamie Fullmer, chairman, Yavapai-Apache Nation. Published in the tribal newspaper Gah'nah/Ya Ti, *April 2004.*

Fearlessness and a sense of presence were key traits of our traditional great leaders. These leaders were elevated to the seat of authority by their previous experiences in which leadership and courage showed through their actions. A record of past successes in warring, raiding, and meeting the needs of the people often were benchmarks that our people gave standing to. Equally important was the possession of spiritual gifts and religious understandings....

The harsh reality of our leadership is this: Most of the traditional leaders with any power or clout were dead before the march to San Carlos in 1875....When the U.S. was at war with our people in the 1860s and 1870s, any individual who seemed radical,

Former chairs of the Yavapai-Apache Nation receive honorary chief's blankets from Chairman Jamie Fullmer

supported resistance, and maintained traditional religious practices was considered to be a threat....and was removed by any and all means necessary....They are gone but their leadership spirit remains with us to this day....

In a quiet....way the men that were leaders remained in charge of their own families, clans, and tribal groups [at San Carlos]....Apache and Yavapai men that were employed by the Army as scouts attained status due to their actions, regular paychecks, and rifles. On the reservation, it was these men who became the community leaders at the family and clan level....Since the 1900s our women have taken more leadership roles within the community as well.

After the Indian Reorganization Act of 1934, Apache and Yavapai people.... returning to their old homeland faced the new economy of a New World....Our leaders adapted to the changes of the modern world and moved our tribal alliance forward ....These leaders have had to prove themselves not only to....our people, but to the non-Indian world as well. These chairmen have demonstrated themselves as our leaders and have taught us to walk confidently as a people.

life in the proper manner. They ruled by consultation rather than order and could be removed if their band's confidence in them waned.

The Canyon Keepers—the Hualapai and Havasupai—occupied a part of the Southwest through which many traders passed, moving between the West Coast and the pueblos. They connected with tribes in all directions through a well-developed network. Red and white mineral pigments from their lands were especially prized as cosmetics and decorative paint; also traded were well-tanned deer and antelope hides and dried food items like pigweed seeds, mesquite pods, Mormon tea, and lima beans. In turn, they sought Hopi and later Navajo weavings, shells from the Pacific, and food to add to their diet such as the peaches grown by the Hopi.

Those who became known as Havasupai, People of the Blue-Green Water, separated from the greater tribe around 1200, according to archaeologists. They farmed the beautiful, watery canyon where they live today. There cottonwood and willow glow green against the walls of a gorge of red sandstone set off by buff-colored limestone cliffs. Each spring the farmers would prepare the soil, direct water from Havasu Creek into the fields with small earthen dams,

Dancers commemorate a time when waters rose until the Big Horn Sheep dug a hole with his horn through which they receded. He still guards the Havasupai.

The *wigleeva,* rocky pinnacles representing a Havasupai family that stayed on top when others moved into the canyon, protect Supai Village.

and plant. As corn, beans, sunflowers, and other crops sprouted and matured, some people would return to the plateau while others weeded, cultivated, and guarded the fields against raiders, both human and animal.

Havasu still is a bountifully beautiful slash in the earth that meets the Grand Canyon. Its floor is bisected by Havasu Creek, which makes its way through Supai, the only village, and over four enormous waterfalls before it rushes into the Colorado River. Mineralization of the water creates white-surfaced travertine terraces that showcase turquoise blue waters. Protected by its twin pillars, the people even today seem isolated within a narrow paradise inhabited by a colorful array of butterflies and wildflowers.

In the old days, however, the lives of the Havasupai were not confined to farming their canyon. They, too, followed the seasons on the plateau, ranging far from their small fields. The 300 or so members of the tribe built dwellings and hunted deer, bighorn sheep, antelope, wild turkeys, and other game up above, stopping at hunting shrines to make appropriate prayers to pay tribute to such sacred sites as Red Butte. The canyon served primarily as a place to grow crops. Portions of each crop were stored by sealing it into caves in the canyon walls for emergencies, each bin sealed tight and identified with a family's mark.

They tilled fields in other places, as well. Indian Gardens, a point along the Bright Angel Trail into the Grand Canyon, was the location of another farm. During the winter, they might visit a storage cave, but between harvest time, which they celebrated with Hopi and Navajo friends in the canyon, and spring planting, Supai village lay quiet, waiting for the sun's return.

Hualapai tribal leaders remember their people's suffering during their forced march to La Paz.

Foreign Contact

Father Francisco Garcés was the first European to describe the Hualapai and Havasupai. He passed through their lands in 1776 on his way between what is now California and the northern pueblos, accompanied by a Hualapai captain.

Garcés' route was to pave the way to the end of traditional life for the Pai peoples. In the next century, explorers and trappers followed the priest along that trail. Then came prospectors, who discovered gold in the Hualapai and Cerbat mountains. Settlers followed. To ease their travel, a road was surveyed and built by the U.S. government. Lt. Edward Beale led the crew. His job included testing camels as pack animals (they didn't work well because they scared the horses). Back then it was called Beale's Wagon Road. Today it is known as Route 66.

By 1860, when construction ended on the Wagon Road between New Mexico and California, wagons were streaming across Indian lands. Neither the Pai nor the Mojave welcomed the travelers. Adding insult to injury, the newly-formed Arizona Territory allowed William Hardy to build another road—a toll road—between Hardyville (Fort Mojave), his steamer port on the Colorado River, and Prescott, then the territorial capital. It also passed through the heart of Hualapai country. Natives of the area sometimes exacted their own toll in the form of traveling livestock and food supplies. Contact and conflict increased as the number of miners and settlers multiplied.

Finally, representatives of the tribes made a deal. For $150 worth of goods, Hardy contracted the right for others to cross Indian country. However, the contract provided for whites to build mail stations and houses at several watering places, graze cattle, and make use of whatever was "necessary for the traveling public." The result was more confrontation. Settlers killed Indians and Indians killed settlers. The Army intervened, first from Camp Beale's Springs, then from Fort Mojave, and later at the tollgate, which became Camp Hualapai.

In 1866 a freighter passing through murdered Wauba Yuma, a Hualapai leader and one of the headmen who had signed the contract. He came to the

---

Cherum: Time-Tested Leader

The story of Cherum, who led the western Pai against the U.S. Army in his native Cerbat Mountains, illustrates how those who survived La Paz learned to live as a conquered people.

Cherum was in line to receive the hereditary and honorable title of *Tokumhet*. He had earned the right to use it while he was in his twenties. Through a series of strategic trades —pigment for weavings, weavings for horses, and horses for guns—he had acquired weapons for his people before the "Hualapai War" began. He also organized 250 western Pai, Havasupai, and Southern Paiute, who were also joined by others over the course of the conflict. At the end of the war, Cherum was sent to prison in San Francisco. On the way, he escaped his guards and returned to his homeland.

Cherum, who led his band through conflict to reservation life in the 1800s. His name and line continue.

The Army soon came to the defeated Hualapai to recruit scouts to help them fight other tribes. Although he did not appear in person, Cherum cooperated by sending six men, as did other Hualapai leaders and Chief Navajo of the Havasupai tribe. These scouts continued to work under the Army until the capture of the Apache chief Geronimo ended fighting in 1886. They thus became instant U.S. allies, since scouting redefined friends and enemies.

Cherum and his family of five wives and children, some of whom walked to La Paz and back, returned to the Cerbat Mountains. There he became an employment contractor for his 24 followers. He found them work at the mines in Chloride. This kind of arrangement seemed the best strategy for adapting to the wage economy in their homeland.

Time passed and a reservation was established for his people. Still pragmatic, Cherum lived to see Pai participate in full regalia in Fourth of July celebrations in Kingman. Almost 100 years after Cherum's birth, his son, called Bob Schrum, took the seat reserved for the hereditary head chief on the Hualapai tribal council.

Adapted from Henry F. Dobyns and Robert C. Euler, "The Nine Lives of Cherum, the Pai Tokumhet," The American Indian Quarterly, June 22, 1998.

freighters' camp to insist that the contract called for continuing payments in the form of horses, mules, and flour—goods that the freighter was carrying. That event is often credited with starting the "Hualapai War," which continued through 1868.

Retaliation for Wauba Yuma's death began with an attack on some miners led by another contract-signer, Hualapai chief Cherum. The war itself was a relentless series of guerilla exchanges punctuated by retaliatory murders and Army missions that destroyed Pai people, food stocks, and settlements. The Army fought out of Forts Mojave and Whipple against Hualapai, Havasupai, Yavapai, and Southern Paiute warriors.

Many took refuge in remote places to avoid the fighting. However, in 1874, those Hualapai who could be found were forcibly marched 125 miles down the road built for the settlers. Their long walk took them from Beale's Springs to La Paz, a mining town on the lower Colorado River where many died from lack of food and disease that ran rampant in the hot climate and unhealthy conditions. One year later, those who survived escaped the camp, recrossing the desert to their homeland only to discover that springs and arable land had been taken over by miners and settlers.

In the old days, the Havasupai people used dwellings in the canyon during farming season and built them up above during hunting and gathering seasons.

The Pai alliance battled hard—officers from Fort Whipple said they would rather fight five Apache than one Hualapai—but they lost the war and a third of their people. They officially surrendered at Fort Mojave in 1878.

Reservation Life

Reservation life began for the Hualapai shortly afterward at a temporary post at Beale's Springs, where an agent issued rations of flour, sugar, and beef to them every 30 days. Their permanent reservation was established in 1883 with Peach Springs as its center. The local water rights, however, had already been sold to the railroad and to cattlemen, so many people continued to have to depend on government-supplied commodity foods.

By the time the Hualapai reservation was formed, the Havasupai had already received their land. In 1880, 518 acres 5,300 feet below the rim of

Most Wanted

No Indian who roamed the Arizona Territory during the last desperate decades of the 1800s outraged authorities more than the "Red Ant," the Yavapai chief called Delshay. In the Tonto Basin, Delshay was feared as southern Arizona feared Cochise, Victorio, and Geronimo.

Delshay rivaled those chiefs in his ability to outwit and manipulate the U.S. Army during the relentless guerilla encounters known as the Indian Wars. Like the southern Apache, he appeared and disappeared, making and breaking deals, changing sides, and frustrating the army and its most devious scouts. Like them, he made a tenacious stand for his besieged land. Gen. George Crook's Tonto Campaign left him both a villain and a hero.

In spite of Delshay's fierce determination and audacious brand of fork-tongued diplomacy, he is best remembered for the strange circumstances surrounding his final disappearance. He rose to the top of commanding general Crook's "Most Wanted" list in 1864, after other renegade chiefs of the north had been defeated. A bounty was placed on his head and, in short order, two heads said to be Delshay's rolled to Crook's feet. Both headhunters were paid their $50 reward and the "Red Ant" was never seen again. To this day, no one is certain whether he was killed. Did his nephew arrange his murder after soldiers threw Mexican pesos into a blanket until they met his price? Was the chief a victim of Apache scouts who ambushed him in his strong-hold? Did a conquered renegade chief do him in? Crook never determined with any certainty. As a message he posted one head at San Carlos and the other at Camp Verde. Given his skill and determination, Delshay may have watched Gen. Crook leave the territory from the safety of a secret cave.

Praising Delshay as a great warrior, Yavapai Mike Burns recalled in his memoir: "He was not the only man who had taken up arms to fight and protect himself, his family, his people, his home, his property, and the country of his ancestors, hoping he might conquer his enemies and be left alone with his people to enjoy the freedom they were used to." He was, however, one whose determination to stand to the end with his land and people belongs alongside the iconic Apache who were the very last of the traditional warrior chiefs.

A Moveable Feast

Mescal was the staple food of the Yavapai. Tall stalks of agave, from which it is taken, are found all over the areas where they gathered food. The hearts of the best plants were removed and roasted in a firepit dug into the ground. After it was cooked, it could be dried and cached for use as the band moved from place to place.

Havasu Canyon was declared theirs. This tiny reservation virtually confined them to a canyon 12 miles long and 5 miles wide. Everything from building materials to mail had to be brought in by horses and mules (to which helicopters have been added in recent years). No road has ever reached them. Intensive cultivation of their land resulted in stress to both plots and farmers, although they successfully grew wheat, corn, vegetables, and fruits. But seasonal migration, with its freedom to live on open land and enjoy socializing with relatives, became difficult under the reservation system. And once and for all, they were differentiated from their relatives, the Hualapai.

In 1974, 160,000 acres was added to the reservation. Much of this addition lies within Grand Canyon National Park and is held as a Traditional Use Area in joint control of the tribe and the Park Service.

An agave roasting pit at Phoenix's Desert Botanical Garden illustrates how this staple of Pai nutrition was prepared.

Times have changed slowly at Supai. A government day school was built in 1895, where children were taught in English about European society. It closed in 1955. In 1975 a new K–8 tribal school was established at which children may speak the Pai language, although after eighth grade they must leave for public or boarding schools. It is the older children now who move up and away from Havasu Canyon at the time of the Harvest Festival.

Gambling has not been a viable source of income for rural tribes, but the passage of the Arizona Indian Self-Reliance Initiative in 2002 brought the Havasu and Hualapai an opportunity to participate in that revenue. In 2003 the Arizona Indian Gaming Association allowed a transfer of the Havasu's gaming rights to Fort McDowell Yavapai Nation and the Salt River Pima-Maricopa Indian Community. The income from the transfer will supplement tourism dollars, the only other major economic and employment source for the 500-plus people who make their home at Supai.

The Yavapai

The Yavapai, with whom the ancestral Hualapai shared almost half of their territorial border, language, and cultural roots, split long ago. They formed bands that spread from the San Francisco Peaks in northern Arizona to the Mazatzal Mountains near Phoenix. Oak Creek Canyon and the area around

A Yavapai cowboy herds cattle across the Verde River near Fort McDowell.

Instant Architecture

A *wahm bunnyah* was the traditional dwelling of the Yavapai near Prescott. These brush shelters could be constructed in about an hour. Frames as large as 10 by 20 feet and as high as 7 feet were made from flexible woods such as juniper, willow, and mesquite. Cottonwood, oak, or sumac were tied on the frame horizontally and then thatched with juniper bark. Thinner material at the top allowed smoke to rise. Doors faced east and were covered with hides and later blankets. Inside spaces were set aside for storage, sleeping, and cooking, although outdoor ramadas often served as kitchens and sleeping areas in summer.

Sedona, the Black Hills near Jerome, the Bradshaw Mountains by Prescott, and southern lands all the way to Yuma bear signs of their presence. How long ago did they arrive? Ancient oral traditions tell of prehistoric mastodons, camels, horses, and bison that were gone from the earth by 6,000 BC, although archaeologists offer varying opinions.

Eventually the Yavapai aligned with certain clans of western Apache, especially those known as Tontos (Dilzhe'e) whose territory bordered theirs near the Verde River in central Arizona. Considerable Yavapai-Apache inter-marriage resulted because, as the story goes, either the Yavapai women were so beautiful that Apache men couldn't resist them or the Apache women were so attractive that Yavapai men found language no barrier to love. In any case, they came together as two distinct tribes who had historically lived in the upper Verde Valley. When they intermarried, they raised their children bilingually and biculturally.

The outside world had difficulty sorting out the result. Over the years they have variously been called Yavapache, Mojave-Yavapai, Yuma-Apache, and Mojave-Apache. Only recently have the tribes formally adopted names that satisfactorily identify related peoples living on three reservations: the Yavapai-Prescott Indian Tribe; the Fort McDowell Yavapai Nation east of Phoenix; the Yavapai-Apache Nation at Middle Verde. The true meaning of Yavapai is Sun People, and in the Pai language the word *a-baya*, which sounds like "Apache," also means "people."

Although Yavapai and Dilzhe'e Apache lived as neighbors and in-laws prior to white settlement, they found themselves allied by necessity when, in the mid-1800s, immigrants began arriving in great numbers. Gold prospectors and miners led the pack. Strikes near Prescott, Wickenburg, and Jerome drew new people like magnets—people who used the natives' rivers, springs, meadows, and soil to survive while they searched for minerals. Soon Indians and settlers were tripping over each other in pursuit of their lives and goals. Conflict grew constant, violence became arbitrary and ever-present, and the U.S. Army was called in. Another bitter chapter in the Indian Wars began.

A *wahm bunnyah,* the traditional dwelling of the Yavapai, could be built in a day.

Forts were established to try to contain the Yavapai and Apache peoples, whose leaders took their bands to remote areas in their enormous territory. Information handed down through generations gave them knowledge of every valley, cave, and spring in the Mazatzal, Sierra Ancha, Bradshaw, Weaver, and other rugged mountain ranges. Fort McDowell, near where the Verde and Salt Rivers meet, and Fort Whipple, north of Prescott, were inadequate to prevent raiding and retaliation strikes that came in response to the loss of their land. Camps Miller, McConnell, Goodwin, Verde, and Reno were maintained in nearly roadless regions. U.S. Army Gen. George Crook was called in to organize the military effort, and he did. Using hostile scouts from their ancient enemies the Pima and other tribes, he ultimately led the force that overcame these native peoples' determination to keep their homeland and their traditional lifeways.

These people, too, were eventually evicted from their homeland. In 1875, the Yavapai and Dilzhe'e Apache walked a long trail to the San Carlos agency, far to the south. The two tribes were separated on either side of the Gila River and were issued government rations to supplement what they raised and gathered from the mountains. The men served their turn as Gen. Crook's scouts, searching for the southern Apache tribes led by the famous chief Geronimo. As an incentive, Gen. Crook promised the Yavapai and Dilzhe'e Apache that they could return to their homelands when Geronimo's band was captured.

Geronimo surrendered in 1886, but not until 1890 were the people formally released from San Carlos. They scattered, mainly over west-central

Patient Advocate

A remarkable advocate of human rights lies at rest in the cemetery at Fort McDowell. As a young child, Wassaja was stolen from his Yavapai family by Pimas and sold to a photographer from Chicago. The man raised him as his own and saw that he was educated. He became a doctor. He returned to his homeland, where he fought for Native American rights, including citizenship. Dr. Carlos Montezuma, as he became known, was also instrumental in helping the Yavapai regain their homeland. Wassaja died in a traditional dwelling in Arizona.

Arizona. One group stopped at Fort McDowell. The Yavapai clustered around the Prescott area and the Verde Valley. Dilzhe'e Apache families returned to the Tonto Basin, along Fossil, Beaver, and Clear Creeks, or settled near Camp Verde. Work was available at the mines around Clarkdale until they closed down in the 1950s. Some workers transferred with the company to Ajo, near the Mexican border, until that mine closed. When the Indian Reorganization Act of 1934 made them independent of the U.S. government, the tribes organized in the locations where their headquarters are located today.

A peaceful side canyon at Havasupai

The Indian Gaming Act has created revenue for all the Pai reservations, directly or indirectly. Fort McDowell, near Phoenix, had the first gaming operation in Arizona. Both the Yavapai-Apache and the Yavapai-Prescott are located in places that give them access to a good clientele. While they work to preserve their language and traditions, the face of the future is changing.

Classic Style

With the coming of western missionaries, the old ways of dress and adornment changed. Today "traditional" dress means the long skirts and loose tops introduced at the turn of the last century. They are distinctively decorated, always in bright calico colors. Yavapai women may wear one-piece dresses with long sleeves, sometimes in layers; Dilzhe'e Apache women are likely to wear two-piece dresses with shorter puffed sleeves. Yavapai-Apache women may compromise by wearing two-piece dresses with the tops tucked in.

Traditional hairstyles meant straight shoulder-length cuts for the Yavapai women and long loose hair for the Apache women. Cosmetic tattooing called for lines of dots, crosses, squares, and circles. This kind of tattooing is rarely practiced now. Nor is face painting, which was done with deerfat-laced red or white clay for special dances and social occasions.

Men and boys, who used to bundle their long hair in back and dress in buckskin and high moccasins, tend to wear cowboy clothes now, which are both traditional and contemporary.

The Annual Gathering of the Pai gives children a chance to dress up for traditional dancing and feasting and to watch a Pai weaver who represents a Mexican branch of the people begin a basket.

Exploring the Pai Lands

Pai reservations are located near Phoenix, Prescott, Camp Verde, and north at the Grand Canyon. Each has its own level and type of tourism development.

Near Phoenix

Fort McDowell Adventures

Fountain Hills • (480) 816-6465 • www.fortmcdowelladventures.com

Follow AZ 87 (Shea Blvd.) north from Phoenix/Scottsdale through Fountain Hills. Turn left (north) at IR 1, where Fort McDowell Casino is located, and follow the road to your destination.

Fort McDowell is surrounded by some of Arizona's most spectacular scenery, including Four Peaks, the prominent mountains east of Scottsdale that look a lot like the image on Arizona license plates. To enjoy it, the tribe offers activities that are more cowboy than Indian, but connect history and the land.

• The Wild West is the specialty of Fort McDowell Adventures. Trail rides along (and through) the Verde River are available for individual tourists. Larger groups can participate in a City Slicker Cattle Drive or enjoy stars over the desert from the comfort of a hay wagon.

Navajo Falls cascades down Havasu Canyon.

• A Yavapai Jeep Tour Experience will take you along 7 of the most spectacular miles you've ever traveled. You're surrounded by mountains—the McDowell, Mazatzal, and Superstition Ranges, Four Peaks, and Red Mountain. Then Sycamore Creek takes you into the backcountry for a desert cookout, or you can go back to the Ranch. Beautiful places in this country are always more beautiful at sunset.

• The Ranch and La Puesta del Sol has interesting settings designed for groups of over 50 people. A saloon, outdoor fireplaces, and covered seating create a comfortable environment. Bands, cowboy games, line dancing instruction, storytellers, dancers, hold-ups, trick ropers and gamblers, "dying" contests, and even a private rodeo can be arranged to add atmosphere. It would be hard to designate these as Native "cultural heritage events," but they're fun.

Planned at the time of this publication is a 247-room Radisson hotel and an RV park.

Deer Valley Rock Art Center

3711 W. Deer Valley Rd., Phoenix • (623) 582-8007
www.asu.edu/clas/anthropology/dvrac • Open: 9 a.m.–5 p.m., Sundays noon–5 p.m.,
October–April; 8 a.m.–2 p.m., Sundays noon–5 p.m., May–September; Closed on
Mondays • Take Deer Valley Rd. west off I-17 at Exit 215B

This site, maintained by Arizona State University, was created at the Hedgpeth Hills Petroglyph Site, an ancient place where many peoples, including the Yavapai, passed through (a map of traditional Yavapai territories is included in the exhibit). Some of the figures pecked into rock stained with black desert varnish have been dated back to the Archaic past, 10,000 years old. Those that appear to relate to the Yavapai ancestors are dated between 300 and 1450. Outlined crosses and figures with large fingers on their hands are typical.

This museum is a good place to understand all about petroglyphs and pictographs, which are well explained and interpreted. The best time to visit is morning or late afternoon, when the sun's rays don't hit the rocks from above.

The museum includes a book and gift shop and traditional plantings along the paths to the site. Guided tours are available. Call to schedule one.

Ancient people left this life-size guard on alert in Yavapai country.

When the Blue-Green Waters Run Brown

Flash floods wash through Supai Village regularly, falling from the plateau over the canyon walls. Some have devastating consequences; others simply stay in the channels of Havasu Creek, then rush into the Grand Canyon. On p. 184–187 of her memoir, People of the Blue Water, Flora Gregg Iliff describes her experience of summer flood:

Suddenly masses of black, heavy clouds boiled in view, rolling and tumbling ominously, the lower folds surging violently upward....The topography of the surrounding country was against us; the plateau spread, like an open fan, to the south, the east, and the west, forming a drainage area of hundreds of square miles which poured its water into our canyon....The indentations in the rimrock were old watercourses, which this drainage had cut through the outer limestone walls on its way to our chasm....

The clouds opened, pouring down water in a solid column....The entire west wall as far up the canyon as we could see was now hidden behind a curtain of water. Then the east wall...was likewise hidden....Those curtains, hundreds of feet high, were pouring tons of water into our gorge each moment....

Then came a new danger....With startling suddenness, a full-grown river, boiling with sand and debris, leaped over the east wall with a force that shot it far out into the canyon....We realized the volume and strength of the current when a large evergreen tree rode its crest and fell, beaten and crumpled, almost at our feet....It hurled

a boulder over the rim, spun it crazily, and smashed it on the ground with an impact that shook the canyon. Our stream of clear, blue water had disappeared. A maelstrom of dirty suds...swept down Havasu's bed, spreading across the canyon from wall to wall....

The talus took us above the flood water....From this point, we watched the water plunging down the canyon bed, striking tree trunks, boulders, or angled walls and shooting long streamers of spray high into the air. It surged against the buildings, ran up the walls, then fell back heavily....

Then quite suddenly...the rain struck with less force. The clouds rolled away and never before had our strip of sky looked so serene, so blue, so beautiful!
(reprinted by permission of Christobel I. Berger)

Flash floods occur regularly in canyon country when rainwater runs from the plateau over immense canyon walls. Some have devastating consequences while others simply rush down into the Colorado River.

Near Camp Verde

Seventy-plus miles north of Phoenix off I-17 are three prehistoric sites with ties to the past of all the Pai.

Tuzigoot National Monument

(928) 634-5564
www.nps.gov/tuzi/home.htm
Open: Memorial Day–Labor Day, 8 a.m.–6 p.m.; September–May, 8 a.m.–5 p.m.; Closed: December 25

Take 1-17 to Exit 287. Travel west about 14 miles on AZ 260 to Cottonwood, where you will turn left at the fifth traffic light (Main St.). Signs along the road will direct you to Tuzigoot National Monument.

This beautifully preserved hillside, stone-walled dwelling was occupied between 1100 and 1400. The monument also has a small, well-organized museum and picnic facilities.

Stone walls and a museum containing artifacts excavated from the Verde River country attract visitors to Tuzigoot National Monument.

Montezuma Castle and Montezuma Well

(928) 567-3323 • www.nps.gov/moca/ • Open: Memorial Day–Labor Day, 8 a.m.– 6 p.m.; September–May, 8 a.m.–5 p.m.

To get to the Castle, take Exit 289, which leaves I-17 just north of Camp Verde. Turn north on the unpaved road across from Cliff Castle Casino. Montezuma's Well is 11 miles north, off Exit 293.

The "castle" is a 5-story, 20-room cliff dwelling that was used between 1000 and 1400. The "well," 11 miles away, is actually a deep, round lake created by a limestone sink. Some dwellings and remnants of early irrigation remain there as well. This serene place is said to be the place where *Kamalapukwia*, First Woman of the Yavapai, was sent off in her boat to begin the world we live in.

Fort Verde State Historic Park

(928) 567-3275 • www.azparks.gov/Parks/parkhtml/fortverde.html
Open: Daily 8 a.m.–5 p.m.; Closed: December 25

From I-17, take Exit 255 onto the General Crook Trail. Follow it toward Camp Verde, where it meets AZ 260. Turn right onto AZ 260 and then left onto Main St. (also called Finney Flat). Brown signs will lead you to the intersection with E. Holloman St., where the fort is located. Or take Exit 287 and follow AZ 260 east directly into Camp Verde. Go left on Main St. to E. Holloman.

This is the best preserved example of an "Indian Wars" period fort in Arizona. It was established in January 1864. Among other duties, the soldiers oversaw the Rio Verde Reservation near present-day Cottonwood, where many Yavapai and Dilzhe'e Apache lived. After 1873, nearly 1,500 people from various bands farmed there on 56 acres, irrigated by ditches dug with any tool they could lay their hands on. In February 1875, these people were marched 180 miles to the San Carlos Reservation near Globe. Many died. Some escaped. Their former reservation was opened to settlers in 1877.

Fort Verde was the primary base for Gen. George Crook's scouts and soldiers, and nearly every Yavapai and Tonto Apache who opposed the Army sooner or later spent some time there. The Crook Trail, now a paved road, follows the Verde River not far from the fort. Today, visitors can see informative exhibits which include artifacts related to military life, Indian Scouts, and "Indian War" history housed in the Fort Verde Administration Building.

Verde Canyon Railroad

300 N. Broadway, Clarkdale
(800) 320-0718 • www.verdecanyonrr.com

Take Exit 287 from I-17. Follow AZ 260 about 14 miles northwest to Cottonwood. At the fifth traffic light, turn left onto Main St. Follow it past Tuzigoot National Monument to the sign marking the railway station.

Unrelated to the tribes but a good way to see the land and the Verde River is to take the 4-hour round trip on the Verde Canyon Railway. It passes red rock cliffs; clear, green water; riparian wildlife, including bald eagle habitat; and ancient Indian pueblos. It's a good way to get a sense of the region where the desert meets the river. A narrator shares history and legend and entertains along the way. Spring brings wildflowers and fall showcases the changing leaves. In winter the eagles are nesting and in summer you can ride in the evening.

Prescott

This area was important to certain Pai peoples and boasts a fine historical museum today.

Sharlot Hall Museum

415 W. Gurley St., Prescott • (928) 445-3122 • www.sharlot.org
Open: May–September, Monday–Saturday, 10 a.m.–5 p.m.; Sunday, noon–4 p.m.;
October–April, Monday–Saturday, 10 a.m.–4 p.m.; Sunday, 1 p.m.–5 p.m.

Leave I-17 at Exit 262, near Cordes Junction. Go west on AZ 69 into Prescott. Follow signs to Gurley St. You will pass the courthouse plaza on the left and the museum is 2 blocks further west, also on the left. Reservation lands and a casino also lie on the outskirts of town.

The Sharlot Hall Museum is the largest museum in central Arizona. It is located on attractively landscaped grounds dotted with historical buildings. Founded by a pioneer poet, it is dedicated to providing educational adventures that explore the rich diversity of regional heritage through festivals, living history events, outdoor theater performances, changing exhibits, publications, and research resources. Each summer the museum hosts an outdoor market of Indian arts and crafts. At the north end of the museum, don't miss the permanent exhibit, "The Baskets Keep Talking: the Story of the Yavapai Prescott Tribe."

Near Sedona

Palatki Heritage Site

(928) 282-4119 • www.fs.fed.us/~3/coconino/recreation.red-rock/palatki-ruins.shtml
Open: Daily 9:30 a.m.–3:30 p.m.; Closed: Thanksgiving, December 25, and when rainy or snowy weather prevents access. The entry gate closes a half hour before the site closes.

While the beauty and significance of the site are well worth the trip, a some-what adventurous spirit is required to get there. Leave I-17 at Exit 298 to get to Sedona. In Sedona, you will come to a Y in the road (89A). Take the left (south) fork. A half-mile south of mile marker 365, you will turn right at a group of mailboxes onto FR 525 to FR 795, both unpaved. Go 8 miles to Palatki. Another unpaved route via Dry Creek Rd. and Boynton Pass Rd. (FR 152C) is bumpier and dustier, but takes you along spectacular red rock buttes to Palatki.

This site, like so many others, was inhabited by a series of cultures, including the Yavapai, whose oral history tells of their first home near what is now Sedona. An unusual reminder of human habitation at the dwelling is an ancient agave-roasting pit, complete with the preserved remains of agave hearts (a Yavapai staple) that have been chewed and spit out.

The rock art, however, tells its story best. Be sure to take advantage of all that the rangers can tell you about these images that relate stories of succeeding cultures as clearly as a book. A few are truly archaic. They may be 10,000 years old. Others tell of post-Spanish times—a horse is pictured with its rider —and you'll find fascinating images of times in between. Taken individually or together, they bring the past to life. Restrooms and a ranger station are the only amenities here.

An unusual reminder of human habitation at the dwelling at Palatki is an ancient agave-roasting pit where preserved remains of agave hearts were chewed and spit out.

Near the Grand Canyon

From these central Arizona spots, you can head north to the Grand Canyon to experience the lands and culture of the Hualapai and Havasupai. Both offer grand outdoor adventure travel as well as rugged natural beauty. While Hualapai lands are the very definition of the "wide open spaces" outside the Canyon, Havasupai Canyon has often been described as a Shangri-La, its greenery and beautiful waters confined out of sight of the rest of the world.

Grand Canyon West

Hualapai Lodge in the town of Peach Springs
(888) 255-9550 • www.grandcanyonresort.com

All trips into the western Grand Canyon begin at Hualapai Lodge in Peach Springs. You may book your room as a package with your adventure. The lodge has a good dining room where you are surrounded by reminders of the local wildlife. Twenty-four hours advance notice is required for tours, but even more notice is better. The high season is April to October.

To get to Peach Springs from Phoenix or Tucson, take 1-17 to Flagstaff, where you pick up I-40 and follow it west to Seligman. From there, follow Route 66 west to Peach Springs. A more complicated shortcut via Prescott Valley is described under Havasu Canyon.

Travelers in search of life on the literal edge won't want to miss Grand Canyon West, a pristine stretch of the Colorado River on the Hualapai reservation. Traveling Old Route 66 to the tribal capital, Peach Springs, you will find a collection of adventures packaged and delivered with a Native touch.

The only way to drive into the Grand Canyon is the 21-mile Diamond Creek Road through Peach Springs Canyon on Hualapai lands.

The only way to get to Supai Village is by horse, foot, or helicopter—and it doesn't fly every day.

The Hualapai have made sure that nothing stands between the viewer and the view at Quarter-master, Eagle, and Guano Points. No railings, warning signs, or commercial ventures block the experience of vast space and geological beauty that spreads out between Diamond Creek and Pearce Ferry. Only your comfort level lets you know when to stop walking, if looking straight over a 5,000-foot cliff is the way you want to experience the river. This is where Evel Knievel's son jumped over the narrowest point in the Canyon on his motorcycle in 1999.

Options for acrophobic visitors to Grand Canyon West include a 7-rapid, 40-mile day-trip river rafting expedition; relatively inexpensive helicopter tours over and INTO the Canyon offered by the tribe through Papillon of Las Vegas; and a driving excursion down Diamond Creek Road, the only road into the Grand Canyon. Graded but unpaved, it gradually descends to the Colorado through Peach Springs Canyon. This 21-mile chasm is a wonder in itself, lined by cliffs and bordered by forests of ocotillo and crown-of-thorns. It is also home to herds of wild burros. Excursions led by Hualapai guides are available, or the road can be driven in your own vehicle. You can ride an ATV to the Canyon rim or combine a number of activities. Most packages include transportation and the relevant meal.

Hualapai Wildlife sells permits to hunt desert bighorn sheep, trophy elk, antelope, and mountain lion that roam the million acres of the reservation. The terrain is diverse, spectacular, and challenging. Call for information on costs, guides, rules, and regulations. Camping or Hualapai Lodge accommodations are available.

Pack horses bring campers' supplies and equipment to the campground at Havasu Creek.

Havasu Canyon

Supai • (928) 448-2120

Visiting the canyon is a two-stage process. First, you have to get to Hualapai Hilltop, where the trail begins. Most people spend the night in the vicinity—Seligman, Grand Canyon Caverns, or Peach Springs—and leave for the trailhead early in the morning. Be forewarned that no gas, water, food, or services of any kind are available at Hualapai Hilltop. Parking is free.

The second stage involves getting into the canyon. The only way to get there is by foot, horse, or helicopter. If you take the helicopter, all you need is a round-trip ticket. If you are riding a horse, be sure to bring water, a hat, and sunblock. If you're hiking, bring water, sustenance of some kind, a hat, sunglasses, sunblock, and good boots. The trail is rocky and dusty and completely open to the sun until just before you reach the village. When you come to rushing water bordered with willows, you will begin to realize that this trip is worth the effort.

Note: Everybody needs to check in at the tourist office when they arrive at the village.

Campground reservations (mandatory) and information: (928) 448-2120. (The line is often busy. Keep calling.) The campground office is open daily. Check-in is 9 a.m.–5 p.m.

The crystal falls and milky turquoise pools of Havasu Canyon are set dramatically against red sandstone and surrounding greenery. Blue-green travertine pools created by Havasu Falls invite swimmers as well as photographers.

The lodge is open daily. Call between 8 a.m. and 5 p.m. for reservations: (928) 448-2111 or (928) 428-2201.

See the Havasupai website (www.havasupaitribe.com) or inquire by telephone about costs and arrangements involved in taking the helicopter into the canyon or hiring a horse or mule for you and/or your baggage.

To get there from Phoenix, take I-17 north to Exit 262 at Cordes Junction. Follow AZ 69 west toward Prescott. In Prescott Valley (not yet Prescott) take Glassford Rd. to its intersection with US 89A and US 89. Turn right (north) and head for Ash Fork. Just before you get to Ash Fork you will intersect I-40. Follow it toward Seligman, Exit 121. You can stay there or follow Route 66 out of Seligman to either Grand Canyon Caverns (25 miles) or Peach Springs (12 miles farther). (For other options, see directions to Grand Canyon West, p. 189.)

From any of these towns, take Route 66 to IR 18, the road to Hualapai Hilltop (ask for directions wherever you stay). The distance between the junction of Route 66 and IR 18 and the Hilltop is 68 miles—each way! Not a single service is available on IR 18 and few cars pass by. Top your tank and carry water!

A man wheelbarrows a little girl down the only street in Supai Village.

This cultural experience is extraordinary, matched only by the natural beauty of the place. Plan to stay a couple of days at the Havasupai campground, which is 2 miles farther than the village (it seems longer when you've hiked in the 8-mile trail). But don't fail to spend some time quietly watching how the people live in Supai. Buy something at the grocery, have a soda at the restaurant, see the little children play and the young men ride down to the stream on their horses. Strike up a conversation.

Beyond the village, however, are four blue-green waterfalls that make you feel as if you are in another world. The pools below them are lined with a mineral that makes them naturally resemble swimming pools. Each of the falls is different, so you can choose to swim, lie on a beach, climb down one like a monkey, or just admire the blue-green beauty. Hikers can follow the stream all the way to the Colorado River.

Tour packages are available if you aren't a regular camper. Even those who are usually have their supplies packed in on horseback, which requires prior arrangements with the tribal tourist office. Fees and permits are required, as are reservations on the helicopter.

Dining and Overnight Accommodations

• **Radisson Fort McDowell Resort & Casino** at the eastern edge of Scottsdale has 247 rooms and a conference center. (800) 333-3333; www.radisson.com.

Two tribal casinos offer lodging and dining close to Camp Verde:

• **Cliff Castle Casino** offers a steakhouse, gift shop, and bowling center. (800) 381-7568 for reservations; www.cliffcastlecasino.net.

• **Bucky's Yavapai Casino and Prescott Resort** in Prescott has 160 rooms that overlook Prescott and the surrounding landscape. (800) 967-4637; www.buckyscasino.com.

Near the Grand Canyon accommodations are available at:

• **Grand Canyon Caverns and Inn**, at mile marker 115 on Route 66. Grand Canyon Inn also offers an RV park, restaurant, gift shop, and real caverns. (928) 422-4565; www.gccaverns.com.

• **Hualapai Lodge in Peach Springs** is very close to the road to Hualapai Hill. (928) 769-2230; www.grandcanyonresort.com.

• **Seligman:** Check online for motels and dining in this Route 66 town near the road to Hualapai Hill. A campground in Seligman is available. www.grandcanyon.worldweb.com.

Shopping

Although older Pai baskets are very collectible, few are being made today. Few shops or trading posts currently exist on Pai lands. However, you might "ask around" if you visit. Occasionally you'll find individuals who are still weaving baskets, beading, or creating other kinds of artwork without placing their creations in retail outlets. Someone at a store, restaurant, hotel, or casino gift shop might put you in touch with people who have art objects for sale.

Recurring Events

All Pai Peoples
- **Annual Gathering of the Pai** (different locations each year)

Hualapai
- **Route 66 Days** (May)
- **Miss Hualapai Pageant** (August)
- **Sobriety Festival** (June)
- **Indian Day** (October)

Havasupai
- **Land Day** (January)
- **Peach Festival** (August)

Yavapai
Fort McDowell Yavapai Nation:
- **Orme Dam Celebration and Powwow** (November)
- **Cultural Festival, Arts and Crafts**

Yavapai-Apache Nation:
- **Exodus Day** (February)
- **Indian Day** (September)

Bird dancers continue a Pai tradition that is shared by other tribes.

Native Voices, Native Lives: Camille Nighthorse

Near the Grand Canyon, I was raised on the Hualapai Indian Reservation by my grandparents, Nellie Jack and Fred Work Mahone. They had taken me in so that my mother could continue on with her college education.

My grandfather's greatest emphasis was education for our people. He said we needed to learn the white man's language to communicate effectively with them, and to become educated and succeed in becoming a self-sufficient people.

My grandfather, having been born in 1888, had served during World War I in France and was able to see other cultures and societies from a different perspective than those who remained on the reservation. During the time that I lived with my grandfather, he was partially blind, not energetic and couldn't get around very well, but yet he had a great mind. He had fought most of his life trying to reclaim our traditional lands from the government. He passed away in March 1971 at the Indian Hospital in Parker. Later that year, the tribe was finally awarded nearly $3 million for the land claim, which came out to a few cents per acre. This represented what the land was worth in the late 1800s.

Camille Nighthorse, dressed in traditional shawl and beaded collar, holds a Hualapai basket.

The first seven years of my life with my grandparents was an experience I will always cherish. They are memories of a world that no longer exists—a world that was in a transitional period. The U.S. government was trying to make great changes in the Native way of life, but my grandmother chose to remain close to her traditional ways of survival.

I was raised in our native language, speaking English only when I needed to. We spent a lot of time out on the reservation gathering piñons, picking squawberries, hunting deer, elk, and rabbit for food. We would get as much as possible to dry and store for the coming winter.

During certain times, we would drive out in her 1950 Ford and gather willows for making Hualapai baskets, or other plants and roots to make cradle boards. She would usually invite a close friend or cousin to accompany us so they could also get the materials needed to make these things. My grandmother, being 20 years younger than my grandfather, had learned to become very independent and we would usually leave him at home for the day. She instilled in me a large part of herself, her inner strength and character of genuine kindness. As their first grandchild, they had given me the love and stability I needed in my formative years to later deal with all of the challenges and sorrow that lay ahead.

From the time I was almost nine years old, I went away to attend school in Garden Grove, California, and would return home for the summers. For six years, I stayed with a foster family who were members of the Church of Jesus Christ of Latter-day Saints while I attended school. I regretted missing those years with my grandmother, but I was a quick learner and realized I could do anything that was expected of me. For the first few years it was really tough to live in a world that was extremely different and with people who I couldn't relate to. I was very shy and pretty much kept to myself.

It was hard to feel comfortable in a home where I didn't feel the love and harmony that I was used to with my grandmother. I viewed the white society as a people who were loud, competitive, and working to gain material wealth. On the reservation, we were just trying to survive, having faith that our Creator would bless us with our needs if we did our part. My grandmother's actions showed me that in order to be blessed with peace and happiness, one must be helpful, have gratitude, and be generous to others. I saw her as the perfect role model.

When I was almost 15, I decided not to return to the placement program in California because I wanted to be with the Indian kids in school. I wanted to go to a boarding school that I always heard so much about from my cousins. I was thrilled when I got accepted to attend the Phoenix Indian High School in my sophomore year. I soon found that love and harmony did not exist at the boarding schools either. I graduated in 1977 and saw that I had no home to return to on the reservation.

During the summers I worked on rafting trips that began on my reservation for tourists going down the Colorado River. My mother, who was working at the Intermountain Indian School in northern Utah, told me they offered classes to post-high students for vocational training. It all sounded good. I went there to study music, theatre, and design for a semester until I met my real father and his other seven children.

At 19, I began my first year of college at Brigham Young University. It had a great program for Native Americans. Their tuition was automatically taken care of. I thought I would major in elementary education so I could become a teacher back on my reservation. But I had always loved writing, acting, and photography. I had so many interests and thoroughly enjoyed learning just about everything.

In my sophomore year I got married and began having children while I was still in school. I focused on raising my own family. Family was something I had always wanted and longed for. By the time I was 32, I had eight children and had lived in many places throughout the country and in Europe. I longed for home.

I moved my family back to the Hualapai reservation so they could get to know their native roots and I could get reacquainted with cousins and relatives. I worked for the special education department in the Peach Springs School. I also did volunteer work for the Hualapai Emergency Services and became an EMT. Later I worked in the Planning Department for the tribe until I moved to the Phoenix area. I attended Scottsdale Community College and began to study film production and photography.

I have produced a couple of Native American calendars to promote Native talent in the entertainment industry. I have worked in major motion pictures for the last 10 years and am a member of the Screen Actors Guild. I photograph models, actors, and musicians for promotional headshots and composites.

With half of my children grown, I have since remarried and now live in Phoenix, but travel frequently back to my reservation to visit my mother, Mabelene Mahone, who retired back home in the mid-1980s. I am researching individual histories of the Hualapai families so that the younger generation can know exactly how they are related to one another.

I am also planning to put together all the information I gather for a film documentary on the history of our people. I recently started a production company, Silver Spirit Entertainment, so I can produce the stories of our Native people in film. I recently lost my younger brother who was named after one of the Hualapai chiefs who was murdered in the 1870s—Wabeyuma. He, too, had a sad story to tell.

Each of us has our story, in every generation, on every reservation, from every tribe that has a similar history. We begin with ourselves, sharing so that we may lift one another, compare the struggles with our brothers, and become one in spirit with our Creator, our God. We can only move forward by knowing from where we have come. Our past is full of great sorrow and pain, but without it we cannot gain strength from the spirits of our forefathers to go beyond what they sacrificed for us. They do wait for us on the other side and have found peace and happiness when they left this world. Let us be grateful to be alive in this new generation and do those things that will make our ancestors proud.

Ndee: The Apache

"...traveling in [their] minds, listening for the ancestors, and studying the landscape..."

—Keith H. Basso, *Wisdom Sits in Places*

Ga'an Dancers, whose regalia includes symbols of the four directions and fire, are the focus of attention of visiting "royalty" on Apache Heritage Day at Fort Apache.

Introduction to Apache Culture

N ame recognition? The Apache tribes have it all over the world. Few and far between are places where the word Apache (whose actual meaning no one really knows) doesn't call up the image of fiercely determined fighting men who give no quarter.

Ironically, the world's most famous American Indian tribe wouldn't have understood the meaning of the word Apache until it came into common use in the 1700s. Like others, they called themselves the People, *Ndee* (nn-DEH). Like others, the tribe was made up not only of war heroes, but of women and children, men who did not raid or fight, and elders. They lived in family groups; prayed and cared for each other; and hunted, gathered, traded, lived, and died across an enormous, diverse region in the Southwest.

Their tribal customs took shape there. The characteristic Apache dwelling was a brush structure called a *gowa*, or wickiup, often covered with bison, cow, or horse hide. They wore buckskin clothing and high moccasins with turned-up toes. They became skilled in the use of stone war clubs and bows and arrows. They developed rituals and amulets and clothing with special powers to protect their men in battle. Their system of smoke signals was universally understood and effectively used to communicate.

Along with hunting and collecting wild food, the Apache also learned to cultivate crops. Women were the primary farmers. They grew corn, beans, squash, and pumpkins near creeks, rivers, and springs. Often they planted and then went off with the rest of the clan to gather agave hearts, cactus fruit, acorns, walnuts, and piñons and didn't return until harvest time. They would come back provisioned for the winter, with goods to trade as well. Meat and animal hides, salt, tallow, and wild food products were often exchanged for corn and woven cotton.

They practiced the rituals that took them through life: blessing their babies in the cradleboard, when they took their first steps, and at the time of their first haircut; telling wintertime stories about Killer of Enemies, who rid the earth of evil monsters, and Coyote, the ultimate bad example. They developed rites of passage to manhood and womanhood, for the curing of illness, and success in war. The mountains, trees, rocks, earth, and wind spoke plainly to the people, sharing their wisdom with each generation. The four-leggeds were on par with the two-leggeds.

Women in traditional attire put the finishing touches on a wickiup, the European name for an Apache dwelling whose construction is a woman's responsibility.

In these ways, the Ndee made the Southwest their home. With their Navajo relatives, they came there from the region around today's Alaska and Northwest Territories, speaking dialects of an Athabaskan language. Their arrival, however, reaches so far back in time that religion and legend situate their sacred places only in the Southwest and northern Mexico. Whether or not (as scholars suggest) they crossed the Bering Strait from Asia, spent time in the Arctic, and then moved halfway down the continent across plains and mountain ranges to the western landscapes, they are a very resourceful and enterprising group.

Their journey, whatever it entailed and whenever it began, undoubtedly occurred over many generations. Although stories and customs have survived, early sites of the Apache have not, because they carried little with them and moved from camp to camp. Scholars say that they began to differentiate into subtribes when their numbers became too great for any one place to support.

Fascinating Facts about the Apache

• Many American Indian names that are internationally recognized belong to Apache people, including Geronimo, Cochise, Mangas Coloradas, and Victorio.

• Few names of Apache women are widely known, although strong women have always played important parts in all aspects of tribal life. Traditionally, inheritance goes through the female line. Women of course carried the primary and ultimate power of reproduction, but those who wanted to be involved in war were welcomed as advisors and warriors.

• The 1886 surrender of Geronimo, whose Chiricahua Apache name was actually Goyahtlay, ended the "Indian Wars" of Arizona. These were the last open conflicts between Euro-Americans and Native Americans in the United States.

• Following Geronimo's surrender, renegade Apache groups who never were willing to come in to reservations lived in secret hideouts in the Sierra Madre of Mexico.

• The word "Apache" does not belong to the culture of the people to whom it refers. Experts disagree on its derivation. It might come from a Pueblo word that refers to an enemy, or it might be related to a Pai word that simply refers to another community, or it might have another source.

• Apache, Navajo, and certain Arctic peoples speak languages that are so closely related that their names for themselves—Ndee, Diné, and Dene—are pronounced nearly identically. The different groups can understand some of each other's speech, as well.

• When horses were brought in by Spanish entradas, Apaches were the first Native Americans to use the animals for transportation rather than for food.

• "Fort Apache," which featured tiny cowboys and Indians in conflict, was a popular board game in the 1960s. Early versions are quite collectible and can be found on the Internet. Ironically, the real Fort Apache was a relatively peaceful place.

Branches and bands developed their own territories, still keeping their identity as a tribe. Perhaps before 1500, they settled into the high country, came to know the valleys within it, and also learned to use foods from the surrounding deserts.

Arizona is home to two of these branches: the Western Apache and the Chiricahua, the branch of Geronimo, Cochise, and other famous cavalry fighters. The Western Apache are further divided into Tonto, or Dilzhe'e; White Mountain, San Carlos, and Cibecue. Before modern times, these and other Apache groups adopted customs of the peoples nearest their territory, learning from the Pueblos, the Plains Indians, from Mexican border groups, and people with whom they traded. They began to differentiate from one another. Even so, the various subtribes of Apache continued to see themselves as one people and shared their land peacefully.

Foreign Contact

Winds of change began to blow with the coming of Europeans. The Apache were quick to adopt horses and use them for warfare, which allowed them to expand this territory they called their own. Almost as soon as the Spanish introduced them into the Rio Grande Valley, horses appeared elsewhere with Apache riding them. (Many tribes used horses for food before they rode them.) Threatened by this advantage, others came to call the Ndee "Apache," a word

Creation Story

Before the days that the speech of one could not be understood by the other, the world was dark, without sun, moon, or stars. Creatures no longer known lived there, among them nameless monsters that destroyed human offspring. They also could speak and be understood.

Eventually two tribes, the birds and the beasts, came into conflict about whether to light the world. The birds, led by the eagle, prevailed, and light began to shine day and night.

One of the humans who survived the conflict was a woman who had many children, whom she hid from the remaining monsters. When her son matured, he ignored his mother's warnings and went out to hunt. He killed a deer and dressed it. Four times, a monster came and took his meat. Four times the boy took it back, and then he called the monster out to fight.

They established rules. Each got four shots with a bow and arrow, the monster going first. Each time the monster shot his enormous arrows, the boy jumped onto a rainbow and the monster's arrows splintered where they fell. When it was the boy's turn, he shot three arrows that exposed the monster's heart. The fourth arrow pierced it, and the beast rolled dead over a cliff, far down into a canyon, where his body still lies.

Then the Creator, *Usen,* taught the boy how to prepare herbs for medicine, how to hunt and fight. He and his descendents became the Ndee, and were given their land forever.

connoting enmity, whatever else it meant. Until then, the Spanish had called them all *coyoteros*.

Of course, the horses that enhanced their lives were accompanied by explorers and colonizers, who, between the late 1600s and the end of the 1700s, began a process of invasion that would produce exactly the opposite result. First Spanish, then Mexicans, then Americans would see the promise of material value in the beautiful and abundant lands of the Apache. They would pursue their interests to the bitter end.

The view from sacred Mount Graham takes in Fort Grant,
the scene of bitter memories for the Apache.

Hide playing cards were used for a game called Mexican Monte. The hide cards were made for about 20 years, between the time the Apache learned the game and when traders began to sell paper decks. Suit and number were the elements that mattered most in the game. The cards often copied pictures from decks used for other games.

As pressure began to increase on their established way of life, the Apache added raiding to their economic activities. They ranged from central Arizona into Sonora and Chihuahua, Mexico, and from the White Mountains to the deserts beyond the Superstitions in search of livestock and other supplies. Winter camps moved constantly, following the availability of cattle and horses in the same way they used to pursue game.

These hide-covered Apache homes were called *gowa*.

Their raiding activities were often exaggerated. Settlers would blame Apache for trouble even when they weren't sure of its source. Other tribes also raided and sometimes raiders were Apache who had been evicted from the tribe because they were judged of bad character. When they committed depredations, everyone was held responsible. The Pima, Maricopa, and Tohono O'odham—settled groups with food stocks and livestock herds—became permanent foes, as did the Hualapai and Havasupai. The Navajo were sometimes friends, sometimes adversaries. Recent raids or vengeance for the death of a relative were determining factors in their status.

The Apache ability to outwit just about everybody provoked a strong reaction from the colonial Spanish in the late 1700s. They wanted to expand their settlements north into territory the tribe considered their own. Using force and violence, the colonizers brought many Apache to forts in Mexico, handing out rations as the Americans would later. During this period, the Apache who complied learned about irrigation, tortillas, a card game called Mexican Monte, Spanish clothing, slavery, and an alcoholic beverage known as *tulapai*.

Mexico's independence from Spain in 1821 put an end to the expensive dependency that the Spanish had encouraged and to any vestige of friendship. The new government instituted a policy of extermination against the Apache, offering bounties as high as $100 a head. They began to raid again, using firearms combined with improved knowledge of the Hispanic culture.

When the Treaty of Guadalupe Hidalgo made the Southwest part of the United States in 1848, the familiar clashes between Indians, miners, settlers, and U.S. soldiers increased for the Apache as well as for other tribes. Freed of Mexican oppression, the tribe at first hoped for a better relationship with their new government. This didn't materialize. A series of incidents in which Americans pretended friendship but killed or poisoned Apache ensued, and eventually ignited the "Apache Wars" that lasted from the 1850s until Geronimo's capture in 1886.

The establishment of Fort Apache in 1870 became a turning point. It was planned as a preventive strategy to keep White Mountain bands from supplying hostile groups with whom the Army was already fighting. Local Apache helped select the site and cooperated with the soldiers. The first non-Indian expedition to cross the Salt River into White Mountain Apache territory, led by Maj. John Green, called the place "a garden spot."

Maj. Green also observed that the Apache "almost worship" their land. This intense attachment to place proved to be the aspect of their culture that elicited consequences beyond what either side could have predicted. They would totally refuse to give it up or leave it, whatever the cost.

The Warpath

Perhaps one reason the Apache are known first as warriors is because, in their own eyes, their wars were always righteous and fought to avenge the death of a relative. While raiding was carried out to get food and supplies, war was an act based on family loyalty.

The Apache planned their attacks strategically. When somebody died in a raid or battle, the family leaders would elect a war leader. He would recruit related bands that might bring their own headmen. The warriors would meet in council to plan their campaign. A medicine man or woman would usually consult with the war leaders to assist in predicting the outcome.

Equipment was prepared, including weapons and items like special caps (which were carried, not worn), arm bands, shields, and other protection. Before they left, a ceremony was held at which dancers demonstrated how they were going to treat the enemy. The women participated by inciting anger and encouraging the warriors' bravery. The clans involved feasted and danced socially until the day to depart dawned.

Stealth and surprise were crucial to successful raids and attacks. Guerilla tactics were a specialty and Apache were known for their ability to disappear. They concealed their tracks by walking in one another's footsteps, scattered so no one could follow their trail, hid camps high in the rocks, built fires in the daytime so that they would be reduced to smokeless coals by night, and put their hands over horses' nostrils to keep them quiet. They sometimes cut the tendons on mules' ears to keep them from sticking up. People on a raid operated as individuals, separating so that they would be harder to capture. They would reconvene following the attack.

It has been said that to be killed in a fight with Apache was better than to be captured. Cruel torture was often the fate of a prisoner. Sometimes he would be turned over to the wife of a person he killed. The warriors knew that she would do her job without inhibition. The story of Gouyen illustrates. After her husband met his death in a raid, Gouyen left her camp with only a little food, water, and tools to care for her moccasins. When she came upon her quarry he was dancing a victory dance with her husband's scalp on his belt. Gouyen joined the dance, seduced the killer, and then murdered him. She returned home with his scalp, breechcloth, and moccasins, which she presented to her husband's parents.

A victorious Apache war party was also welcomed back with a feast and dancing. Victory dances lasted four days and nights. The warriors came dressed for battle. Each man danced as he had before going on the warpath, while singers proclaimed the significance of his actions.

However, from that time on the Ndee began to lose material and spiritual control of that land. Originally estimated to be at least 14 million acres, it was reduced to 5 million acres when the first reservation was established in 1871. Ultimately, the entire Western Apache reserves added up to only 4 million acres. How could newly arrived strangers lay claim to the place of their ancestors? That question was unanswerable to the Apache.

Adding insult to injury, the same newcomers mined it, logged it, hunted, fished, and redirected its water resources. They drove the Apache trout nearly to extinction. The top predator, the wolf, whose power the tribe invoked for their own hunts, vanished. Elk, deer, and other game had to compete with domestic animals. Their livestock overgrazed the grasses. In the language of the Ndee, one word, *ni'*, means land and mind. To them, overusing the land and its inhabitants seemed mindless.

Reservation Life

Reservations prevailed by the late 1800s. Many Apache people had voluntarily moved to them because the harsh alternatives seemed to be extermination or starvation. Others were forcibly removed from their homes by the military.

Geronimo's Gift

John Vicker, a Quaker who owned the Chiricahua Cattle Company, which was near Tombstone in the 1880s, allowed Geronimo to hide in his barn from U.S. cavalry soldiers who were tracking him. He also brought him food and dressed his wounds. After the Apache leader recovered, he quietly slipped away. The Vicker family then found this Western Apache basket in the hay where he had slept. It is now in the collection of the Museum of Northern Arizona.

Goyathlay, known as Geronimo, a member of a Chiracahua band, held out with his people in the Sierra Madre Mountains of Mexico until the end of the "Apache Wars."

They were called renegades. White Mountain came first. A reservation was created briefly at Camp Grant; however, when a group of about 100 people, primarily women and children, was massacred or kidnapped by settlers while under the protection of the military, it closed. That event is still remembered on Apache Memorial Day.

In 1872, San Carlos was established. Members of different subtribes as well as Yavapai from the Verde River area and later Quechan and Mojave were forced to live together, which resulted in friction and often violence. The people endured overcrowded conditions in a climate many were not accustomed to and were given inadequate and unfamiliar food to eat. Men were not allowed to use weapons, which meant that women had no hides from which to make clothing. Frustration and despair led to a virtual state of war between the Apache and the Army.

Reservation land was reduced many times during the 1870s, as deposits of copper, silver, coal, and timbered land were handed over to settlers. During these years, the famous warriors Cochise, Mangas Coloradas, Victorio, and others were making their stand. All of these men were Chiricahua, from southern bands. The wild Sierra Madre range near the border with Mexico provided them with a place to escape that was not available to northern bands.

A Foot in Each Camp

Alchesay was born a White Mountain Apache in 1853. He expected to become chief, rather than scouting his own people on behalf of the U.S. Army. He was given the Congressional Medal of Honor in 1875 for gallant conduct during his service in the winter of 1872–1873.

During Alchesay's service as a scout, he was able to maintain cordial relations with the U.S. soldiers. A frustrated Gen. George Crook selected him to contact Geronimo in 1886. Alchesay was instrumental in Geronimo's surrender, which ended the Indian Wars.

Amazingly, in Alchesay's day, the Apache were given names that matched numbers stamped onto metal tags. The tags were distributed by Gen. Crook to Indians who lived on the reservation and were meant to assure fair distribution of rations. Alchesay was known as A-1, a reflection of his status with the Army.

AL-CHE-SAY----Chief of the White Mountain Indians. 1886. Has 1886 model Winchester.

Until the late 1920s, trails to hidden Apache camps in those mountains were still used. Geronimo, whose real name was *Goyahtlay*, used them the most and was the last warrior to surrender.

In 1896, 10 years after Geronimo's final surrender, the Apache reservations were fixed as they remain today. The section above the Salt River is still called the Fort Apache or White Mountain Apache Reservation and the southern section is the San Carlos Apache Reservation. (The Tonto Apache later received 85 acres.) The dispiriting practice of rationing eventually ended and troops departed. But Apache still had no control of their lands and resources, and no economy.

In order to live, many became wage laborers for road construction, mining, and farms. The Indian agents hired them out. They provided much of the labor for the dams that were built on the Salt and Verde Rivers and for Coolidge Dam on the Gila River. Ironically, when this dam was completed, the old village of San Carlos was inundated and had to be moved upstream. It did, however, provide irrigation water for the reservation.

Cattle raising and farming did not provide an adequate base for the reservation economy during the Depression. Many Apache remembered the old ways and gathered wild acorns, walnuts, and agave to supplement their food supply. It took the Indian Reorganization Act of 1934 to create the beginnings of self-government. Apache were among the first to provide job training to adults and youth and to establish a justice system and police force of their own.

Family Ties

Family lies at the heart of Apache heritage. A traditional household centered on a woman, her husband, her married daughters and their families, and any unmarried daughters and sons. They would all live close to each other, if not in the same place. Certain men were allowed more than one wife, who were normally sisters. A married man's obligation was to support his mother-in-law's family.

Although no formal marriage ceremony developed outside an exchange of gifts, marriage was a respected institution. Men and women took their respective contributions to the household seriously. Fidelity was expected and children were cherished.

Clans consisted of groups of people who considered themselves descended from a single female ancestor. They were often named for their place of origin, such as "red rocks people." Before reservation days, clans united Apache in groups that occupied farm sites and had rights to hunting territories. They were also responsible for carrying out ceremonial obligations. Aunts and uncles were called mothers and fathers. Cousins were sisters and brothers.

Each clan group operated independently under a respected family leader, resolving its own problems under its own rules. No one could marry within their clan. By the 1800s, about 60 clans existed. Certain personality types and behaviors were said to be associated with each one.

Today the White Mountain Apache Reservation and the San Carlos Reservation are home to more than 20,000 tribal members who live in communities scattered on just under 2 million acres of land. The Tonto (Dilzhe'e) Apache, with a population of about 200, live near Payson. Cattle raising, timber sales, outdoor recreation, some farming, and the mining of peridot—a beautiful lime-green semiprecious stone found in only two other places worldwide—provide employment for San Carlos. White Mountain has a ski resort and a number of fishing lakes, plus fine hunting resources. Since the mid-1990s both reservations have operated successful casinos that allow them further economic development as well as health and social programs.

Tourism provides both jobs and revenue to the tribes. The reservation lands are beautiful, covered with pine forests and lakes, more than 20 of which the tribe created in the 1950s in spite of opposition from the downstream Salt River Water Users' Association. A tribal fish hatchery stocks them. Hunting, fishing, and camping are very popular on both reservations. Historic and prehistoric sites lure cultural heritage tourists, as well.

Raising cattle is an important business for the White Mountain Apaches.

Ceremonial Customs

Traditional Apache rites related to curing, becoming an adult, agriculture and hunting, personal power, and protection. Spiritual guidance is still provided by medicine men and women, whose powers may be specialized or general. They conduct ceremonies, counsel individuals, and heal illness. The creator is called Usen, Life Giver. White Painted Woman, Child of Water, and Killer of Enemies play important parts which are detailed in Apache origin myths. (Not surprisingly, Navajo and Apache creation myths are similar.)

Mountain spirits called *Ga'an* originally provided the people with their ceremonial customs and rituals. Men become those spirits as they dance. They appear with black hooded faces, their bodies painted with symbolic designs. They wear highly decorated headdresses that gave rise to the name outsiders sometimes give them, "crown dancers." The bull roarer and Apache drum accompany them. The eerie sounds that the dancers make seem to come from another world. When they dance at night, they appear and disappear suddenly, making no sound after the echo of their calls dissolves into silence.

Today, some of the Apache people are exclusively Christian while others are Christian and also participate in the Apache religion. Some practice only the old ways. The Apache Survival Coalition has led an international struggle to try to preserve their traditional sacred sites.

The Mountain Spirits called *Ga'an* originally provided Apaches with their ceremonial customs and rituals.

• **The Sunrise Dance Ceremony:** The most important community ceremony today is the girl's maturation ceremony—*Na'ii'es* in Apache, Sunrise Ceremony in English. It is frequently performed and usually takes place in the summer following a girl's first menstrual period. The family selects a sponsor who will stay with her for the entire four-day ceremony. Her godmother cannot be related to the girl by blood or marriage. She acts as a role model and creates

The Sunrise Dance Ceremony celebrates White Painted Woman's powers of creation, birth, and renewal.

a bond of mutual support between the girl's family and her own, which they consider as strong as blood relationship.

Besides celebrating White Painted Woman's powers to give birth and renew, the Sunrise Ceremony reaffirms traditional values for everyone who attends. In imitation of Changing Woman, the young woman performs a series of symbolic actions. One is for the attainment of a healthy old age, for which it is necessary to be in harmony with the supernatural forces of life. As the girl is transformed into Changing Woman during her four-day ritual, she receives the power of longevity. The cane which she circles four times represents a life lived through all four stages. Tossing four buckskins in the four directions casts away illness.

Oriole feathers decorate her cane, expressing a harmonious disposition. Morning runs on each day of the ceremony and the massaging of her body by her godmother symbolize endurance and physical strength as well as figuratively molding her into the ideal Apache woman. Prosperity and freedom from hunger, the fourth and last objective, are symbolized by her walk in the sacred footsteps outlined in pollen on buckskin, and by the corn, candy, and fruit that are cascaded over her head.

On the final morning, the singer (a ceremonial specialist) paints the girl's face white, blesses her and her sponsor, and puts a sun symbol in her hair just as the sun's rays strike her. He then leads her by two eagle feathers through a bower that symbolizes the tent of White Painted Woman. Guests follow, and receive her powerful blessing.

One indication of its importance is that the cost of a Sunrise Ceremony is significant. A singer conducts the ceremony, which is accompanied by drumming and sacred songs. Social times during the ceremony call for secular music, food, and drink for guests. A perfect buckskin dress, beaded adornments, ritual substances and the services of singers, musicians, and food are all expensive. Often families pool their resources to usher their child properly into her role as a woman.

This antique doll's beaded and fringed buckskin clothing looks like that worn in today's Sunrise Dance Ceremony.

Ornamented carrying baskets decorated with long fringes of buckskin finished with rolled-up tin have long been made by Apache weavers.

Pouches held U.S. government-issued ration cards in reservation days.

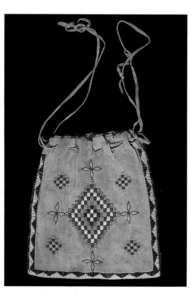

Beaded pouches carried objects important or sacred to the owner.

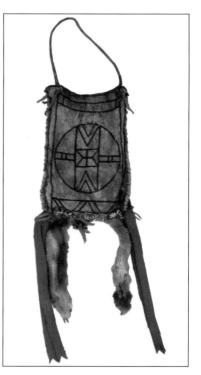

Fur and red flannel cloth decorate this White Mountain Apache pouch.

Western Apache were noted for their high moccasins with turned-up toes.

Beading is a highly-developed Apache art, whether created on a loom or applied to clothing or other adornment.

The Apache violin is made from a hollowed-out plant.

This moccasin, decorated with glass beads, was made around 1900.

Exploring the Apache Lands

The lands of the Apache people cover a lot of territory. Opportunities for a brief experience of their culture are concentrated in museums, while the past is evoked at historic and prehistoric sites.

A rich trove of archaeology can be found on Apache lands, although most of it likely predated their arrival. Their ancestors may have occupied these places for a time, but did not construct them. Still, they lie on lands that this tribe holds dear and have been part of their history far back into memory.

Although outdoor recreation may not ring of cultural heritage tourism to some, a relationship exists between understanding the lands and understanding a people for whom land lies at the heart of living. If hunting and fishing represent recreation to you, these activities have deep roots in tribal experience and are well organized. Visitors who simply enjoy wilderness will also find it here, along with abundant silence and solitude to enjoy it and consider the people who are inseparable from it.

Activities like golfing, skiing at Sunrise, or rock-climbing, require a more imaginative connection with culture, but they're fun and, in their own ways, they "touch the earth."

The Amerind Foundation museum lies in the heart of Chiricahua Apache country. The mountains in the background are in Mexico.

Along with the three forts and a presidio that are interpreted for visitors, a short list will suffice to remind you that most of Arizona became an Apache battleground before the tribe was forced to turn over the land it had depended on. A partial list of sites where major conflict between Apache (often along with Yavapai) and whites occurred includes:

Fort Buchanan, Patagonia; Camp Grant, at the confluence of Aravaipa Creek and the San Pedro; Cochise Stronghold, near Willcox; the site of Geronimo's surrender, near Douglas; Fort Goodwin/Thomas, near Bylas; Bloody Tanks, near Miami/Globe; Fish Creek in the Superstitions; Wheatfields; Picket Post Mountain and Queen Creek Canyon, near Superior; Apache Leap, near Superior; Skull Cave, near Canyon Lake; Turret Peak, near Cordes Junction; Cibecue; and Big Dry Wash.

Any library or bookstore offers hundreds of choices of books that will fill you in on the details. Websites abound.

East of Globe

Besh-Ba-Gowa Archaeological Park and Museum

(928) 425-0320; (800) 804-5623
www.go-arizona.com/Besh-Ba-Gowah-Archaeological-Park
Open: Daily 9 a.m.–5 p.m.

From Phoenix, take I-10 east and merge onto US 60, which you will follow about 90 miles to Globe. Continue on US 60 south through Globe. Just before you leave town, you will come to the first sign for Besh-Ba-Gowa. The rest of the route is well marked. Shaded picnic tables are available.

This combination museum, ethnobotanical garden, and partially restored prehistoric pueblo offers a unique way to experience aspects of life around the thirteenth century, when it was built and used by a culture that archaeologists call Salado.

Visitors walk into the plaza of the pueblo through its original entrance. From that level, they see a kiva-like underground ceremonial chamber and enter ground-floor storage rooms. A ladder leads to the upper stories, where people lived. A number of rooms are restored and furnished with replicas of tools and pottery that were excavated there. The rooftops were gathering places and they, too, are accessible.

Besh-Ba-Gowa (BESH-buh-go-ah) means "House of Metal" in Apache. This was actually the name they gave to Globe. Metal referred to the mining on which the town depended. Besh-Ba-Gowa and its predecessors—which go back to 9300 BC, when this was a paleo-Indian campsite—were not occupied by Apache, who didn't make this region their homeland until about AD 1600. It's possible that they joined the Yavapai who re-occupied this and six other pueblos related to it.

Water-smoothed rocks from nearby Pinal Creek were used to construct Besh-Ba-Gowa, a 700-year old pueblo that occupies a site where human habitation dates back over 10,000 years.

The museum is unique in that the items it displays were all excavated from the site it adjoins. The Salado people who built the pueblo made beautifully decorated pottery, wove cotton cloth, and created stone tools that are exhibited. It is set in an ethnobotanical garden of the plants that grow between desert and mountains which supplied food, fibers, dyes, and construction materials to the people. Nearby Pinal Creek provided water, which was directed into irrigation canals, and the smooth river stones for masonry.

Timelines in the museum illustrate the influence of peoples there from earliest times through trapping, mining, the coming of the railroads, and modern life.

San Carlos Apache Cultural Center

Peridot • (928) 475-2894 • www.apachegoldcasinoresort.com/Things_to_DO.htm
Open: Tuesday–Saturday, 9 a.m.–5 p.m. Subject to seasonal changes. Call to confirm hours.

Follow directions to Globe under Besh-Ba-Gowah (p. 215). Pick up US 70 in Globe. The small cultural center is in Peridot, about 20 miles east of Globe.

This small museum offers the advantage that only tribal cultural centers can. It tells the story of the southern Apache from their own point of view. Its "Window on Apache Culture" uses archival photographs to look at history. It also explains the tribe's spiritual beginnings. Some artifacts are exhibited, including a man's necklace with tweezers that were used to remove facial hair.

A life-size diorama illustrates the Changing Woman Ceremony, also known as the Sunrise Ceremony (see p. 209). It explains the role of the Ga'an dancers and displays some of their regalia. Other exhibits show life on the reservation and tell of the tribe's vision for its future.

Near Pinetop-Lakeside

To get to Pinetop-Lakeside, follow directions from Phoenix to Globe (p. 215) and take US 60/AZ 77 north to Show Low. At its junction with US 60, take AZ 260 southeast to Pinetop-Lakeside (where you will find services, food, and lodging), about 20 minutes away. To visit the White Mountain Apache locations, go to Hon-Dah Casino in Pinetop, which is located at the junction of AZ 260 and AZ 73. Take AZ 73 south through Whiteriver to Fort Apache Historic Park, about 45 minutes away.

Fort Apache Historic Park

Information: (928) 338-1392; Tourism Office: (928) 338-1230. Call to arrange a walking tour. • http://www.wmat.nsn.us/fortapachepark.htm Open: Daily 8 a.m.–sunset

Fort Apache was built in 1870, the year before the White Mountain reservation was established, to prevent local bands from supplying other hostile Indians. Initial interaction was cordial; however, the Army soon became involved in gathering Apache and other Native people onto the San Carlos Reservation. During that process, relationships deteriorated, although the frustrated, displaced Apache attacked the fort only once, in 1881.

Geronimo came in to the fort after his first surrender in 1884, as did Naches, Nana, Mangas, and, on an earlier occasion, Cochise. A group of about 150, including Geronimo, bolted again in 1885. When the dust settled after his final surrender in 1886, Fort Apache became a self-sustaining post and a relatively peaceful cultural meeting place. It remained active until 1922, when one of the buildings was converted to Theodore Roosevelt Indian Boarding School. Remaining Apache scouts were moved to Fort Huachuca. The last retired in 1947. At Huachuca they patrolled the boundaries of the military reservation and took part in ceremonial functions.

Not until the 1960s was Fort Apache's historical significance publicly recognized. It was placed in trust by the government and the White Mountain Apache Tribe built its first cultural center there. In the 1970s, Fort Apache was listed on the National Register of Historic Places, but by the 1990s the World Monuments Fund recognized it as one of its 100 Most Endangered Places. Since then, the tribe has taken the lead in designing a master plan and successfully seeking funds to restore its 26 buildings on 288 acres. Nine of them are completed, and the Fort appears cared for and authentic. It is now an official Save America's Treasures project.

Each year the tribe holds a Heritage Reunion on its grounds. This event is meant to be a time when individuals work on transforming a symbol of conflict into a celebration of cultural survival.

Walking tours are available through the Cultural Center with advance reservations. Visit the Office of Tourism in a log cabin; the Commanding Officer's, Captain's, and Officers' Quarters; and many more original buildings that surround the Parade Ground.

White Mountain Apache Cultural Center

Nowike Bagowa (*House of Our Footprints*)
(928) 338-4625 • *www.wmat.us/wmaculture.shmtl*
Open: June–August, 8 a.m.–5 p.m., Monday–Saturday;
Closed: Sunday. Call to confirm hours.
The museum is adjacent to the grounds of Fort Apache.

This contemporary museum, built on the site of the old Fort Apache army hospital, exhibits culturally significant objects selected by the tribe that are well-displayed and clearly explained. It also interprets Fort Apache from the tribal point of view. Outdoors you can visit a park where traditional structures have been recreated. Fine Apache arts and crafts, books, and souvenirs are available at the gift shop. This is not to be missed.

The contemporary White Mountain Apache Cultural Center, called House of Our Footprints, stands next to a park where traditional dwellings have been constructed.

Kinishba Ruins

(928) 338-4645 • *www.centerfordesertarchaeology.org*
Open: Daily 8 a.m.–5 p.m. • Required permit available at
Fort Apache Cultural Center. Ask for directions there.

Not far from Fort Apache, this Ancestral Puebloan structure provides an excellent example of the masonry skills of the people who built it. A perennial spring once ran in the nearby wash, and a variety of plant food and game thrived at altitudes that range from warm low areas to distant pine-forested mountains that are visible from the pueblo. The main plaza and rooms can be discerned within what was once a 3-story structure, although the ruins are not stabilized or restored.

To one side of the ruins is a historical building that was constructed in the 1930s, when Dr. Byron Cummings of the University of Arizona was directing restoration that he was not able to complete. Dr. Cummings hoped that the site would become an archaeological teaching facility as well as a source of revenue for the tribe.

Reaching the site requires a 2-mile drive down a dirt road, IR 41. It has

Kinishba Ruins, an ancestral pueblo archaeological site near Fort Apache, was once a 3-story structure.

no interpretive signs and attracts few people, which somehow gives you the feeling of having come upon a lost civilization.

Because this site is somewhat isolated, it is very important to respect its integrity and not disturb it in any way.

East of Tucson

Presidio of Santa Cruz de Terrenate

Take AZ 80 south from Benson (I-10, Exit 203) toward Tombstone and turn right (west) on AZ 82 (or you can get to AZ 82 via AZ 90 to Sierra Vista). On the west side of the San Pedro River look for Iron Horse Ranch Rd., a gravel road on your right (north). Turn right and go a couple of miles. The trailhead is on your right (east), and is marked with a large Bureau of Land Management (BLM) sign. The hike to Terrenate is about a mile and the trail is well marked.

Near the San Pedro River west of Tombstone stand the ruins of the Spanish Presidio de Terrenate, established in 1775. Today, traces of buildings and adobe walls remain, including the gate and fortified wall, the chapel, the soldiers' barracks, and the commandant's quarters. Traditional Spanish fort warfare was ineffective against the refined guerrilla tactics of the Apache. In 1780 the Presidio was abandoned in defeat.

Amerind Foundation

(520) 586-3666 • www.amerind.org
Open: Daily 10 a.m.–4 p.m., October–May; Wednesday–Sunday,
10 a.m.–4 p.m., June–September; Closed: Major holidays.
Exit I-10 at Dragoon Rd. (Exit 318). The turnoff is 1 mile south, and well marked.

The Amerind Foundation is beautifully located in the Dragoon Mountains (known locally as Cochise Country) between Benson and Willcox, about one hour south of Tucson. It was founded by a family with intense archaeological

interests and resembles a hacienda rather than a museum. In addition to an exhibit about the Apache people—in particular the Chiricahua, whose territory it lies within—the Amerind (American + Indian) displays a variety of objects from its large collection. Exhibits include "Images in Time," which features Native American art and expression from

The Amerind Foundation is in Chiracahua Apache territory. A permanent exhibit there interprets aspects of Western Apache culture.

prehistoric to contemporary eras; "The Pottery of Silas and Bertha Claw," clay vessels and figures that recall traditional Navajo life; and "Hopi Paintings on Paper: Drawing on a Life of Ritual and Community." A library, extensive research collection, and gift shop are part of the museum.

Cochise Stronghold

Sunsites • (520) 826-3593 (Forest Service Ranger Station)
www.cochisestronghold.com or alysion.org/Cochise/CochiseTrail.htm
      Leave I-10 at Exit 331. Follow AZ 191 south 18 miles to Sunsites. Take
Ironwood Rd. west toward the mountains. The pavement ends partway down
the 8-mile road (FR 84) to the campground.

Approximately 39 miles southwest of Willcox is the natural granite fortress used by the Chiricahua Apache under the leadership of Cochise. It is believed that the burial site of Cochise is located somewhere in the canyon (only his friend Tom Jeffords knew for sure). Visitors can picnic, hike, and camp there. For more civilized accommodations, there is also a bed-and-breakfast (see p. 228).

Chiricahua Regional Museum and Research Center

127 E. Maley, Willcox • (520) 384-3971
Open: Monday–Saturday, 10 a.m.–4 p.m.; Closed: Sunday

A small museum with a well-interpreted collection of Apache artifacts. It also boasts a wickiup built there by Cochise's great-granddaughter.

The Revenge of Cochise

Cochise worked as a woodcutter at the Apache Pass stagecoach station of the Butterfield Overland line. In 1861 a raiding party took cattle belonging to a rancher and abducted a child belonging to one of his hands. An inexperienced army officer, Lt. George Bascom, was called to the scene and ordered Cochise and five other Apache to appear for questioning. They asserted their innocence, but were arrested. When they resisted, soldiers killed one man and subdued the others. Cochise suffered three bullet wounds but escaped through a hole in the side of a tent.

Following the Apache way, he organized the abduction of a number of whites to exchange for the Apache captives. Bascom retaliated by hanging six Apache, including relatives of Cochise.

Cochise and his uncle, Mangas Coloradas, were then obligated by Apache morals and customs to avenge their deaths. During the following year, the attacks of Apache bands were so fierce that most troops, settlers, and traders left the region. At the same time, the army troops were called east to fight in the Civil War.

Cochise and his band of 200 hid in the Dragoon Mountains for 10 more years, until Gen. George Crook arrived in Arizona in 1871 and used Apache to scout Apache. Cochise was captured in 1871 but escaped in the spring of 1872. He surrendered again when the Chiricahua Reservation was established that summer. He died there in 1874 and was entombed at an undisclosed location near the place that is now called Cochise Stronghold in the Dragoon Mountains.

Cochise Stronghold lies deep within granite formations of the Dragoons that protected the Apache leader and his band. He is said to be buried somewhere in these mountains. The famous rock formation below is known as Cochise Head.

Museum of the Southwest

1500 N. Circle I Rd., Willcox • (520) 384-2272; (800) 200-2272
Open: Monday–Saturday, 9 a.m.–5 p.m.; Sunday, 1 p.m.–5 p.m.

The museum offers "Travel the Magic Circle of Cochise," a plan and directions for taking a self-directed driving tour of the county.

Chiricahua National Monument

(520) 824-3560 • www.nps.gov/chir
Open: Daily 8 a.m.–4 p.m.; Closed: December 25.
Exit I-10 at Willcox (Exit 336) and follow AZ 186 southeast from Willcox to AZ 181 which leads to the Monument.

The Apache called this "Land of the Standing Up Rocks," for reasons that become immediately clear. A drive along Bonita Canyon Drive takes you 8 miles to Massai Point, which offers restrooms, picnic tables, and an excellent view of Cochise Head, a formation that some say resembles the face of Cochise.

Hikers can take trails of various lengths and difficulties that add up to about 20 miles of adventure through the rocky wilderness. Echo Canyon and Heart of Rocks Trail pass balanced rocks, pinnacles, and spires that defy description. Wildlife abounds, including some very unusual hummingbirds. The visitor center has an audiovisual program and exhibits, as well as books and maps for sale.

Fort Bowie National Historic Site

(520) 847-2500 • www.nps.gov/fobo; www.desertusa.com/bow/
Open: Daily, 8 a.m.–4:30 p.m.; Closed: December 25. The Ruins Trail is open sunrise to sunset. • The park is located 12 miles south of Bowie (I-10 Exit 364) on Apache Pass Rd.

Fort Bowie was constructed in Apache Pass in 1862 to head off Confederate incursions into New Mexico. A second fort replaced it in 1868. Between then and 1886, when Geronimo surrendered, the U.S. Army sent troops and scouts out from here to fight the Chiricahua Apache. It guarded Apache Pass, which was a vulnerable spot along the Butterfield Stage route. Fort Bowie was later abandoned in 1894.

Fort Bowie served as a base of operations against southern Apaches. Geronimo and his band were sent from here to Florida and then to Oklahoma following their surrender in 1886.

You have to want to visit this national monument, but the experience is worth the effort. It's a 30-minute drive over gravel roads followed by a 1-hour hike on the Ruins Trail. The good news is that the trail is easygoing and interesting. It winds past the post cemetery, a replica Apache wickiup, the Chiricahua Apache Indian Agency, Apache Springs (the essential water source), the site of the first fort, and ends at Fort Bowie.

Here you will come to a visitor center and ranger station that offer park brochures, books, maps, historical memorabilia, a reconstruction of the second Fort Bowie, and a bust of Cochise. This is a place to linger and to remember history while you picnic at the available tables.

You can take an alternative trail back that gives you a higher perspective of Fort Bowie and Apache Pass. It is a little bit longer and less well interpreted, but still a piece of history.

East of Phoenix

Tonto National Monument

(928) 467-2241 • www.nps.gov/tont/
Open: Daily 8 a.m.–5 p.m.; Closed: December 25.
The Lower Cliff Dwelling Trail closes to uphill travel at 4 p.m.

Take Shea Blvd. (AZ 87) northeast from Phoenix/Scottsdale. Follow it to AZ 188 and turn right (southeast) toward Roosevelt Dam. The monument is 4 miles east. Travel time is 2.5–3 hours, each way.

Another Salado dwelling, built and occupied around the same time as Besh-Ba-Gowa (see p. 215), is built into a cave overlooking the high desert toward Roosevelt Lake (which of course was a well-populated stretch of the Salt River when people lived there). A half-mile footpath, Cactus Patch Trail, interprets plant life as it leads to the monument. Your climbing efforts are rewarded by the 20-room lower ruin. You will see how Salado builders first located a site with construction material littering its floor; mortared the quartzite rocks together with clay; collected wood, saguaro ribs, grasses, and reed for beams, and finished the ceiling with mud to allow for a second story. Many left their handprints in the plaster. The 40-room upper ruin is open only between November and May, when temperatures permit the exertion required for the 3-mile round trip hike up. Guided tours to the upper ruins are available with advance reservations.

The Visitor Center displays tools and pottery of the Salado people and offers an audiovisual program that discusses their lives and still-unexplained disappearance from the area.

Outdoor Recreation

People from all over the world come to pursue their favorite outdoor activities at both the San Carlos (1.8 million acres) and adjacent White Mountain (1.7 million acres) Apache Reservations. Together, they comprise an enormous, pristine wilderness. The active sportsperson can fish for bass or trout, hunt some of the world's largest elk, or simply hike and explore. Those who prefer to be more passive observers of the beauty and variety of the land can camp undisturbed by lakes where the forest reaches the shoreline. Wildlife is very plentiful: large and small, furred and feathered. Eagles, owls, deer, wild turkeys, beavers, and badgers are there to photograph or just to enjoy quietly. Wildflowers and berries color the landscape when in season.

This 16-pound bass, caught in San Carlos Apache waters, is displayed at the Office of Recreation and Wildlife.

These lands offer some of the best wilderness experience available. More than 1,000 campsites exist, many with pure spring water nearby. However, be aware that camping is definitely self-sufficient—you're on your own. Pack it in and pack it out. A permit is necessary, so you need to apply to San Carlos (see opposite page) or White Mountain (see p. 226) and to request a copy of rules and regulations when you do. Lakes and rivers are perfect places to view and photograph wildlife, including (in season, at the right places) exotic migratory birds that are found in Chiricahua territory farther south than San Carlos and White Mountain—although they have their share. Hiking is extraordinary, mostly off-trail. Mountain biking and rock-climbing, canyoneering, and river running, too. You can even rent your very own lake. Think of an outdoor activity and it is available somewhere on these reservations, as well as in southern Arizona Apache territory.

Be Prepared

A word to the wise: *preparation is essential* if you are going to enjoy this country. Distances are enormous. Forests can be dense. You may be at high altitude. No services exist and your cell phone doesn't work. If you have a GPS unit, use it. If it is hunting season, know it. You don't want to be the object of a search and rescue team, so be sure to provision yourself with maps, water, food, appropriate clothing, shelter, and —most important—information. Weather, road conditions, and rules and regulations are available at the tribal Department of Recreation and Wildlife, which should be your first stop. Well prepared, you are in for a rare experience.

San Carlos

San Carlos rises from a land of desert sage, cactus, and mesquite at its lowest points through seven biotic communities to ponderosa pine, spruce, and fir north of the Black River that designates its border with White Mountain.

For a taste of what's out there, visit the San Carlos Office of Recreation and Wildlife. There you'll see a small zoo of taxidermied animals that used to roam the wilderness, including the head of an elk that is believed to be the world's largest (Boone & Crockett is still checking) and a rare albino Merriam's turkey. Also preserved is a 16-plus-pound bass, possibly the third-largest known to have been caught.

People who love the outdoors and enjoy a land nearly free of man's influence marvel at the rare and beautiful places that have produced these and other creatures. Here, you'll find adventure in all directions.

Wildlife abounds. San Carlos has its Big Ten game animals: Elk, of course, three herds of some of the world's largest (elk on the reservation are related to the Yellowstone herd and may possibly have genes of Merriam's elk, thought to be extinct); mule deer and white-tailed Coues deer; Rocky Mountain and desert bighorn sheep; mountain lions; black bears; Merriam's wild turkey; pronghorn antelope; and javelina. Smaller game includes birds such as dove, quail, blue grouse, waterfowl, and migratory birds; bobcats; badgers; foxes; rabbits; and other assorted creatures.

All species except mule deer may be hunted by non-tribal members. Most hunts are not guided, although trophy hunts for elk and bighorn sheep require a guide to be present. Permits are limited to keep hunter densities low. All hunters must have a San Carlos Habitat Stamp, available through the Wildlife Department, which also provides a list of tribal-licensed guides, rules and regs, and all the information you need. Combination hunts may be arranged by adding a small game, predator, or mountain lion permit to your tag.

• **Hunting:** A variety of licenses and tags are offered, including elk trophy hunts, javelina, and predators. San Carlos manages its three elk herds for hunting. Bull permits are limited to an older age class and antlerless hunts are

---

Recreation at San Carlos

(888) 475-2343; (928) 475-2343 • www.sancarlosrecreationandwildlife.com
Open: Monday–Friday, 8 a.m.–4:30 p.m., Saturday; 7 a.m.–3 p.m.

Tags may be purchased by mail. You may also obtain permits at Apache Gold Casino Resort.

The San Carlos Recreation and Wildlife Department is located at US 70 and Old Moonbase Rd. in Peridot. (See directions to San Carlos Apache Cultural Center on p. 216. The department is located a few miles farther.)

Some of the largest elk in the world roam Apache forests. This one may have set a world record at 503 inches.

held in early November. Two of the herds are resident but a third comes down from the north and east in winter.

Bull elk in the Malay Gap management area average 310–330 inches, but some have scored up to 400 inches. Hilltop and Dry Lake herds have the largest animals. A bull believed to be the largest ever taken grossed 503 inches. Trophy hunts are held in September. Archery or rifles may be used. The revenue generated by these tags goes into the tribe's Conservation Fund.

• **Fishing:** San Carlos has both cold- and warmwater fisheries. Its largest lake —San Carlos—is actually the largest lake in Arizona when it is full. It nurtures largemouth bass, flathead catfish, and crappie. At the northern end of the reservation look for rainbow and brown trout, smallmouth bass, and—if you are lucky—Apache cutthroat trout. Dry, Phillips Park, and Point of Pines Lakes are also up there. In between are hundreds of tanks and ponds to fish as well. The Black, Salt, San Carlos, and Blue Rivers round out the water resources. Maps are available.

White Mountain

At the White Mountain reservation, another 1.5 million acres of wilderness continues at higher altitude. Spectacular canyons slash through both lands. At White Mountain, there are at least 2,300 acres of reservoirs, 800 miles of trout streams, two major rivers…and few humans. The reservation controls one-third of Arizona's coldwater resources.

• **Hunting:** Big game hunting at White Mountain is also impressive. Think Big Ten, but elk rule! Since the inception of the tribe's program in the late 1970s, the Wildlife and Outdoor Recreation Division has guided clients to more than 100 Rocky Mountain bull elk that are officially in the Boone & Crockett record books. The year 2001 may have set a single-season record for the greatest number of bull elk to be eligible, with 10 Rocky Mountain bulls having antlers that (still unofficially) exceeded the minimum scores.

Recreation at White Mountain

White Mountain Apache Wildlife and Outdoor Recreation Office
P.O. Box 220, Whiteriver, AZ 85941 • (928) 338-4385
http://162.42.237.6/wmatod/index.htm (includes a weekly fishing report)
Open: Monday–Friday, 8 a.m.–5 p.m.

Licenses, tags, permits, and information. Permits are also available at the Hon-Dah Resort Casino. See directions to Fort Apache (p. 217). AZ 73 passes tribal headquarters in Whiteriver where the office is located.

Trophy elk are hunted out of three camps between early September and early October, when the rest of the reservation is closed. Antlerless hunts follow.

Upland game birds include grouse and quail.

• **Fishing:** Rivers, lakes, and streams harbor an abundance of fish, including the rare Apache cutthroat trout. Species range from warmwater largemouth bass to varieties of trout and smallmouth bass. Hawley, Pacheta, Christmas Tree (which is managed for trophy Apache trout), and nine other reservation lakes offer fine fishing. Every year the Division hosts a fully outfitted fishing camp at Christmas Tree Lake before the lake officially opens in late May.

The White Mountain Apache Tribe rents cabins to visitors who come to enjoy the lakes, streams, and forests on their lands.

Streams, of course, hold rainbows and brown trout that are smaller than their lake-dwelling cousins but just as feisty. The Black River has both warm- and coldwater fish, depending on its elevation. Lake or stream, the farther you go from the road, the better the fishing, so locating a fairly remote spot is worth some map study.

Sunrise Park Resort

Greer • (928) 735-7669; (800) 772-7669 • www.sunriseskipark.com • Open all year
Drive to Pinetop-Lakeside according to the directions for Fort Apache (p. 217); however, you will continue through Pinetop on AZ 260. Turn right (south) at its junction with AZ 273. Sunrise Park Lodge is 4 miles south and Sunrise Ski Area is 3 miles past the lodge.

In winter, skiers can explore three mountains that boast 65 runs of varying difficulty. Its Express High Speed Detachable Quad Chairlift can handle 16,000 skiers per hour. A separate Snowboard Park, cross country ski trails, and a childrens' "ski-wee" area complete the picture.

Sunrise Park Lodge is a 100-room hotel with two restaurants, a lounge, gift shop, indoor pool, hot tubs, sauna, and game room. Located on Sunrise Lake, it provides a great base for summer and winter activities.

Just outside Pinetop, Hon-Dah Ski and Outdoor Sport has rentals of all kinds available: camping, ski equipment, boat rentals, hunting, rafting, and canyoneering.

Dining and Overnight Accommodations

Sites related to the Apache peoples are scattered all over Arizona. Globe, Pinetop-Lakeside, and Willcox offer accommodations if you don't base your activities out of the big cities. Try www.azcentral.com/travel as a source of both overnight and restaurant accommodations in the state.

• **There is a small bed-and-breakfast near Cochise Stronghold** (see p. 220). For reservations call (520) 826-4141 or (877) 426-4141.

Accommodations on the Apache reservations include hotels associated with the casinos. Both have RV parks. They are:

• **San Carlos Apache Gold:** (800) 272-2438; www.apachegoldcasinoresort.com; 5 miles east of Globe on US 70

• **White Mountain Hon-Dah:** www.hon-dah.com; located just east of Pinetop-Lakeside at the junction of AZ 260 and AZ 73

Shopping

Beautiful baskets, traditional clothing, and beading created by Apache people are not easy to find. **The cultural centers** are always a source of authentic items, but do not often have a large inventory. It is always possible to ask around, both on the reservations and in surrounding towns. Individual artists can sometimes be located this way. The **Heard Museum**, in Phoenix (see pp. 39 and 91), carries beautiful Apache art and crafts.

An interesting exposure to the culture can be found at the unexpectedly named **Anasazi Trading Post**, a tiny store at 3142 Highway 260 in Pinetop-

Willow baskets woven at San Carlos and in the White Mountains are recognized for their excellence. They can be distinguished by such details as the intricate interlocking designs, as seen in the two examples below.

Lakeside, (928) 368-5060. It is stocked not only with crafts but also supplies for traditional practitioners and herbalists, Ga'an dancers, and artists. The inventory includes blankets, bells, beads, beeswax, drums, snake root tobacco, hides, earth paint, and feathers. Owners Allen and Renée Barraza can answer all your questions and some you didn't think to ask.

Recurring Events

White Mountain

- **Canyon Day Open Show** (April)
- **Sunrise Dance Ceremonies** (May–September)
- **Junior Rodeo** and **Headstart Rodeo & Parade** (May)
- **Apache Heritage Days:** Fort Apache (May)
- **Intertribal Powwow in the Pines** (June)
- **"Old Timers" Junior Rodeo** (July)
- **Tribal Fair and Rodeo** (September)

San Carlos

- **Apache Gold Casino's Annual Powwow** (February)
- **Indian Festival at St. Charles School** (March)
- **Annual Mt. Turnbull Rodeo** (April)
- **Sunrise Dance Ceremonies** (May–September)
- **Apache Independence Day** (June 18)
- **Independence Day 10K Run** (July)
- **Indians in Sobriety Annual Campout** (August)
- **Holy Ground Blessing: People Helping People Gathering and Youth Leadership Conference** (October)
- **All Indian Rodeo and Fair:** Veterans Memorial Parade, rodeo, and queen pageant (November)
- **Anniversary of opening of San Carlos Apache Tribe's Cultural Center** (September)

Apache Heritage Days present an opportunity for participants to experience traditional dancing, food, and games.

Native Voices, Native Lives: Laurel Endfield

I was born in Miami, Arizona, but returned to the reservation when I was two, so I grew up inside my tradition. As a child, the Crown Dancers and the Sunrise Dance Ceremony were part of my life. My grandmother was the backbone of my extended family. She passed away when I was 16 and left a void in my life. I didn't appreciate her until I was older.

When I was 15, I found myself a pregnant teenager. I dropped out of high school. I got my GED at 16, was married at 17, and had four kids by 22.

My parents never gave up on me. They believed that education is very important. Although I was a non-traditional student, I never dreamed of not pursuing a degree in higher education. I enrolled at Northern Pioneer College and for eight years studied different things I was interested in; basically, I changed majors constantly and ended up with four associate degrees. It wasn't until I became an assistant in a Head Start program that I discovered my true love: education. So I went on and got bachelor's and master's degrees from Northern Arizona University (NAU).

I was able to do that because my advisor nominated me for the Gates Millennium Scholarship Program. I didn't understand it very well, but signed everything. She sent in the paperwork. The program was in its inaugural year and I was one of 230 graduate-level students selected from a pool of 63,000. I was one of only 20 Native Americans and the only Apache at the graduate level.

I received a check for $800, but I didn't understand the full extent of the program until the end of the year when I went to the Gates Leadership Conference. We all came together and I heard the stories of other recipients. Their stories were amazing! I was honored to be among them.

Leaders from many organizations, including the U.S. Department of Education; the Native American, Hispanic, United Negro, and Asian-American College Funds; and others were there, bragging about how wonderful we were! I found out that the rest of my bachelor's, master's, and doctoral degrees would be paid for. I haven't been able to go to another conference, although they're held every year, always in the East.

I finished my undergraduate degree, a Bachelor of Arts in liberal studies with an emphasis in learning and pedagogy; my master's in Educational Technology; and I'm working on an Ed.D. in education leadership and change at the Fielding Graduate Institute. I'll graduate in February 2006.

I am a single mother, so I have to work, too. I'm the center manager for Northern Pioneer College (NPC) in Whiteriver, on the Fort Apache Indian Reservation. I am the first tribal member to manage NPC. I also teach early childhood education there and at Yavapai College and Prescott College, both in Prescott.

I also do some public speaking (although I hate to do it), but if I can make a difference in a child's life it's worth it. I use my story to inspire single mothers and other students who want to return to a higher educational setting. I go to high schools, to welfare-to-work programs, and to freshmen orientations. I want others to know that they should never give up on their dreams. If I can do it, so can they.

I'd like to become a superintendent in a reservation, public, or Bureau of Indian Affairs (BIA) school. I'd like to see a tribal member in that leadership position. I want to effect positive change—better grades in school, better performance, more Native American teachers. I'd like to encourage multi-cultural education and programs for the perpetuation of indigenous language. I'd like to see Indian education teach responsibility for the environment—the approach is so different from Western thinking. I'd like to include technology with traditional teachings and to help students become lifelong learners. They need to be able to seek and use knowledge, to find what they need and know how to use it.

The schools need to create more of a mesh with traditions, or they could be lost—classes in Apache, traditional sewing of camp dresses, beading, basket-weaving, building a wickiup. Currently teacher aides are the ones who pass along the culture in most reservation elementary schools.

I know. I grew away from all that in my rebellious stage, at 16, when my grandmother died. I lived off the reservation for 10 years. The most amazing thing happened to me when I witnessed my own daughter's Sunrise Dance. I was involved in every aspect of it. It pulled me back totally into my culture. How beautiful and incredible it was! I felt we had lost the family leadership with my grandmother's death, but this pulled us all back to the close-knit way my grandmother had us. I have a deeper appreciation of my culture now and a great respect for the importance of family and tradition.

ON THE LOWER COLORADO RIVER

Mojave, Quechan, Cocopah, Chemehuevi

*"You're not really in the desert
when you're on the river."*

—Curtiss Martin, Mojave
quoted by Stephen Trimble in *The People*

The landscape along the lower Colorado River is distinguished
by its desert climate and unusual rock formations.

Introduction to the Colorado River Peoples

The Mojave is the most extreme of all North American deserts. Summer temperatures in this region can exceed 120 degrees, while in winter they drop below freezing. Its floor descends to 282 feet below sea level, the lowest point in the North America. Its highest mountain reaches 11,000 feet. At the foot of jagged mountain ranges lie the plains, dunes, marshlands, and sinks that characterize its landscape. Strong winds are legendary. Annual rainfall averages 2 inches. Of the 250 plant species that live there, 90 are unique to the region. It is favored by the deadly Mojave rattlesnake. Why would the benevolent creator of the people whose name it bears give them such a place?

Creation Story

He made this land habitable by adding the gift of water. By thrusting his staff into the ground, the Creator caused one of North America's great rivers, the Colorado, to run along the eastern boundary of the desert. The tributaries that are now called the Bill Williams and the Lower Gila also fed the Colorado

Fascinating Facts about the Colorado River Peoples

• The Mojave Desert is one of the most extreme environments in North America. It holds records for the lowest point, the least rain, and the highest temperatures on the continent.

• Most tribes believed that battles should not start before sunrise or continue after sunset. The Mojave did not, and took advantage of their enemies by attacking at night.

• Out of a single cottonwood tree, the Colorado River tribes made canoes big enough to hold 20 people.

• An important Chemehuevi ritual song, the Salt Song, is composed entirely of Mojave words pronounced so that they cannot be understood by either Mojave or Chemehuevi. The intention and story are understood without words, so the effect is humorous.

• The first Spaniards thought the Colorado River people were giants. The average Spaniard then was 5 feet 3 inches; the average Native man in the area was 6 feet or over, and powerfully built.

• In the nineteenth century, the last of an ancient guild of Colorado River region runners still survived. They specialized not only in speed, but in conveying important messages with precise accuracy.

• The Cocopah, traditionally desert people who enjoyed traveling to hunt, gather, and trade, had no word for village.

• Cocopah tradition held that people needed to have their faces tattooed in order to follow the trails to peace in the next world.

• The Mojave year begins in the middle of summer, the time of pounding the mesquite beans. It is not counted in moons or suns.

• The "mud volcanoes" by the Mexicali Geothermal Plant once constituted the dividing line between the Cocopah and the Quechan peoples.

• The artist Ted de Grazia created a pastel called *Little Cocopah Indian Girl.* Its sales raised $30,000 for the tribe during a time of great need.

• The Chemehuevi, whose creator is Ocean Woman, follow a strict taboo against eating fish.

The first Spaniards thought the powerfully built Colorado River people were giants.

• The honey mesquite tree, which is native to the Lower Colorado River valley, bears fruit with more sugar than the sugar beet.

• The word "Mojave" is spelled with a "j" when it directly refers to the tribe—Fort Mojave, Mojave Desert, Mojave Indians. It is spelled with an "h" for everything else— Mohave Mountains, Mohave Road.

within his peoples' territory. These waters brought from the north plenty of rich, silted earth to feed, clothe, and shelter not only the Mojave (moe-*HAH*-vee), but other groups as well: the Quechan (Kwt-*SAHN*), Cocopah (*KO*-ko-pah), and Chemehuevi (Cheh-muh-*HWAY*-vee) among them.

The people were precisely taught in the First Times how and where to live on their land. A century ago, a Mojave elder related his version of the original coming together of the tribes. He told how they positioned themselves around a house built for winter in the proper manner. The Mojave stayed inside with the Quechan and other Yuman language speakers, while the Chemehuevi, who received their own language, sat outside with their relatives the Hualapai and Yavapai. Their places reflected the relative positions of the land they would occupy.

From there they went into the world. The river peoples were given farmlands with corn, beans, and pumpkins to plant on them together with tools and containers for preparing food. Hunting and gathering groups like

Winter temperatures in the Mojave Desert can drop below freezing. In summer they can rise above 120 degrees.

Decorative collars were a feature of Colorado River women's dress and adornment before European clothing was introduced. They evolved from natural materials such as seeds and shells to metal and glass beads.

the Chemehuevi were given the right to use foods from the farmlands. Social rules and values were also defined. Instructions included how to fight correctly using mallet-headed war clubs—skills that came into frequent use as time passed. The people were told that warring would keep them close and strong.

So for many generations, the ancestors fought, cultivated their fields, and built seasonal dwellings along the course of the Colorado River, whose channel was dependent on a range of upstream conditions. Rainfall, snow melt, and silt accumulated and picked up speed as the river flowed more than 1,000 miles from its headwaters high in the Colorado Rockies into the Gulf of California. Tributary rivers and climate changes added complexity to the environment. When the channel and delta of the Colorado changed, the people had to adapt. For them, "home" was a dynamic concept and regular relocation a necessity.

Tribal relationships changed along with the river. At various times at least eight other groups joined the tribes named by the Mojave storyteller. Most

The Chemehuevi-Mojave Alliance

Although the Chemehuevi people came to the river from dry desert lands, they recognize Ocean Woman, the personification of great waters, as their prime creator. They joined the Mojave as allies against common enemies and were known to be fast runners. During nonfarming seasons they lived in the country between the Panamint and Serrano Mountains.

Though their fields lay to the north and east of the river, the Chemehuevi are related to the Southern Paiute rather than to the Yuman peoples. They wove excellent baskets and in the old times were known to have carried crooks, which were used for pulling gophers, rabbits, and other small animals from their burrows.

spoke a language of the family called Yuman, including the Mojave, Quechan, and Maricopa, who belong to the River Branch of Yuman speakers. The Cocopah belong to the Delta Branch. The Upland Yuman still occupy the plateau where the Colorado flows west through northern Arizona. Still others have merged beyond recognition with different groups in different places.

Enduring Lifeways

Despite associations of blood, trade, and intermarriage, conflict prevailed among these people. By the nineteenth century, the Yuman tribes on the Colorado had been reduced to three: the Mojave, to the north; the Quechan, centering on the confluence with the Lower Gila; and the Cocopah in the Delta country where the river meets the sea. Each tribe maintained a strong sense of identity without a great deal of formal organization.

Warfare and constant adaptation to places and people is a way of life that archaeologists associate with even the distant prehistoric ancestors of today's Cocopah, Quechan, Mojave, and others. The ancestral Hokan or Patayan people are known to have moved around with the climate and the configuration of the river's channel and delta. Scientists say that the climate grew hotter and drier as the first century progressed. They believe that ancestral groups came from the deserts to the river around 700. These people are more difficult to trace than many ancient Southwestern cultures since, like other mobile groups, they had few possessions and built temporary structures. Although they settled in by the river for seasonal farming, floodwaters carried away most of the evidence of their lives there.

Farther from the river channels, the presence of the ancients is associated with sites where they left sleeping circles of stones, *manos, metates* (grinding stones), roasting pits, utilitarian pottery, and extensive trail systems marked with rocky trail shrines. Influenced by the Hohokam to the east, they developed irrigation canals and check dams. Clay figurines like those of the Hohokam have also been found. These signs of their lives survived the ages.

The people and the river lived in a constantly shifting relationship.

Around 1050, the people fanned out: north to southern Nevada, south to Sonora, east to the Phoenix basin, and west to a vanished freshwater sea created by a natural dam in the Colorado River. Called Lake Cahuilla, it grew to the size of Delaware, attracting game and providing fish and other foods. This Eden in what is now California's Imperial Valley dried up little by little until it was reduced to insignificance just before Europeans began to head

The mesquite war bows of the Quechan were almost as tall as the men who carried them.

west. Today it is a sink called the Salton Sea, an extremely saline body of water. Other lakes near the Mohave River receded about the same time. The Lower Colorado became the place to go.

This situation pressured the people who already lived along the Colorado and the Lower Gila, since access to the best flood plains assured good food supplies. Any change in the hierarchy of rights to these places disturbed the balance of power among the tribes. Control of the ford called Yuma Crossing was another important key to power.

Even before the demise of Lake Cahuilla, warfare with neighbors was common, whether it came in the form of raiding for plunder, settling old scores, or ritual fighting. In fact, material gain was often not its purpose. Conducted according to traditional prescription, it was believed to strengthen a tribe and demonstrate power to others. Herman Grey, a Mojave, explains that "…going on war parties was a favorite outdoor sport…like a profession or occupation." Over time, the Mojave and Quechan aligned with the Yavapai, Chemehuevi, and Western Apache. The Cocopah, Maricopa, and Pima allied against them.

Battling to the death characterized this warfare. A warrior was physically imposing, vigilant, alert, totally focused, prepared to kill or be killed. Men whitened their powerful bodies and painted their faces black and red. Their long hair signaled defiance, since it could become a trophy of battle. A warrior

The Mojave take their name from the word *hamakhava*, meaning "three mountains" in English. These mountains lie on the west side of the river and are referred to as "The Needles" today.

might be an archer, lance man, or clubber. Mesquite war bows were almost as tall as the men who carried them. Rawhide shields offered little protection and were carried only by war leaders.

An encounter might start with a long distance communication to the enemy warning that attack was imminent. Then warriors assembled and one or two leaders came out to provoke the opposition and incite violence. Feathered standards announced their intentions. Champions backed them up, followed by perhaps 200 warriors who fought hand-to-hand to the death with clubs made of mesquite or ironwood.

The prevailing tribes ruled the field after the battle. To the victor belonged the spoils, which included scalps. Part of the ritual of warfare involved taking them from members of the losing tribes. The warrior who killed kept the enemy

The Mountain's Spirit

Although Spirit Mountain is recognized as the place where the Colorado River tribes had their spiritual beginnings, few destinations for the cultural heritage visitor lie in its direction. It is the home of their creation stories, songs, myths, and legends and its power belongs to them. There are other mountains for travelers to explore, such as the nearby Black Mountains, which allow hiking, off-road vehicles, rock-hounding, and hunting.

There are no archaeological resources and no trail up Spirit Mountain. The area has been designated a Traditional Cultural Property and is also listed on the National Register of Historic Places. Spirit Mountain is monitored by a Fort Mojave group which collects medicinal plants there.

Spirit Mountain is said by the Mojave to be the place where their Creator gave the people instructions for living.

scalp with him at all times during the purification period that was required before he returned to his family. Scalps taken would later be displayed to the community, who celebrated victory in their presence. Afterward they would be kept by a specially appointed scalp-keeper in a sealed container that remained underground until the next battle. Violent as these encounters were, warriors traveled far and wide to engage in them. Eventually, chronic conflict drove the Maricopa and other groups away.

Ceremonial Customs

Warfare also meant the constant presence of death, which was greeted with cremation and an elaborate ceremony. As soon as possible after death, the body was prepared and all the things that he or she had cared for were placed on the funeral pyre. Once they were burned and the ground covered over, no one could ever speak the name of that person again.

A Cry or Mourning Ceremony might occur months afterwards, perhaps even on the anniversary of the death. The Colorado River people lived in widespread rancherias, so bringing bands together involved planning and travel. Runners might be sent out carrying a string that was knotted to indicate the amount of time that would pass before the gathering would be held. The family prepared food and gifts for their guests. The guests gathered what

Anytime, Everywhere: Dreamings

Dreaming, in the sense of the word used by the Mojaves and other Colorado River peoples, afforded gifted individuals the power to transcend ordinary limitations and access spiritual and historical truths. All truly important knowledge, the Mojaves believed, came through dreaming.

A dreaming was not a vision, like those experienced through solitary vigils by Plains people. Dreamings were associated neither with sleep nor with hallucinatory herbs or plants. Rather, they represented a different state of consciousness—one that offered the dreamer means to transform ageless wisdom into song and story for the community.

Dreamings conveyed information in layers: Like holy written texts, they revealed their truths through multiple forms and interpretations. They were not memorized; however, elders could assess them by references to sacred sites and ceremonies. Dreamings were expected to cure illness, lead to victory in war, assist the spirit in death, and accomplish practical results related to other significant events. The dreamer was discredited if they were ineffective.

A dreamer was carefully observed as he sang or orated. A family, clan, or entire group might attend a singing or oration. It was not considered religious, so no special regalia were worn. Herman Grey, in his 1970 book *Tales from the Mojaves*, explains: "[Dreamings] are still potent forces in Mojave life, although their outward expression through Sings and Great Tellings has greatly diminished, and with it the closeness and unity of Mojave life."

they needed for the memorial ceremony. They were allowed full expression of their grief both at the funeral and at the memorial.

The most important element of the Cry involved the presence of a specialist with the knowledge and power to deliver the requisite message in a sequence of song or speech. These men were the keepers of eternal information which was passed from one generation to another by means of experiences that ethnologists call "dreaming."

The Songs or Tellings presented on significant occasions had their origin in a state of consciousness for which Western civilization probably has no word. They were not visions nor did they necessarily occur while sleeping. More specific than insight but less conscious than thought, they required the listeners' total concentration. Each individual was free to interpret what he heard, yet they created closeness and community. They were timeless, having come from the creator, but exact and identifiable details and locations were woven into them. Elders knew when a song or story cycle needed correction, but they were not memorized. In fact, the idea of conscious learning was as puzzling to these people as this psychic state seems to a fact-oriented Western culture.

The Mourning Ceremony might last for a day and night or longer, and more than one person might be memorialized. After the orator delivered his message, a mock battle and the re-creation of cremation offered another opportunity to openly grieve the departed. Afterwards, dancing, gambling, athletic games, and other activities allowed the community to socialize together before they returned to their homes or camps.

Daily Living

Return to daily life meant going back to the river farms during the growing season or to winter camps near mountain springs in winter. Summer homes consisted of brush shelters while in winter the people built more substantial dwellings, often partially underground. Roofs were thatched with arrowweed, brush, and earth. Baskets of staple foods were stored on top of the roof or on a special storage platform. Some baskets were 6 feet high, and filled with mesquite beans or seeds. The Cocopah built shelters of closely woven willow for protection from mosquitoes and placed smudge pots in and around them. The Mojave lived in adobe-style homes with access to a large tepee-like lodge made of thatch. Everyone could sleep inside on cold nights.

The hot climate required few clothes in summer—none, in the case of men who preferred not to wear them. Some wore breechcloths made of the inner bark of the willow. Women wore aprons or willow bark skirts. Woven robes of rabbit skin and hide blankets provided warmth in winter. Travelers protected their feet with sandals. In cooler weather, the Chemehuevi donned moccasins, antelope skin shirts, and white caplike headdresses decorated with feathers.

Face-painting had special significance for people along the Colorado River.

Cocopah women adopted European fashion, layering collars and shawls over long cotton garments.

Cosmetic adornment was very important to both men and women. They decorated their bodies, faces, and hair with paint and tattooed their faces. The Cocopah considered special tattoos necessary for achieving peace in the next world, since they mapped trails to the place where the ancestors would be waiting. The tattoos were created with mesquite thorns and blackened with charcoal. Men wore jewelry in their nasal septum and ears.

Long, thick hair was an asset to both sexes. Women (and sometimes men) cut theirs into bangs in front and painted it with white striping. In the old days, men used white mud to stiffen theirs. Later they rolled it into ropes, using mesquite gum and clay. A haircut was an expression of mourning.

Life for these people was relatively unstructured. They traded and traveled for fun and profit, exchanging agricultural products for feathers and shells from the ocean people, and brokering barters with tribes to the north and east. Religion was life, and life was religion. The deities had performed the work of creation and explained how to live, so petitioning them was not ordinarily necessary. The people accepted the rhythm of farming, fishing, hunting, and gathering. Ordinarily, survival did not present major difficulties. Marriage and divorce were easy and family relationships not closely prescribed. Pottery and basketry were purely functional. Clans had no political function and permanent chiefs were only designated after the white man needed to find a spokesman for the tribe.

Foreign Contact

Their lives began to be transformed, however, when the Spanish started to arrive, which occurred for the Colorado River peoples sometime during the sixteenth century. By the 1540s, Spanish had traveled to the confluence of the Colorado and the Gila, where Yuma now lies, and sailed as far as present-day Parker. They wrote reports describing the people who lived there as "tall and muscular as giants." While these were not the first Indians the Spanish encountered, the Cocopah, Quechan, and Mojave had not seen Europeans before. Did they go back to their camps talking of midget-sized men who traveled on top of large, four-legged beasts? What did they make of clerical robes and armor, swords and guns? How did they react to bushy beards and hair that must have seemed thin and pale in comparison to theirs?

Whatever the shock of strange men and animals, initial contacts were friendly and cooperative. Mojave guides led the Spanish travelers to the Pacific Coast, and along their other travel routes. Quechan leaders befriended Franciscan priests on their way to coastal missions, hoping to be rewarded by promised gifts and partnerships in war. Cocopah accepted gifts of new foods.

This auspicious beginning, however, soon deteriorated into vicious competition for Spanish trade among the groups along the river. The newcomers

Control of Yuma Crossing by the Quechan was a significant source of power. Here the de Anza expedition is shown heading for California after escorting Father Garcés to Quechan territory.

recognized the political value of intertribal conflict and often encouraged it. The Quechan deity *Kwikumat* noted that they were aloof and stingy and drove them away, for a time.

In the late 1770s, Franciscan Tomas Garcés traveled from San Xavier in Tucson to prepare for and later establish two missions: Puerto de la Purisima Concepcion and San Pedro y San Pablo de Bicuner near what is now Yuma. Spanish colonizers did not follow in significant numbers until 1779. When they came, settlers and soldiers brought cattle that battered the land and ruined the wheat crop, and diseases to which the Indians had no immunity. Smallpox, measles, influenza, syphilis, mumps, and tuberculosis trailed the Europeans. The newcomers had few supplies and no idea how to farm the floodplains. The crops of the native peoples failed that year, food became scarce, and in 1781 the Quechan attacked the missions and killed many of the immigrants, including Father Garcés.

Traditional life got a reprieve. Non-Indians didn't return in great numbers to the territory until the 1840s, when travelers daring the deserts hoping to make a fortune in California gold were funneled to Yuma Crossing, where the river is reduced to a manageable ford. Wagon trains and stagecoaches following the Southern Overland Trail ended up there as well. The Quechan people still controlled the ferry service, which consisted mainly of human assistance, rafts, ropes, and the occasional dugout cottonwood log. Swimmers would sometimes ferry loads by pushing them across the river in large pots.

But as numbers of travelers and resulting profitability increased, the settlers began to establish rival services and the "ferry wars" began. The discovery of gold 20 miles east on the Gila and 50 miles north on the Colorado fueled the fires, but the Quechan held their position until after Fort Yuma was established in 1852.

Permanent disruption of their cultures arrived relatively late for the river peoples, but when it came it hit like a bolt of lightning. Forts quickly led to reservations, although the idea of restricting movement was absolutely opposed to traditional lifestyles. The land the people received was only a small portion of

In dress typical of her time, a Mojave woman returns home with dinner.

First in Time, Last in Line

A timeline of social and economic transformation on the Colorado:

1848: Mexico ceded most of the territory where the Colorado River tribes lived to the United States. The Mexican government had never really exerted control over the region. Due to an administrative oversight, the Colorado River delta, home of the Cocopah, was not included.

1849: The Gold Rush drove prospectors and settlers to brave daunting deserts to get to California. Most crossed the Colorado at Yuma Crossing, making control of that ford very profitable. Dr. Able Lincoln, who launched a ferry there in 1850, raked in $60,000 in three months.

1852: Steamboats came to the lower Colorado River. They took over the river's freight business until the railroad arrived in **1877.** Business consisted of distributing food, supplies, and livestock by horse and mule from Yuma's Quartermaster Depot to all the military posts in Arizona, Nevada, Utah, New Mexico, and Texas. Capt. George Johnson's paddle wheeler was said to earn him $20,000 in a month.

Fort Yuma developed from smaller military camps into a real fort that was built to help protect emigrants to California.

1858: Fort Mojave built for the same purpose.

1865: Colorado River Indian Reservation (referred to now as CRIT, the acronym for Colorado River Indian Tribes) established for "Indians of said river and its tributaries," which included the Mojave, Chemehuevi, Quechan, and Cocopah. A minority of Mojave came to live there. No Cocopah came; it was not their home territory and the Mojave were traditional enemies.

the land they depended on, and generally the least productive. In this desert, soil without water is meaningless and the rules were always manipulated in favor of the newcomers. The Native peoples could muster no effective opposition.

Within a few years, the wisdom that had served the people so well since the First Times would be turned on its head. Where would they find guidance to deal with a society whose values were often in total opposition to theirs?

As new people arrived, first in a trickle and then a steady stream, they wanted to

After the Colorado River people could no longer live traditionally, men like this Mojave boatman found wage work that utilized their knowledge of the river.

1870: Fort Mojave Reservation established within Mojave homeland. Mojave people came, but the people were divided between those who joined CRIT and those who didn't.

1870s–1880s: The Chemehuevi were forced onto reservations. Many began to move their homes to the oasis at Twentynine Palms.

1879: Colorado River Boarding School opened with the purpose of assimilating the people from the Colorado River Indian Reservation. Haircuts, Western dress, religion, and English language were required. Parental influence and use of their own language were discouraged, often by punishment.

1884: Fort Yuma Reservation established for the Quechan. It encompassed only a small part of the territory the tribe had historically controlled. (**1978:** Acreage created by movement of the river channel in **1920** was returned to the Quechan, minus water rights.)

1917: Western part of the Cocopah Reservation established, without access to water. In the **1980s,** the eastern part of the reservation was added, with access to water; this allowed for more leaseable farmland, housing, and, later, a casino.

1942: 25,000 acres of CRIT land appropriated for Japanese internment camp. Irrigation facilities promised as compensation.

1945: "Surplus" (as defined by the government) Hopi and Navajo families relocated onto CRIT lands, nearly doubling the population. They worked on irrigation projects.

1952: Order for colonization rescinded by the tribe and ignored by the Department of the Interior.

1970: Chemehuevi Indian Reservation set aside in the Chemehuevi Valley of California. Chemehuevi awarded $82,000 for land taken by Parker Dam when it was built in **1939**.

Steamboats on the Colorado River fueled settlement
that changed Native life forever.

control what the Indians had: land and water. The Quechan were forced to
give up Yuma Crossing. The Mojave won battles (which occurred regularly
among both Natives and immigrants) but had vision to understand that they
would lose the war against wave after wave of settlers and soldiers. The lot of
the Chemehuevi was automatically thrown in with the Mojave. Some Cocopah
found themselves Mexican citizens while others became United States citizens
because their river delta had been forgotten in U.S. political dealings. At first,
this quirk of fate meant little to them. Later, relatives would have to deal with
border-crossing formalities and language differences.

Reservation Life

In a single generation, all the river peoples were engaged in a struggle to
survive. As the stream of immigrants grew, the Colorado River shrank and the
good land was taken. The next 100 years would overturn lives, divide families,
clans, and tribes, and combine unrelated peoples. Time tested tradition in
every possible way.

The people moved on to life in a world that had shaken their traditions
to the roots. Damming the river changed their agriculture beyond recognition.
As they adapted to Western culture, some tribal members transitioned to wage
work on the steamboats, for they knew the river and made excellent pilots.
They later found work with the railroads and at labor and domestic jobs.

Although the Colorado River tribes' water rights were theoretically in
place because they used it first, the entire 5 trillion gallons of water that
run down the river have been appropriated since 1922. Damming, draw-off,
concentration of pollutants, and the end of seasonal flooding all negatively

affected the quality of their share. Poverty prevailed. As time passed, a number of people left for places where making a living was easier.

Two positive influences finally arrived: the anti-poverty programs of the 1960s and the introduction of legal gaming on Arizona reservations in 1993. Tribal income began to bring in funding for capital projects, health, social services, and education. Education increased the tribes' ability to create and pursue a legislative agenda. Successes in this arena encouraged other proactive initiatives.

The tribes continue to build on this potential. CRIT opened an administrative complex during the reservation's centennial in 1965. A complete judicial system is in place, which was successfully tested in 1989 when the

Mojave Traveler

In about 1860, a physically imposing Mojave headman called Irataba became the first among leaders of the river tribes to experience and understand the full impact of Euro-American society on the Native peoples.

Irataba was among those who guided U.S. Army Lt. A. W. Whipple in his travels through Mojave country. Through this early contact with the whites, Irataba learned ways to make good relations pay dividends while reducing the costs associated with raiding. Once, when his men proposed a food raid, Irataba simply approached the proposed target and told him that his people were hungry. The proprietor of the store proceeded not only to provide bacon, flour, and other foods; He showed how to prepare them. The cause of peaceful relations was thus advanced on both sides.

The chief developed a friendship with John Moss, a successful prospector who dressed him in a black suit and took him to San Francisco where the newspaper there described "a big Indian...standing some six feet in his moccasins...broad shoulders and granitic in his appearance...with a head less in size to a buffaloe's [sic] and a lower jaw massive enough to crack nuts or crush quartz...." [*San Francisco Daily Evening Bulletin,* Dec. 2, 1863, p. 62, in Fulsom Charles Scrivner, *Mohave People* (San Antonio: The Naylor Co., 1970), p. 136, n. 18.]

A year later Moss took Irataba through the Isthmus of Panama to New York, Philadelphia, and Washington, D.C., cities considered more sophisticated than the West Coast towns of the Gold Rush era. In Washington, Irataba was presented to President Lincoln, a leader of similar height, who gave him a silver-headed cane.

He returned to California to find his people in conflict with settlers, Chemehuevi, and Paiute. He negotiated on their behalf for as long as he could, but he was growing old. Irataba died in 1878, leaving as his legacy vastly increased Mojave land claims and a deep understanding of the necessity for cultural transformation in the face of Euro-American encroachment.

Irataba was cremated according to Mojave custom. Photographs from his travels, his horses, home, and the silver-headed cane that was given him by President Lincoln accompanied him to the next world. His name is spoken only by those for whom such reference honors his memory. His own people do not utter it, lest he be called back from the beautiful world of the spirits.

city of Parker attempted to supercede the jurisdiction of the tribe on Indian lands within Parker. The multitribal CRIT community has a housing authority, health care system, and supports educational programs that combine public schools, a Bureau of Indian Affairs (BIA) school, and funding for vocational and higher education. The CRIT museum and library is active in preserving the traditional culture. Tribal documents and oral histories are archived and available for study.

The Fort Mojave reservation is also preserving its past while managing for its present and future. The Aha Makav Cultural Society offers classes in the Mojave language and traditional learning. The tribe has built a master-planned community that offers affordable housing on the reservation to non-Indians. In addition, it owns businesses ranging from resource development and energy to retail and communications, including a newspaper, radio stations, and television channels. Agriculture is still an economic factor even though the reservation's 32,000 acres are checkerboarded with private land, which creates challenges related to the allocation of irrigation water.

With more than 80,000 acres of farmland, agriculture is also an important element of the economy for the Fort Yuma–Quechan people. Fertile bottomlands and available water produce cotton, alfalfa, wheat, feed grains, lettuce,

The peoples of the Colorado River and the Gila River shared customs such as men's wearing of turbans over long, bundled hair.

"Fertility Rocks" in the Mojave Desert suggest their powers.

and melons. In 2000 the Supreme Court affirmed the tribe's right to 1 percent of the Colorado River outflow, so their allocation now exceeds their immediate needs. It represents almost one-third of Arizona's portion. The tribe also operates light industry that employs community members. Tourism-related enterprises include parks for mobile homes and RVs and a department of fish and game. The tribe has its own utility company.

The Cocopah tribe, located in the southwestern corner of Arizona, also benefits from agriculture through leasing farmlands to large agricultural enterprises. Tourism activity related to the river, to its proximity to the Mexican border, a casino, and cultural visitation all bring in revenue.

The people who live along the river continue to refashion lifeways that honor their ancestors and their pre-contact relationship to the river and the land. Surrounded by pressures and outside influences, this is a difficult task. How can native languages, traditions, myth, and legend be made relevant within the context of today's world? The pace at which cultural regeneration can progress is slow, since life must be lived and an array of recollections and points of view must be integrated.

The complexity of renewal explains at least in part why the development of tourism has not held a position of high priority within these tribes. Though reservation-based cultural activities are few, one of the best ways to experience their roots is to appreciate the land as you drive north and south along the Colorado. The combination of river, desert, and mountain speaks of lives spent following the ancient trails in harmony with the rhythm of the seasons.

Exploring the Lands of the Colorado River

The reservations along the Colorado River are no exception to the rule that the homelands of the people, even reduced in scope by a reservation, constitute an enormously important part of their cultural heritage. To those who honor them, the land is inseparable from traditional lifeways. It is a living thing that holds both ancient history and the seeds of what is and will be, for better or worse.

The best way to understand the unique lands of the Colorado River tribes is to map out activities along the river between Yuma and Needles, California. That path will include the reservations of the Cocopah, CRIT, Chemehuevi, and Mojave. You will experience low and high desert, the river itself, riparian marshes, and farmland, always set against a background of serrated mountain ranges and improbable rock formations. It isn't impossible

The Mojave Rocks jut from the Colorado River near Topock Gorge.

to experience all these ecosystems at once. Plan to get out of your car.

Travel between November and the end of March. Summer here is hot and long. Temperatures rise to dangerous levels. The climate is home to native Indian peoples, but unless that includes you, your goal during the hot months is likely to be finding the next air-conditioned building. Much natural beauty will be lost to the harshness of the season.

Another reason to travel during these months is that winter sunlight transforms the desert and its mountains. The direct sun of late spring and summer flattens geography and geology. The indirect sunshine of winter mornings and evenings enhances them. While you may miss the deep greens that edge the river during the farming season, you chance witnessing cactus dusted with snow and sunsets turning the mountains incredible purples.

Pictographs, like petroglyphs (see p. 276), have survived the ages in the dry climate of the Mojave Desert.

An additional benefit to winter is that snakes and lizards are hibernating, freeing those who appreciate nature to concentrate on the view instead of the path or trail.

Limits of Cultural Tourism

Organized cultural tourism on tribal lands along the Colorado is limited to tribal museums and special events. Side trips to wildlife refuges and other natural attractions are not to be missed as part of the Native heritage, even though they aren't related to tribal enterprises.

Tourism unrelated to cultural experience abounds on and near the reservations in the form of casinos, RV parks, overnight accommodations, and water sports facilities. The casinos usually have good restaurants, rooms, and sometimes access to the river, although they don't really qualify as a cultural experience.

The Native people live in residential areas that are not tourist destinations. Much ancestral land surrounding the reservations is part of the either the U.S. Army Yuma Proving Grounds (YPG), the Marine Corps Air Station, or the Barry M. Goldwater Air Force Range—not exactly travel destinations.

Yuma and Somerton

Yuma is located on I-8, once part of the ocean-to-ocean highway and still a popular route from Arizona to southern California. I-10 and the "Mother Road", Old Route 66, lead to AZ 95, the north-south road that follows the Colorado River.

Yuma is a good place to start. Of course you can easily reverse the order and travel from north to south from the Needles area, or begin anywhere in between.

Quechan Museum

Yuma • (619) 572-0661 • Open: Monday–Friday, 8 a.m.–5 p.m.; Saturday 10 a.m.– 4 p.m.; Closed: Major holidays; Call to confirm.

Admission fee to the museum is minimal. Donations beyond admission are appreciated and appropriate.

The museum is located off CA S-24, which is easily accessible from I-8. Signs indicate the exit for the Territorial Prison. Cross the bridge near the prison, drive toward the casino, and look for a sign for the museum.

Fort Yuma Indian Reservation, located just across the old bridge on the California side of the river, belongs to the Quechan people (pronounced Kwt-*SAN*, not *KWEH*-chan, which is sometimes heard outside the community). The Quechan Museum is housed in a pink adobe building built in 1851 as the officers' mess for Fort Yuma. It is set on high ground overlooking the river. Behind it is Saint Thomas, a white mission church built in 1922, which is still

Chemehuevi desert country

Yuma and Umo

The first explorers called the Quechan people Yuma, probably after the Spanish rendering of the Quechan word *umo*. The Quechan used smoky smudges to keep insects away from their dwellings. Their name for themselves, Quechan, is derived from *xamkwacan*, which refers to the ancient trail they followed to their homeland.

active. This reportedly stands on the site of one of the missions destroyed in the violent summer of 1781.

The museum exhibits feature relics of Spanish missions, military artifacts from Fort Yuma, and finally a cultural interpretation section. *Kumastamxo* brought the people from Avikwame Mountain and gave them instructions for life and religion. Among other teachings, he showed the people how to conduct funeral ceremonies and orations. Tribal cremation grounds lie below the museum site.

Musical instruments include gourd rattles and courting flutes made from *axta* cane. A young man would sit outside a girl's home and play the flute to draw her to his side.

Examples of traditional dress show both willow skirts and the long skirts and tops later required by Europeans. Before air-conditioning, it wouldn't be hard to choose between them.

Beads decorate cradleboards, belts, necklaces, and other personal adornment. You can also see a few examples of pottery, including the Quechan dolls that resemble figurines of the ancient Hohokam. These are no longer being made.

Two small gift shops carry local work and art. Conversations with the people who staff them offer an opportunity to hear more about the culture. One store is in the museum and the other lies across a courtyard. Most of the items in the latter are for sale, although some excellent works are simply displayed there.

The Quechan reservation extends to the border with Mexico. The tribe operates a seasonal parking lot at Andrade—outside Algodones, a port-of-entry community—and an RV park.

Yuma Crossing State Historic Park

Yuma • 201 N. 4th Ave. • (928) 329-0471
Open: Daily 9 a.m.–5 p.m.; Closed: December 25

The Crossing, for centuries a base of power for the Quechan, is a state park today. It is hard to imagine its strategic position before the town of Yuma grew around it, with its bridges and canals. Little is left to suggest the ford where settlers and Forty-Niners crossed to California. There are two exhibits that relate directly to Quechan days. One is a drawing that shows travelers crossing the river on horseback, escorted by Native men chest-high in the water. References are also made to Native history in a 30-minute video that profiles the history of the Crossing.

The remainder of the park illustrates the history of the river tribes only as it relates to the U.S. military presence. A six-month supply of clothing, food, and ammunition was stored here at the Quartermaster Depot during its tenure. Nearly 1,000 mules were kept to deliver goods brought in by steamboat until the railroad arrived in 1877. The goods were then delivered to Army posts in the West. Below the park is a riverside trail that leads to the Territorial Prison.

Century House Museum

Yuma • 240 S. Madison Ave. • (928) 782-1841 • www.arizonahistoricalsociety.org
Open: Tuesday–Saturday, 10 a.m.–4 p.m.; Closed: Major holidays

Built in the 1870s, Century House displays material related to the history of Yuma Crossing and the lives of Native Americans, explorers, missionaries, soldiers, miners, riverboat captains, and early settlers. Adobe Annex, next to Century House, offers local crafts and an excellent selection of books on regional history.

Yuma Valley Railway

Yuma • (928) 783-3456
The train departs from 2nd Ave. and 1st St. behind City Hall

On Saturdays and Sundays between October and May, a 1952 diesel-electric locomotive pulls a 1922 Pullman coach on the 34-mile, 3.5-hour round trip through acres of farms, Cocopah lands, and riverside scenery, then back to Yuma. A historian tells the story of the region.

Cocopah Museum and Cultural Center

Somerton • County 15th St. and Avenue G • (928) 627-1992
Open: Monday–Friday, 9 a.m.–4 p.m.; Closed: After 2 p.m. on the last Friday of the month. Admission is free but donations are accepted at the gift shop. Etiquette suggests contributing if you visit.

Take US 95 south and west to Ave. G in Somerton. Turn right (north) and continue through the fields of the Yuma Valley. You will see the reservation water tank on your left. Turn left (west) on County 15th. The road is not paved. Follow it about 2 miles as it curves across railroad tracks to the museum, located near tribal headquarters. About 30 minutes from Yuma.

The lands of the Cocopah (*Kwapa*, or River People, in their language) extend across the Mexican border south of Yuma near Somerton, Arizona. Visitors to the museum cross acres of fertile land that contrast strikingly with the surrounding desert. Neat crop rows, glittering irrigation ditches, and homes within their own tiny oases line the roads.

The lands of the Cocopah lie in a sea of agriculture made possible by Colorado River irrigation.

In this sea of agriculture, surrounded by a park landscaped with native plants, is the carefully organized Cocopah Museum and Cultural Center. Exhibits interpret pre-contact daily life through objects and realistic life-size dioramas. In them, models dressed in bark skirts and rawhide sandals engage in traditional activities like grinding mesquite beans and netting fish such as the pike minnow, mullet, and humpback chub that once populated the river.

European-influenced women's clothing is also shown, each mannequin wearing beautifully appliquéd long skirts and overblouses, intricate beadwork collars and necklaces, and a chain holding a Jew's harp—a simple, ancient musical instrument found in many world cultures which is held against the mouth and plucked with the fingers.

A highlight of this museum is an entire wall dedicated to masks showing traditional facial tattoo designs. The designs are deeply symbolic, relating to the trails people must follow to reach the place where they will be greeted by the ancestors at death. They reflect a person's clan and are done with special ceremony. The expressive masks on which the tattoos are displayed were modeled from life.

Arrowweed baskets, red and black pottery, and intricate contemporary beadwork display the artistry of the Cocopah. Beading decorates jewelry, belts, dolls, cradleboards, and knife handles. At its best it is made into elaborate collar-necklaces that are loomed or sewn.

The warrior section of the museum reminds us that such culture is still ongoing. Displays range from war clubs and black and red face paint to a

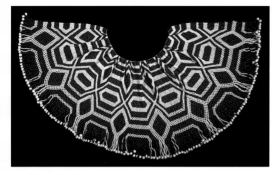

Exquisitely sewn or loomed beaded collars are a unique hallmark of the Colorado River tribes.

wall devoted to Sgt. Bravie Soto, who lost his life in Viet Nam. The U.S. Army Yuma Proving Ground Armament Operations Center is named in his honor. Go online to http://paddyslogger.250x.com/lostsquad/lostsquad.htm to view a personal remembrance of Sgt. Soto.

A non-circulating library and repository of tribal cultural information as well as a gift shop that offers soft drinks and snacks round out the Museum's services.

The tribe operates a casino, an RV park, resort, and golf course which are located on the north part of the reservation. The Museum brochure includes a map and information about the facility.

North of Yuma

Birders, nature-lovers, and wildlife-watchers will appreciate visiting any or all of the national wildlife refuges that they pass between Yuma and Needles. These areas recall the lands that supported the River People. They serve as reminders of the days when the riverbanks were lined with cottonwood and willow forests, sustained by the river's natural periodic flooding. Birds and animals depended on this habitat for breeding, resting, feeding, and shade. Humans also depended on its floods, birds, animals, water, and shade.

Imperial National Wildlife Refuge

(928) 783-3371 • southwest.fws.gov/refuges/arizona/imperial.html
Boats depart from Fisher's Landing (928-783-4400, www.yumarivertours.com)
From Yuma, take US 95 north for 25 miles to Martinez Lake Road. Turn left (west) and follow the signs for 13 miles to the visitor center.

This 15,000-acre refuge protects 30 miles of the Colorado River, including the last unchanneled section north of the border with Mexico. It harbors backwater lakes and marshes set against the ever-present desert and mountains. It lies on the flyway of thousands of migrating birds, which are most abundant during the winter. Egrets, muskrat, jackrabbits, mule deer, wild burros, and bighorn sheep thrive year-round.

All of its lookout points can be reached by car. Mesquite, Ironwood, and Smoke Tree Points offer vistas of the valley and wildlife viewing. The 1-mile-long self-guided Painted Desert Trail interprets the surrounding desert, taking you through multicolored rocks left by 30,000-year-old volcanic activity. It features a panoramic view of the Colorado River valley. You will leave with a clearer impression of how this land once supported thousands of original residents.

Another way to see the refuge is to take a narrated jet boat tour on which you will see, among historical and natural sights, petroglyphs left by the ancient Indians.

Wetlands along the Colorado River's wildlife refuge shelter a wide diversity of animals.

Blythe Intaglios

Follow signs on I-10 west across the Colorado River toward Blythe, California. At the junction of I-10 and CA 95, go right (north) and take the road about 17 miles. On your right you will see a historical marker titled Giant Desert Figures *and on your left, across the road, a sign for the Blythe Intaglios. The road west to the intaglios is graded but not paved. Return to Arizona by reversing these directions.*

Here you will see shallow indentations on the desert that outline figures designed on a grandiose scale. Unlike petroglyphs, intaglios (geoglyphs) are

At 167 feet, the largest figure of the mysterious Blythe Intaglios dwarfs people and automobiles.

quite uncommon. A series of them lies along the Colorado River. They can't be dated with exactitude, but they certainly predate airplanes by hundreds of years. They are best seen from above, but no nearby landform rises high enough to explain how the builders positioned them.

The intaglios (from the Italian word meaning "to incise") are truly enormous, as the marker suggests. The largest is 167 feet long and the smallest 95 feet. According to Native oral histories, the human figure represents the creator. The animals are mountain lions who assisted with creation. A serpent is incorporated in another figure.

Geoglyphs are made by scraping away natural desert pavement to create a design or figure. Here the pavement is quite dark, almost black, while the underlying desert is tan, providing clear contrast.

Those who drive to the top of the road and walk to the site of a geoglyph enclosed in a fence will notice that, even though the figure is recognizable, the relationship between one form and another are difficult to make out. How were they envisioned? How were the images executed on the ground with such precision? Take in your surroundings and you'll also notice a feature of the site that a photograph from above misses: it's surrounded by mountains and overlooks fields that line the river. Since place is always significant in meaning, does this location shed light on the mystery of the intaglios?

They were entered on the National Register of Historic Places in 1976.

The Old Mohave Road

The area around present-day Needles, California, is home to the Old Mohave Road, once the main trade corridor between the Southwest and the coastal Indians and the former site of numerous Mojave villages. Active traders, the Mojaves lent not only their industry but their name to the system of trails between present-day Prescott, Arizona, and the Pacific coast.

The route also served trappers, miners, missionary priests, and, later, Euro-American entrepreneurs as they moved west. Lieutenant Edward Beale surveyed the road in 1857, famously using camels to transport material across the desert. (They frightened the horses so badly that his experiment was called to a halt. Mules and pack horses had to suffice.)

When the Mohave Road was improved between Prescott and the Colorado River following Beale's survey, Native peoples along the route found their lands commandeered by settlers. Since the road crossed Yavapai, Hualapai, Chemehuevi, and Mojave territory, attacks on travelers were common. The U.S. military responded by establishing forts and outposts along the entire corridor.

Industrialization eventually spelled the demise of the Old Mohave Road. Steamships came into use along the Colorado River, followed by the railroad, which made river transport—and the Mohave Road—obsolete. Abandoned, the ancient trail began to fade back into the desert. Today, however, traces of it remain, faintly visible as it crosses the Mojave Desert toward the ocean.

Mohave Road

Also known as the Ehrenberg-Parker Highway, IR 1 takes you to Ehrenberg, once a thriving town where "Big Mike" and Joseph Goldwater, grandfather and great-uncle of the late Arizona Senator Barry M. Goldwater, ran a general store. You are now entering the land of the Mojave.

There are few vehicles along this road, which bisects the Colorado River Indian Reservation. Nor is much left of Ehrenberg that recalls its heyday as a river city (although you might explore the cemetery). It is, however, a lovely way to follow the river to Parker and observe interesting sights along the way.

The fields you pass are mostly leased by the Colorado River Indian Tribes (CRIT) to non-Indian farmers who grow alfalfa, cotton, melons, lettuce, and other crops. Irrigated now, they once received both water and natural fertilizer from annual flooding.

Driving north, you'll come to a monument at Poston that memorializes three internment camps that housed Japanese Americans during the ill-famed hysteria that accompanied World War II. It is dedicated to those who were confined there.

Colorado River Indian Tribes Museum

Parker • (928) 669-1335 • Open: Monday–Friday, 8 a.m.–5 p.m.;
Closed: Lunchtime and major holidays • The museum is about
2 miles east of Parker off of AZ 95, at Mohave and 2nd Ave.

Like most tribal museums, this one is designed to educate the people whose heritage it represents and to act as a repository for books and other documents and artifacts that belong to the tribe. At the museum, a section is devoted to each of its four tribes: Mojave, Chemehuevi, Hopi, and Navajo. Displays depict basic aspects of the cultures: dress, traditional housing, and arts and crafts. A small gift shop offers crafts for sale. A historic Presbyterian church that served the community has been restored nearby.

Ahakhav Tribal Preserve

Parker • (928) 669-2664 • www.ahakhav.com; www.geocities.com/critfishngame
From the Colorado Indian River Tribes Museum, take Mohave south to Rodeo Dr.
Turn right (west) and follow it to Levee Rd., which leads to the preserve.

Park area is open during daylight hours only. Permits to fish are available from CRIT Fish and Game, located at the Tribal Offices. Boating is limited to canoes and trolling motors. No off-road vehicles, alcohol, or drugs are permitted. Carefully observe signs posted to protect flora and fauna.

A work in progress is CRIT's 1,000-acre preserve, set aside to restore the natural ecosystem of the lower Colorado and disseminate environmental research. Invasive salt cedar that has replaced so much native vegetation is giving way to cottonwood, willow, and mesquite—native habitat that encourages regional plants, fish, birds, and animals, some of which are currently endangered. The preserve sets an example and provides education for the community and others. It includes a native plant nursery and back-water areas that serve as nurseries for fish and wildlife.

Visitors may fish, picnic, and visit a beach area that is accessible by a trail. Bird-watching is excellent in season. Restrooms are available. Canoes may be rented from the tribe. Since the park is occasionally used for special events, be considerate and do not interrupt community activities.

Buckskin Mountain State Park

5476 Hwy. 95 • (928) 667-3386
www.pr.state.az.us/Parks/parkhtml/buckskin.html
Off of AZ 95, about 12 miles north of Parker

The spectacularly eroded volcanic terrain of the Buckskin Mountains offers a taste of the places where the native peoples of this area spent time when they were not raising crops. Several trails lead to a panoramic view of the area. Parker Dam is visible from higher ground. Archaeological sites are scattered around the area.

The park lies between the mountains and the river. Water recreation is very popular. Facilities include a large campground, beach, trails, restrooms, showers, boat ramp, picnic area, cabanas, basketball and volleyball courts, playground, camp store, restaurant, gas dock, and ranger station.

The Colorado River Today

The Colorado River starts in the Colorado Rockies and flows into the Gulf of California—in good years. In dry years, little water makes it to the delta. The 1922 compact that divided the river into two basins gave half the water flow to the upper basin, which includes New Mexico, Wyoming, Colorado, and Utah; and half to the lower basin which includes Arizona, California, and Nevada. Cities like Los Angeles, Phoenix, and Las Vegas use every drop of their allocation and continue to grow.

The results downstream have been devastating. The lower Colorado River basin has lost almost all its native willow and cottonwood habitat. Soil and water are too salty to re-establish them, and the tamarisk trees that tolerate the salty environment do not support the wildlife of the historic plant communities. The Colorado River delta is a major stopover for birds on the Pacific flyway. Can it continue to exist under these conditions?

Agriculture also suffers. Less silt, fewer nutrients, higher salinity, and greater concentration of pollutants make the water far less valuable for irrigation purposes.

For these reasons, Native Americans have begun to take a more proactive role in Colorado River water management issues. CRIT is at the forefront with its Ahakhav Preserve, more than 1,000 acres of riparian habitat. Ten other research plots are spread throughout the reservation, providing data on ecological conditions that contribute to a better understanding of the lower Colorado's ecology.

Bill Williams National Wildlife Refuge

60911 Hwy. 95 • (928) 667-4144
www/southwest.fws.gov/refuges/arizona/billwill.html
Between Mileposts 160 and 161 on AZ 95, about 17 miles north
of Parker and 23 miles south of Lake Havasu City.

This area claims the distinction of having a floodplain that's 1 mile wide. The rare sight of such bottomlands recalls how the Mojave, Quechan, Cocopah, and others farmed before giant dams and diversions were engineered. Geological formations and an ecosystem that forms a transition between the Sonoran and Mojave deserts provide a unique setting along this Colorado River tributary.

Grassy bottomlands in Bill Williams National Wildlife Refuge recall the wide floodplains once farmed by the peoples of the Colorado River.

Topock to Kingman

The traditional homelands of the Mojave and Chemehuevi continue up the river toward the sacred mountain, Avikwame. The Mohave Mountains rise on the east side of the Colorado. The lands of the Chemehuevi are memorialized on the west side in the names of the Chemehuevi Valley and Mountains, both in California. The Chemehuevi Reservation, also west of the river, runs a casino but the tribe has not organized a program for cultural heritage visitors. The ruins of Fort Mojave lie west of the river, in Nevada.

Topock (Mystic) Maze

Topock • http://digitaldesert.com/mystic-maze/ • I-10, Exit 1

The Topock Maze is another form of earth figure, although quite different from the Blythe Intaglios (see p. 259). It is hard to know its original relationship to other geoglyphs because it has been cut up and divided by highway and railroad construction until only 9 acres remain.

Mystic Maze is not actually a maze. It is a series of furrowed ridges arranged in a pattern. It was obviously a site of major importance, although scholars say that no one knows with certainty what it meant to the Native people who built it. Mojave oral history represents it as significant to warriors returning from battle. Another source suggests that turtles were raised there. What does it suggest to you?

The Mystic Maze in Mojave country is said to have been used for ceremonial purposes.

The Tale of Olive Oatman

Oatman is a ghost town whose existence memorializes the extraordinary story of two girls who, in 1851, were taken as slaves as their family crossed the desert from the Pima villages to Fort Yuma on their way to California. The town itself, however, like the girls' parents, lived for and died of Gold Fever.

The Oatman family included a baby, 13-year-old Olive, her 14-year-old brother, and 7-year-old sister, Mary Ann. They were traveling alone when their wagon was accosted by Indians—some say Apache, some say Yavapai—who demanded food. The family had barely packed enough for themselves, so could spare little. As a result, the family was attacked and the girls were taken away by the Indians.

Olive and Mary Ann were walked to a camp 100 miles away, where they were put to work as slaves—not an unusual fate for Indian women and children of the time.

What happened next makes their story extraordinary. After one winter, their captors traded the girls to some Mojave. They were adopted into the family of a headman whose home lay on the Arizona side of the Colorado River. Olive and Mary Ann were treated as adopted children, tattooed and dressed as Mojave, and told they were free to leave—which, of course, they were not able to do.

Olive Oatman lived for a time with a Mojave family who tattooed her face, as was their custom.

A year later, a terrible famine struck the tribe and Mary Ann died, as did many Mojave children. In a gesture of respect, the family buried her body rather than follow their own custom of cremation. They mourned her sadly. Olive maintained her sister's grave as a link to her now-distant past. She didn't know that her brother had survived the attack on her family until the day a Quechan man arrived at camp acting as his emissary. He paid for her release with horses, beads, and blankets. Olive's departure saddened the Mojave family who'd raised her as one of their own.

Olive later married a man in Texas who became a wealthy banker. She also adopted a daughter whom she named Mary Elizabeth after her sister and mother. It was said that she always kept a jar of hazelnuts, a food favored by the tribe with whom she lived. She died in 1903.

The town of Oatman was named for the family whose story exemplifies the complex and violent conflicts of cultures that occurred in the 19th century.

Havasu National Wildlife Refuge

(760) 326-3853 • www.southwestfws.gov/refuges/arizona/havasu
Look for a marked exit off I-40 near the Arizona-California border
and follow the signs.

Another beautiful reminder of the river in freer days lies in the wetlands of Topock Marsh and the walls of Topock Gorge. Here, Havasu National Wildlife Refuge protects about 300 miles of shoreline between Lake Havasu City and Needles, California.

Mojave Museum of History and Arts

400 W. Beale St., Kingman • (928) 753-3195
www.ctaz.com/~mocohist/museum/index.htm (Click on "Arizona Memories",
then on "Mohave Sketches") • Open: Monday–Friday, 9 a.m.–4:30 p.m.

Kingman, another Route 66 town, is handily located for a return to Phoenix via AZ 93 or Flagstaff via I-40, and this small museum makes an interesting stop along the way.

The museum is quite eclectic (its exhibits range from portraits of all the First Ladies to a military collection) but its Indian-related exhibits are carefully interpreted and include a sensitively illustrated timeline that runs from prehistoric days through the onslaught of mining and tourism. Well-informed volunteers enthusiastically discuss the objects exhibited and are the first to explain what is and isn't regional Native art.

It includes a research library of historical maps, photographs, documents, and newspapers, and a gift shop.

Trading trails that linked the Colorado River peoples with tribes to the east passed through the mountains near Kingman.

Dining and Overnight Accommodations

From Yuma to Needles to Kingman, you will find roadside diners, chain motels, and restaurants. However, for predictably good food and comfortable rooms plus some resort-type amenities, the tribal casinos are good bets (so to speak) regardless of whether gambling is your idea of fun. Most have RV parks adjacent to the hotels. They include, south to north:

• **Somerton: Cocopah Bingo and Casino**
15318 South B St.; (800) 237-5687; www.cocopahresort.com

• **Yuma: Paradise Casino**
Fort Yuma Quechan
450 Quechan Dr.; (928) 572-7777; www.paradise-casinos.com

• **Parker: Blue Water Casino**
Colorado River Indian Tribes
11300 Resort Dr.; (888) 243-3369

• **Mojave Valley: Spirit Mountain Casino**
Fort Mojave Indian Tribe
8555 S. Hwy. 95; (888) 837-4030 or (928) 346-2000
Exit I-40 on AZ 95 to Bullhead City

• **Needles, California: Avi Resort and Casino**
Colorado River Indian Tribes
(702) 535-5555 or (800) 430-0721; www.avicasino.com
Take I-40 to River Road Cutoff which becomes Needles Highway. Go north 14 miles to Aha Macav Parkway. Turn right and continue 2 miles.

Also see:

• www.kingmantourism.org

• www.go-arizona.com/yuma

• www.allstays.com/us-arizona-hotels/parker-hotels.htm

Shopping

Few crafts are produced by the Colorado River people today, although Chemehuevi basketry is revered by knowledgeable collectors as some of the finest in the world. The tribal museums are the best places to find authentic arts and crafts. Beaded objects, especially elaborate and beautiful collar necklaces, are often sold there. Pottery and basketry are not likely to be created by these tribes, nor is silver jewelry; on the other hand, ask about anything you're interested in. An artist may produce a one-of-a-kind piece. And it's a good way to encourage a resurgence of interest in the arts.

Little art is created now along the Colorado River; however, the fine basketry of the Chemehuevi is collected worldwide. This tray was made by Leroy Fisher in 1985.

This clay figurine from the 1960s was created by Annie Fields, a Mojave artist. The frog is said to have introduced fire.

Recurring Events

- **Miss Cocopah Pageant:** Cocopah (February)
- **Casino Anniversary Days and Powwow:** Fort Mojave (February)
- **Mojave Days:** Colorado Indian River Tribes (March)
- **Land Acquisition Celebration:** Cocopah (March or April)
- **National Indian Days Celebrations:** Beauty Pageants, All Indian Rodeos; Colorado Indian River Tribes, Fort Yuma Quechan, Fort Mohave (September and October)
- **Fort Mojave Indian Days** (October)
- **Annual Veteran's Day Parade and Powwow:** Cocopah and Colorado Indian River Tribes (November)

Native Voices, Native Lives: L. D. (Louie) Lomavitu

Louie is Hopi-Tewa. In 1945 his grandparents were moved to the Colorado River Indian Tribes reservation, where the government had set aside land for Hopi and Navajo in Mojave country. He says they got "40 acres, a sack of seed, and a plow." Both sides of the family stayed, and Louie was born there. He is a musician who ran for the position of tribal chairman in 2004-2005.

The first time I played on stage, I was 11 years old. I played the drums and guitar. I got tired because I could barely reach the pedals of the drums, so the guitar player and I traded off for four hours. I made $20.

In 1971 I joined the group XIT. I'm the only original member left. They were into mainstream and Native American music, playing the California scene. Red Bone was playing at the same time and they really made it commercially.

I was in school studying electronics when I started with them. I saw a flyer for someone to sing and play keyboard for a new album. I called, got the job, and have been with them ever since, except for when I was in Viet Nam.

I have known traditional music all of my life, but I am even more into mainstream since Native American music got into the Grammys. Indians are proud people. Pride is silent. Arrogance is loud. When one of us accomplishes something, we tell them they did, but we don't plaster it all over the place. If I were awarded one, I would decline.

I'm on a lot of albums. I do vocals, bass, and guitar. People ask me, "How can you play bass like that?" How I think and feel all come out in the form of music. I've written a lot of songs. Someday I'll make my own CD.

Native Medicine Today

by John Hoopingarner, Ph.D., D.D.

Today, medicine goes from an ailment to an herb, or a shot, or a treatment program and hardly ever gets into the cause of disease at the spiritual or psychological level. In traditional medicine, we come from the other direction —the psychological or spiritual level. Eventually we get to the place where we may give herbs or even refer someone to a white man's doctor. The modern doctor may spend 15 minutes with you but the medicine person could spend hours or days. A Navajo medicine man might have a Sing that lasts two or three days and nights, just for one patient. It's a different orientation.

Most non-Indians' concepts of traditional Native medicine are based on what they've read or been told, which is probably only a little bit accurate and usually relates only to Plains Indians. Often these people have a single concept of medicine people (who can be male or female), not knowing that every tribe has different customs.

Healthy foods are still prepared from native cactus, agave, and seed pods of mesquite trees.

People within the culture know which kind of practitioner is appropriate for a particular case. For instance, on the Navajo reservation there are quite a few different kinds of medicine people who deal in specific things. The Hand Tremblers primarily deal in diagnostics. A Hand Trembler would determine your problem and then refer you to somebody else.

Sometimes people come to the Southwest wanting to make immediate contact with a medicine person. They are not likely to be referred because they don't understand how the healers work. A visitor who wants to see a medicine person without going through the proper process may find somebody professing to be something he really isn't. The idea of coming in and saying, "I want to see a medicine man" is not really appropriate. The people reading this book need to understand that Native American medicine people should be respected the same as any other professional within their culture and not as an oddity to be sought out for experimentation.

The basic healing power that these practitioners use is energy. Everything has its energy, and one energy is not better or worse than another—it is just different. The energy of the bear is different from the energy of the man. When you combine those energies, they can be utilized for healing. That's where prayers and ceremonies come into being.

All things have reminders of their energy. When a ceremony is related to the bear or hawk, you ask those creatures to share their energy with you. Rituals and artifacts call energy to use. I wear a necklace with the bear claw as a reminder of the power that a bear shared with me. Apache Ga'an Dancers bring the energy of the mountains, clouds, and lightning.

Medicine people also ask for help for treatment from the plant world. At some point somebody was able to short-circuit the trial-and-error process by talking to the plant. The plants let them know that this was what should be used for a particular problem. I was on a trip one time and people got sick from something we ate. The girl who was leading the trip walked up the canyon, found a tree, and made tea from it. We drank some, and within hours we were all well. I asked her how she found that plant and she said that it seemed as if an energy just pulled her up that canyon and to that place. Those things require an ability to understand another dimension.

Traditional people believe that the energy from all of these things combined —creatures, trees, wind, humans—are the Great Creator. We are all part of the creation, which combines all this energy. Particular beliefs, however, vary greatly from person to person and tribe to tribe.

I believe that we could eliminate the cause of a lot of the illnesses and problems that we have if we followed what's called the Red Road. But that's a very hard road to follow in our day and age. For example, traditionally you would get up and say your prayers as the sun came up. In the modern world we get up, have our coffee, and watch TV. We don't know whether the sun's come up or the sun's gone down, we're so out of contact with the earth. In order to reach the level we need for healing, we must have time by ourselves —away from cars, and airplanes, and boats, and everything else.

For years, society tried to suppress this kind of knowledge. There was actually a movement in the United States to take the healing traditions away from Native people. Some were kept secret, like sweat lodges. They were a very, very secret thing until 20 or 30 years ago. If the government found out about one, they'd arrest everybody. Now they're legal. But a lot of knowledge was lost—often along with the family unit that passed it down. As a result, traditional medicine may not go from father to son or mother to daughter

now. It may go from someone on a reservation to a whole different family, a different tribe, or even a member of the Anglo culture. Dr. Carl Hammerschlag practices traditional medicine. He's a New York–raised psychiatrist.

The other side is that conventional medicine is beginning to learn that medicine people can have a very strong impact on the healing process. I've been asked to come to the Indian Hospital to heal people who were in critical situations in the emergency room. The doctor stepped aside and allowed me to practice. Some hospitals around the country employ medicine men and women on staff. Prisons are using sweat lodges as healing for some of their Indian inmates. If you have an open mind, you see a back-and-forth between the two.

Native Americans come from a very powerful lineage that has many things to offer to the world. We need to impress young Native Americans with a sense of pride in their culture and ancestry. They need to study their own history and incorporate it into their lives today.

Deep, verdant tributaries of the Grand Canyon nurtured early peoples.

The "Indian Wars"

by Loren Tapahe, Diné

Publisher, *Arizona Native Scene*

Seasoned travelers often find that visiting places where history was made causes them to think about events and people in new ways. Loren Tapahe shares his viewpoint on the subject of the military encounters that are usually termed the "Indian Wars."

In the middle of the 1800s White people on the eastern seaboard were enjoying tea as, pushing westward, the notion of Manifest Destiny continued to take its toll on Native Americans. The "Indian Wars" continued on the Great Plains and in the Arizona Territory.

While most Native people were killed by diseases to which they had no immunity, carried to America by immigrants from European countries, others died through acts of genocide, the so-called Indian Wars. Although battles between Indian warriors and the U.S. government were recorded in history, they were few. The term "Indian Wars" was created to quiet the conscience of the White man.

They began on the eastern side of the continent of North America, where some Native tribes barely survived the onslaught of White people who considered the New World ripe for anyone's taking. As a result, some tribes are completely gone. Many others are left without land to call their own. Native people consider themselves inseparably connected to the land, through life and death. It is where they lived from the start of time and it is where their ancestors are buried. It is sacred ground. It gives the breath of life and keeps the body after death. Losing it is devastating.

As the wars proceeded west, the tribes of the Great Plains and Arizona Territory were hunted in attempts to eradicate their existence. The wars of Sioux, Arapaho, Cheyenne, Cherokee, Apache, Navajo, Yavapai, Pima, and others may have been described as noble "Indian Wars," but events tell another story. When the U.S. cavalry could not find the warrior bands of certain tribes, they turned to indiscriminate killing of women, children, the elders, and livestock to try to lure the warriors back into their traditional land. A well-known example of this happened in the case of Geronimo, of the Apaches. The cavalry said they would stop the killing when the leader or chief of the tribe surrendered, and would call this an "Indian War."

Some warriors and tribal chiefs were willing to fight to the death because of the atrocities committed against their brothers and sisters in the name of warfare. Some did die. Some lived. Those who lived were beaten into submission and told to take what the U.S. government offered in order to survive, which often meant being forcibly removed from their homeland. Hence, many tribes have stories of a "Long Walk," like the Navajo, or a "Trail of Tears," like the Hualapai and Apache.

An American Holocaust, one section of Navajo artist Steven Yazzie's mural at the Heard Museum in Phoenix

On these forced marches, many died of hunger and exposure to the cold because the U.S. government marched the "savage Indians" at the beginning of winter. They were herded under guard to areas where crops or even grass could not grow. They were denied arms for hunting, or tools for weaving to make clothes. But their numbers did not decline fast enough. Captives were given disease-infested blankets and spoiled raw bacon to eat. Although many died in captivity, there were still too many Indians to exterminate completely.

Congress began to realize it was unprofitable to kill them all, so new methods for dealing with the Indian began. The government developed a policy to Americanize the Indian through programs of assimilation. Strip them of their culture, language, beliefs, their Indian clothing, cut their hair, and make them look like the White man—this became the new policy. "Kill the Indian, save the man." Young Indian children, sometimes infants, were taken to live in White men's homes and the new era of Indian boarding schools emerged. Congress supposed the older Indian could not be changed, but they had a chance with children.

We know today that no policy developed by Congress to change the Indian has ever worked. Indians thrive today with their own identities. Their numbers are rising. Languages are being taught to the young. Native Americans are entering the American political and justice systems, to assure that the Indian is not forgotten and to demonstrate that they survived the so-called "Indian Wars."

Rock Art

by Peter H. Welsh

Associate Professor, Department of Anthropology, Arizona State University, Tempe
Director, Deer Valley Rock Art Center, Phoenix

Rock art is a term commonly used for the designs and other intentional marks that people have made on natural geological surfaces. It refers to marks made—and left—*in situ*. Rock art is not meant to be portable.

The markings take many different forms. Figures pecked into boulders and bedrock (petroglyphs), paintings on cliff faces and cave walls (pictographs), designs made by reconfiguring gravel on the ground surface (geoglyphs)— all of these are rock art. Rock art is found on every inhabited continent, and the time span of its production is huge. Cave paintings in parts of Australia and Europe were created tens of thousands of years ago, and rock art is still being made today in central Africa, western Australia, and parts of the United States.

In North America almost all rock art is Native American. The art has been created continent-wide by people of many different cultures and traditions, beginning thousands of years ago and continuing into the present. In the southwestern United States alone, there are many thousands of rock art sites. Every year more are rediscovered after many decades—or even centuries— during which no one seems to have been aware of their existence. You might come across them in the backcountry, at a national park, or even in your own neighborhood. At some sites, designs are bold and prominently situated. Elsewhere, they are tiny, concealed in hidden places. Technique is sometimes

Canyon de Chelly within the Navajo Nation is a virtual gallery of rock art. Although most petroglyphs do not tell a story, this panel clearly depicts mounted horsemen and a robed man holding a cross that probably chronicle a Spanish entrada.

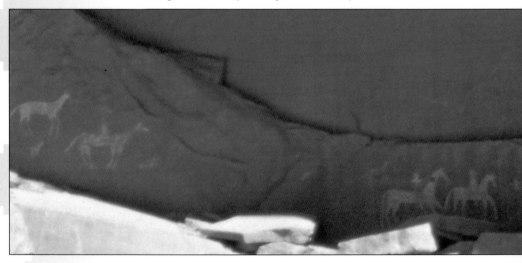

rough and rudimentary. Some is the work of a skilled and practiced hand. Imagery may be identifiable or utterly enigmatic.

Although rock art appears in a wide range of settings, these locations were certainly not chosen arbitrarily. Researchers believe that most was made at places of cultural or spiritual importance. Today, we consider these places significant because of the petroglyphs or pictographs that are there. In the past, however, recognition of the importance of these locations likely preceded the production of the rock art. It was made because of the site's special nature—perhaps as part of an activity associated with its importance. Thus, an underlying significance seems to define rock art sites. One clue we have to a place's value for past peoples is the presence of the rock art.

There really is no single best way to approach an understanding of the places where petroglyphs and pictographs were made. However, a fundamental first step is to overcome the tendency to "decipher" the marks as though they represent a language or code. Your appreciation of rock art will be powerfully enriched by enlarging your view—literally. Resist the tendency to look at it as pictures on a gallery wall against a neutral backdrop. An essential step toward gaining deeper enjoyment and understanding of rock art is to look carefully and thoughtfully at its site and surroundings.

The setting for Southwestern rock art may send a message on both a large and a small scale. It may include the particular surface on which a design or mark was made, the rocks and landforms that constitute the site, as well as everything in the surrounding landscape. Careful observations will take you beyond "pictures" to reveal its complex and fascinating relationship to the surrounding area.

Peter and his wife, Liz, co-authored Rock-Art of the Southwest: A Visitor's Companion, published by Wilderness Press. It is available at the Deer Valley Rock Art Center.

Arizona's Antiquities Act

by Todd Bostwick

City Archaeologist, Pueblo Grande Museum

Arizona is blessed with an abundance of archaeological sites that are protected, in various degrees, by federal and state laws. The federal Antiquities Act of 1906 was the first government regulation of archaeological sites in Arizona, but it applied only to federal lands and was rarely enforced. Vandalism and unauthorized excavation of archaeological materials in Arizona were common in the late nineteenth century, and due to the absence of archaeological institutions in Arizona there were few advocates for the protection of these sites. All that changed in 1915 when Byron Cummings was hired

"Montezuma's Castle" is actually a five-story dwelling sheltered under a chalky limestone alcove on Beaver Creek. It was occupied between AD 1000 and 1400.

as the director of the Arizona State Museum at the University of Arizona in Tucson. Although largely self-trained, Cummings had been exploring and digging archaeological sites in Utah and northern Arizona since 1906. His early work at Betatakin and Keet Seel in northeastern Arizona later led to their designation as a national monument.

Cummings became concerned not only with the vandalism to Arizona's archaeological sites but by the fact that the vast majority of the excavation taking place was by museums located in the eastern United States, where entire site collections ended up in storage.

Ever since he moved to Arizona, Cummings tried to get an archaeological law passed. It was not until 1927, when he was president of the University of Arizona, that Cummings was able to use his new clout to get the legislature to pass an Arizona Antiquities Act. The 1927 act was the first state archaeology law in the western United States.

It was flawed, however, because Cummings attempted to take control of archaeology on federal land. The act required, among other things, that one half of all collections from all excavations, whether on state or federal land, must be deposited at a museum within the state.

Throughout the 1930s, Cummings unsuccessfully tried to get an improved Antiquities Act passed. When one of Cummings' students, Emil Haury, took over as director of the Arizona State Museum in 1938, he, too, attempted to get revisions in the Antiquities Act. It was not until 1960 that the legislature passed a new Antiquities Act that remains today, with some modifications, the state law governing archaeology on state land in Arizona.

This act, following Cummings' original intentions, requires that archaeological permits be obtained from the Arizona State Museum and that only professional archaeologists can obtain those permits. In 1990, the Arizona Antiquities Act was revised to include restrictions on the treatment of human remains in Arizona, as well as the procedures for the repatriation of human remains and funerary objects.

Recommended Reading

Police mystery readers will enjoy the reservation settings of Tony Hillerman's fiction as well as *Cry Dance* and others by Kirk Mitchell.

■ O'ODHAM: PIMA, MARICOPA, TOHONO O'ODHAM

Erickson, Winston P. *Sharing the Desert: The Tohono O'odham in History.* Tucson: University of Arizona Press, 1994.

Fontana, Bernard L. *Of Earth and Little Rain: The Papago Indians.* Flagstaff: Northland Press, 1981.

Manuel, Frances and Deborah Neff. *Desert Indian Woman: Stories and Dreams.* Tucson: University of Arizona Press, 2001.

Nabhan, Gary Paul. *The Desert Smells Like Rain: A Naturalist in Papago Indian Country.* San Francisco, CA: North Point Press, 1982.

Shaw, Anna Moore. *A Pima Past.* Tucson: University of Arizona Press, 1974.

Webb, George. *A Pima Remembers.* Tucson: University of Arizona Press, 1959.

Zepeda, Ofelia. *Ocean Power: Poems from the Desert.* Tucson: University of Arizona Press, 1995.

■ YO'EMEM: THE YAQUI

Choate, Harris S. *The Yaquis: A Celebration.* San Francisco, CA: Whitewing Press, 1997.

Evers, Larry and Felipe S. Molina. Y*aqui Deer Songs/Maso Bwikam: A Native American Poetry.* Sun Tracks: An American Indian Literary Series. Vol. 14. Tucson: Sun Tracks and University of Arizona Press, 1987.

Flores, Enedina, et al. *The Yaquis of Scottsdale, Arizona.* Scottsdale: Concerned Citizens for Community Health, 2002.

Kelley, Jane Holden. *Yaqui Women: Contemporary Life Histories.* Lincoln, NE: University of Nebraska Press, 1978.

Painter, Muriel Thayer. *With Good Heart: Yaqui Beliefs and Ceremonies in Pascua Village.* Tucson: University of Arizona Press, 1986.

Spicer, Edward A. *People of Pascua.* Tucson: University of Arizona Press, 1988.

■ THE HOPI

Bassman, Theda. *Treasures of the Hopi.* Flagstaff: Northland Publishing, 2000.

Bird, Gail, et al. *Be Dazzled! Masterworks of Jewelry and Beadwork from the Heard Museum.* Catalogue from Heard Museum exhibit. Phoenix: Heard Museum, 2002.

Clemmer, Richard O. *Roads in the Sky: The Hopi Indians in a Century of Change.* San Francisco, CA: Westview Press, 1995.

Courlander, Harold. *The Fourth World of the Hopis.* Albuquerque, NM: University of New Mexico Press, 1971.

Day, Jonathan S. *Traditional Hopi Kachinas: A New Generation of Carvers.* Flagstaff: Northland Publishing, 2000.

James, Harry C. *Pages from Hopi History.* Tucson: University of Arizona Press, 1974.

Kosik, Fran. *Native Roads: The Complete Motoring Guide to the Navajo and Hopi Nations.* Tucson: Rio Nuevo Publishers, 1996.

Masayesva, Victor and Erin Younger. *Hopi Photographers/Hopi Images.* Tucson: University of Arizona Press, 1980.

Nequatewa, Edmond. *Truth of a Hopi: Stories Relating to the Origin, Myths, and Histories of the Hopi.* Flagstaff: Northland Publishing, 1967.

Page, Susanne and Jake Page. *Hopi.* New York: Abradale Press, Harry N. Abrams, 1982.

Sekakuku, Alph H. *Following the Sun and the Moon: Hopi Kachina Tradition.* Flagstaff: Northland Publishing, 1995.

Wright, Barton. *Hopi Kachinas: Complete Guide to Collecting Kachina Dolls.* Flagstaff: Northland Publishing, 1977.

▓ DINÉ: THE NAVAJO

Bahti, Mark, Joe Bahti, and Eugene Baatsoslanie. *A Guide to Navajo Sandpaintings.* Tucson: Rio Nuevo, 1978; reprint, 1999.

Bassman, Theda. *Treasures of the Navajo.* Flagstaff: Northland Publishing, 1997.

Fielder, John and Rich Clarkson, eds. *Navajo: Portrait of a Nation.* Englewood, CO: Westcliffe Publishers, 1992.

Iverson, Peter. *A History of the Navajos.* Albuquerque, NM: University of New Mexico Press, 2002.

Kosik, Fran. *Native Roads: The Complete Motoring Guide to the Navajo and Hopi Nations.* Tucson: Rio Nuevo Publishers, 1999.

Preston, Douglas. *Talking to the Ground.* New York: Simon & Schuster, 1995.

Reichard, Gladys. *Navajo Shepherd and Weaver.* New York: J. J. Augustin, 1936.

▓ NUWUVI: THE SOUTHERN PAIUTE

Dutton, B. P. *The Ranchería, Ute, and Southern Paiute Peoples.* Englewood Cliffs, NJ: Prentice-Hall, 1976.

Holt, R. L. *Beneath These Red Cliffs: An Ethnohistory of the Utah Paiutes.* Albuquerque, NM: University of New Mexico Press, 1992.

Spicer, E. H. *Cycles of Conquest: The Impact of Spain, Mexico, and the United States on the Indians of the Southwest, 1533–1960.* Tucson: University of Arizona Press, 1962.

Trimble, S. *The People: Indians of the American Southwest.* Santa Fe, NM: School of American Research Press, 1993.

Recommended Reading

◼ PAI: HUALAPAI, HAVASUPAI, YAVAPAI

Dobyns, Henry F. and Robert C. Euler. *Wauba Yuma's People: The Comparative Socio-political Structure of the Pai Indians of Arizona.* Prescott: Prescott College, 1970.

Hirst, Stephen. *Life in a Narrow Place.* New York: D. McKay, 1976.

Iliff, Flora Gregg. *People of the Blue Water: A Record of My Life Among the Walapai and Havasupai Indians.* Tucson: University of Arizona Press, 1985.

Ruland-Thorne, Kate. *The Yavapai: The People of the Red Rocks, the People of the Sun.* Sedona: Thorne Enterprises Publications, 1993.

◼ NDEE: THE APACHE

Debo, Angie. *Geronimo: The Man, His Time, His Place.* Norman, OK: University of Oklahoma Press, 1976.

Goodwin, Grenville. *The Social Organization of the Western Apache.* Tucson: University of Arizona Press, 1969.

Haley, James L. *Apaches: A History and Culture Portrait.* Norman, OK: University of Oklahoma Press, 1981; reprint, 1997.

Iverson, Peter. *When Indians Became Cowboys.* Norman, OK: University of Oklahoma Press, 1994.

Mails, Thomas E. *The People Called Apache.* New York: BDD Promotional Book Co., 1993.

◼ MOJAVE, QUECHAN, COCOPAH, CHEMEHUEVI

Alvarez de Williams, Anita. *Travelers Among the Cucupa.* Los Angeles, CA: Dawson's Book Shop, 1975.

Bee, Robert L. and Frank W. Porter III, Gen. Ed. *The Yuma Indians of North America.* New York: Chelsea House Publishers, 1989.

Casebier, Dennis G. *Mojave Road Guide: An Adventure Through Time.* Essex, CA: Tales of the Mojave Road Publishing, 1999.

The Editors of Time-Life Books. *People of the Desert.* Alexandria, VA: Time-Life Books, 1993.

Grey, Herman. *Tales from the Mohaves.* Norman, OK: University of Oklahoma Press, 1970.

Laird, Carobeth. *The Chemehuevis.* Banning, CA: Malki Museum Press, 1976.

McNichols, Charles. *Crazy Weather.* New York: Macmillan, 1944.

Emergency Information

◼ O'ODHAM: PIMA, MARICOPA, TOHONO O'ODHAM

Urgent situations on the reservations are handled by calling the local police: Tohono O'odham Police, (520) 383-3275; the Gila River Reservation Police, (520) 562-7115; the Salt River Reservation Police, (480) 850-8200; the Ak-Chin Police, (602) 268-9477; or 911. The Indian hospitals stabilize emergency cases, but if you are not a community member you will be transported to the nearest non-Indian hospital.

◼ YO'EMEM: THE YAQUI

Call 911 in case of emergency.

◼ THE HOPI

In the event of an accident or emergency, call the Hopi Police Department, (928) 738-2233. Headquarters are located between Polacca and Keams Canyon, but patrol units are always in radio contact. The Hopi Health Care Center, (928) 737-6000, is open 24 hours a day. The Public Health Service Hospital, (928) 738-2211, is open 24 hours a day. Critical emergencies receive stabilizing care and are evacuated by helicopter to Flagstaff or Phoenix. An ambulance is available at (928) 738-0911.

◼ DINÉ: THE NAVAJO

Determine your location and call the nearest Navajo Police Department or 911.

◼ NUWUVI: THE SOUTHERN PAIUTE

The National Park Service at (928) 643-7105 is the best source of emergency information if you visit Pipe Spring. The nearest town is Kanab, Utah. No cities are in proximity.

◼ PAI: HUALAPAI, HAVASUPAI, YAVAPAI

Call the Hualapai Tribal Police, (928) 769-1024, or the Indian Health Service, (928) 769-2207, in Peach Springs. Kingman is the nearest town and Las Vegas, Nevada, is the nearest city.

In Havasupai, the Indian Health Service will provide emergency stabilization (the village is so small that no phone number is available). Helicopter evacuation links the village with Phoenix and Las Vegas.

◼ NDEE: THE APACHE

The locations described in this chapter are situated both on and off Apache lands. In an emergency, call 911 or determine your location and call the local or tribal police to determine the nearest and most appropriate facility.

◼ MOJAVE, QUECHAN, COCOPAH, CHEMEHUEVI

These reservations are not far from sizable off-reservation communities. Call 911 or be aware of appropriate facilities in the vicinity.

Photo Credits

p. 1: *(Bottom and top right)* Anne O'Brien, © 2004; *(Top left)* Courtesy of the Museum of Northern Arizona, Flagstaff.

p. 3: Jess Vogelsang, © 2004

p. 5: John Running, © 2004

p. 8: *(Both)* Courtesy of the Heard Museum, Phoenix.

p. 9: Courtesy of the Heard Museum, Phoenix.

p. 10: Courtesy of the Desert Botanical Garden, Phoenix; Ross Conner, photographer.

p. 15: Anne O'Brien, © 2004

p. 17: Joe McAuliffe, Desert Botanical Garden, © 2004

p. 18: Courtesy of the Scottsdale Historical Museum, Scottsdale, from Mesa Public Schools Collection of the Arizona Pioneers' Historical Society.

p. 19: Terroll Dew Johnson, © 2004

p. 22: Diane T. Liggett, © 2005

p. 23: Anne O'Brien, © 2004

p. 24: Edward McCain, © 2004

p. 26: *(Both)* Courtesy of the Desert Botanical Garden, Phoenix; Michael Gardner, photographer.

p. 27: Courtesy of the Desert Botanical Garden, Phoenix; Steve Priebe, photographer.

p. 28: Diane T. Liggett, © 2005

p. 29: Terroll Dew Johnson, © 2004

p. 30: Courtesy of the Heard Museum, Phoenix.

pp. 31, 32, 33: Terroll Dew Johnson, © 2004

p. 34: Roger Young, © 2004

pp. 36, 37: Courtesy of the Pueblo Grande Museum and Archaeological Park, Phoenix; Bob Rink, photographer.

p. 38: Courtesy of the Heard Museum, Phoenix. *(Middle photo)* Ida Redbird and Mary Juan, artists (Maricopa).

p. 39: Courtesy of Starwood Hotels & Resorts Worldwide, Inc.

p. 41: Anne O'Brien, © 2004

p. 42: Courtesy of Starwood Hotels & Resorts Worldwide, Inc.

p. 43: Anne O'Brien, © 2004

p. 44: Courtesy of the Cline Library Special Collections and Archives Dept., Northern Arizona University, Flagstaff (24371); Josef Muench, photographer.

p. 46: Patrick Smith, © 2004

pp. 47, 48: Anne O'Brien, © 2004

p. 50: Courtesy of the Cline Library Special Collections and Archives Dept., Northern Arizona University, Flagstaff (30223); Josef Muench, photographer.

pp. 54, 55: Terroll Dew Johnson, © 2004

p. 56: Courtesy of the Heard Museum, Phoenix.

p. 58: Courtesy of the Arizona State Museum, University of Arizona (PIX 353x23); Ray Manley, photographer.

p. 59: Anne O'Brien, © 2004

p. 62: Courtesy of the Scottsdale Historical Society, Scottsdale.

p. 63: Anne O'Brien, © 2004

pp. 65, 66, 67, 68: Anne O'Brien, © 2004

p. 70: Courtesy of Guillermo Quiroga.

p. 72: Lee Hyeoma, © 2004

p. 74: Courtesy of the Denver Public Library, Western History Collection (P-738).

pp. 77, 78, 79: Courtesy of Alph Secakuku.

p. 81: Courtesy of the Denver Public Library, Western History Collection (P-1111).

p. 82: Tony Marinella, © 2004

p. 84: Jerry Jacka, © 1993

p. 86: Courtesy of Alph Secakuku.

p. 87: *(Top)* Roger Young, © 2004; *(Bottom)* Courtesy of Alph Secakuku.

p. 89: *(All)* Courtesy of the Heard Museum, Phoenix.

p. 92: Diane T. Liggett, © 2005

p. 94: *(All)* Courtesy of the King Gallery of Scottsdale.

p. 95: *(All)* Courtesy of Al Qöyawayma; Chris Marchetti, photographer.

p. 97: Courtesy of Alph Secakuku.

p. 98: Anne O'Brien, © 2004

p. 99: Courtesy of the Heard Museum, Phoenix; Marvin Pooyouma and Mike Gashwazra, artists (Hopi).

p. 100: Courtesy of the Heard Museum, Phoenix; Charles Loloma, artist (Hopi).

p. 102: Lee Hyeoma, © 2004

p. 103: Roger Young, © 2004

p. 104: Courtesy of the Cline Library Special Collections and Archives Dept., Northern Arizona University, Flagstaff (25571); Josef Muench, photographer.

p. 106: Jess Vogelsang, © 2004

p. 108: Courtesy of the Cline Library Special Collections and Archives Dept., Northern Arizona University, Flagstaff (L542); Josef Muench, photographer.

p. 109: Courtesy of Paul Carson.

Photo Credits

p. 201: Courtesy of the Cline Library Special Collections and Archives Dept., Northern Arizona University, Flagstaff (30632); Josef Muench, photographer.

p. 202: *(Top left)* Courtesy of the Heard Museum, Phoenix; *(Top right)* Courtesy of the Amerind Foundation, Dragoon; *(Bottom)* Courtesy of the Arizona State Museum, University of Arizona (32023).

p. 203: Courtesy of the Arizona State Museum, University of Arizona (32023).

p. 205: *(Left)* Courtesy of the Museum of Northern Arizona; *(Right)* Courtesy of the Arizona State Museum, University of Arizona (PIX215).

p. 206: Courtesy of the Arizona State Museum, University of Arizona (PIX778X17).

p. 208: Anne O'Brien, © 2004

p. 209: Lee Hyeoma, © 2004

p. 210: Anne O'Brien, © 2005

p. 211: Courtesy of the Amerind Foundation, Dragoon.

p. 212: *(Top left)* Courtesy of the Arizona State Museum, University of Arizona (C20829); *(Top right and bottom right)* Courtesy of the Amerind Foundation, Dragoon; *(Bottom left)* Courtesy of the Heard Museum, Phoenix.

p. 213: *(Top left)* Courtesy of the Amerind Foundation, Dragoon; *(Top right)* Courtesy of the Arizona State Museum, University of Arizona (C20861); *(Bottom left and right)* Courtesy of the Heard Museum, Phoenix.

p. 214: Courtesy of the Amerind Foundation, Dragoon.

pp. 216, 218, 219: Anne O'Brien, © 2004

p. 220: Courtesy of the Amerind Foundation, Dragoon.

pp. 221: James A. Mack, © 2005

pp. 222: Diane T. Liggett, © 2005

pp. 224, 226: Anne O'Brien, © 2004

p. 227: Diane T. Liggett, © 2005

p. 228: *(Both)* Courtesy of the Heard Museum, Phoenix.

p. 229: Anne O'Brien, © 2004

p. 232: Walter Feller, © 2004

p. 234: Cavins Collection, Mojave Desert Archives, courtesy of Dennis Casebier.

p. 235: Walter Feller, © 2004

p. 236: Courtesy of the Mohave Museum of History & Arts, Kingman (3645).

p. 237: Courtesy of Paul Carson. Photogravure by Edward S. Curtis.

p. 238: Courtesy of the Mohave Museum of History & Arts, Kingman (252).

pp. 239, 240: Walter Feller, © 2004

p. 243: *(Left)* Courtesy of the Denver Public Library, Western History Collection (X-32880); *(Right)* Courtesy of the Sherman Library, Corona del Mar, CA.

pp. 244, 245: Courtesy of Wade Cox, with permission of the National Park Service.

p. 246: Cavins Collection, Mojave Desert Archives, courtesy of Dennis Casebier.

p. 247: Courtesy of the Smithsonian Institution, National Museum of the American Indian archives; Col. Frank Churchill, photographer (N26523).

p. 248: Courtesy of Arizona State Parks.

p. 250: Courtesy of the Society of California Pioneers, San Francisco (1219).

pp. 251, 252, 253, 254: Walter Feller, © 2004

p. 257: Courtesy of the Cline Library Special Collections and Archives Dept., Northern Arizona University, Flagstaff (30138); Josef Muench, photographer.

p. 258: Courtesy of the Heard Museum, Phoenix.

p. 259: *(Top)* Walter Feller, © 2004; *(Bottom)* National Geographic Society Image Collection; Richard H. Stewart, photographer.

p. 263: John Crossman, © 2004

p. 264: Walter Feller, © 2004

p. 265: *(Top)* Public domain; *(Bottom)* Walter Feller, © 2004

p. 266: Walter Feller, © 2004

p. 268: Courtesy of the Heard Museum, Phoenix. *(Top)* Leroy Fisher, artist (Chemehuevi); *(Bottom)* Annie Fields, artist (Mojave).

p. 269: Courtesy of L. D. (Louie) Lomavitu.

p. 270: Courtesy of the Desert Botanical Garden, Phoenix; Elaine McGinn, photographer.

pp. 272, 273: Courtesy of George Billingsley, USGS, Flagstaff.

p. 275: Courtesy of the Heard Museum, Phoenix; Steven Yazzie, artist (Navajo).

pp. 276, 277: Diane T. Liggett, © 2005

pp. 278, 279: Diane T. Liggett, © 2005

p. 296: Jim Hornaday, © 2004

Index

About the Author

Anne O'Brien has traveled Indian lands since 1948, when she first visited the pueblos of the Rio Grande. Her personal interest in Indian tourism, therefore, might be said to fall into the category of modern history.

Although she is a cultural outsider, O'Brien has participated in a portion of this history both as a recreational and a serious visitor to Indian lands. She has made numerous visits to Hopi since the 1960s, explored Navajo country by car and on horseback, hiked the desert country of the O'odham and the mountains of the Apache, walked in honor at an intertribal powwow, and mentored Native American teenagers in the city. As an independent scholar and writer she has read and researched American Indian subjects and recorded oral histories. She's visited and stumbled upon ancient history around Arizona and the Four Corners area and has written about contemporary Indian culture, ancestral sites, and artifacts.

The author has considered the dilemmas of cultural ownership and public display in her capacity as a volunteer at the Heard Museum, the Denver Museum of Nature and Science, the Museum of Natural History on the University of Colorado campus, and the Museum of Northern Arizona. She is a member of Pueblo Grande Museum and the Arizona Historical Society and Foundation and has served on the board and executive committees of the Indian Arts and Crafts Association in Albuquerque and the Museum of Northern Arizona in Flagstaff.

O'Brien developed an appreciation of the interaction of language and culture after receiving a bachelor's degree in French at the University of Colorado in Boulder. Her later studies and experience in the field of social services and psychology helped her learn how to approach human behavior from an appropriate emotional distance. She earned a master's degree in counseling at Arizona State University and practiced in Phoenix. (She recently discovered that Dr. Ruth Underhill's interests progressed from the study of languages through social work to ethnology as well.) She has worked as a writer and editor since the 1980s and is a member of the American Association of Journalists and Authors (ASJA).